W9-DBY-527

ABOUT ISLAND PRESS

Island Press is the only nonprofit organization in the United States whose principal purpose is the publication of books on environmental issues and natural resource management. We provide solutions-oriented information to professionals, public officials, business and community leaders, and concerned citizens who are shaping responses to environmental problems.

In 1994, Island Press celebrated its tenth anniversary as the leading provider of timely and practical books that take a multidisciplinary approach to critical environmental concerns. Our growing list of titles reflects our commitment to bringing the best of an expanding body of literature to the environmental community throughout North America and the world.

Support for Island Press is provided by Apple Computer, Inc., The Bullitt Foundation, The Geraldine R. Dodge Foundation, The Energy Foundation, The Ford Foundation, The W. Alton Jones Foundation, The Lyndhurst Foundation, The John D. and Catherine T. MacArthur Foundation, The Andrew W. Mellon Foundation, The Joyce Mertz-Gilmore Foundation, The National Fish and Wildlife Foundation, The Pew Charitable Trusts, The Pew Global Stewardship Initiative, The Rockefeller Philanthropic Collaborative, Inc., and individual donors.

ABOUT THE NATURAL LANDS TRUST

The Natural Lands Trust (NLT), located in Media, Pennsylvania, is a nonprofit regional land trust, dedicated to working with people to conserve land in the greater Philadelphia region and nearby areas. Created in 1961, the Trust maintains approximately 50 preserves and 125 other properties under conservation easement. During the late 1970s the trust began a significant shift in its operations by providing professional planning assistance to conservation-minded landowners and becoming actively involved in "limited development" projects. By the late 1980s, the Trust began to work closely with communities to help them apply new approaches for managing growth and conserving land. The concept for conservation subdivisions has evolved from the Trust's efforts to help municipalities add significant land protection standards to their existing land-use ordinances, so that conservation approaches will become institutionalized within the local planning framework.

Conservation Design for Subdivisions

Conservation Design for Subdivisions

A PRACTICAL GUIDE TO CREATING OPEN SPACE NETWORKS

Randall G. Arendt

With Site Plans and Perspective Sketches
by Holly Harper, Stephen Kuter, and Nicole Keegan

Natural Lands Trust, American Planning Association, and American Society of Landscape Architects

ISLAND PRESS

Washington, D.C. ■ Covelo, California

Library of Congress Cataloging-in-Publication Data

Arendt, Randall.
    Conservation design for subdivisions: a practical guide to creating open space networks / Randall G. Arendt.
      p.   cm.
    Includes bibliographical references and index.
    ISBN 1-55963-489-8 (paper)
    1. Land subdivision—Planning. 2. Planned communities. 3. Real estate development—Environmental aspects—Planning. 4. Land use—Planning. 5. Nature conservation. 6. Building sites—Designs and plans. I. Harper, Holly. II. Title.
    HD1390.2.A73   1996
    333.77'13—dc20   96-20454
                                                     CIP

"A thing is right when it tends to preserve the integrity, stability, and beauty of the biotic community. It is wrong when it tends to do otherwise."

—Aldo Leopold

Contents

Appendices

Preface

Since the publication of my two earlier books on rural planning principles,[1] I have received numerous enquiries for more detailed information describing the actual techniques that are available to landowners, developers, local officials, and conservation organizations who are interested in conserving land through the development process so that their communities may enjoy the benefits of an interconnected network of open space in years to come.

Although many of the principles advocated in this handbook are not particularly new, they have been articulated and illustrated here in a way that makes them understandable to the majority of participants in the subdivision process—most of whom are typically nondesigners. I have found that this information is most accessible and usable for these participants when it is presented in a simplified manner that brings the various elements down to their fundamentals.

---

[1]*Dealing with Change in the Connecticut River Valley: A Design Manual for Conservation and Development* (Yaro, Arendt, Dodson, and Brabec), 1988. Cambridge: Lincoln Institute of Land Policy; and *Rural by Design: Maintaining Small Town Character,* 1994. Chicago: Planners Press.

The essence of this handbook is therefore a four-step process for laying out residential development around the central organizing principle of land conservation.

However, by far the greater message is that *the open space that is conserved in this way can be required to be laid out so that it will ultimately coalesce to create an interconnected network of protected lands.* Viewed from this perspective, the conservation subdivision potentially functions as a building block within a community-wide system of open space, which is an uplifting concept that goes well beyond the ideas normally found in either the planning literature or in most conservation publications.

Indeed, one of the more exciting aspects of this approach is the possibility it holds for land-use planners to work much more closely with conservation professionals—with developers and landscape architects being the principal bridging members of an emerging "greenspace alliance" in which all these parties could collaborate to produce a more balanced pattern of conservation and development. The current imbalance is directly related to the fact that conventional planning and zoning documents are essentially legal instruments for development, without any significant conservation components (except for unbuildable wetlands, floodplains, and steep slopes).

There are no comparable instruments for land conservation, but the good news is that local plans and zoning ordinances can be recast so that conservation goals no longer proceed on a hit-or-miss basis and are no longer dependent on chance and charity. Fortunately, this shift can be accomplished in a way that respects the rights of landowners and the equity of developers, who would continue to be able to build at *full density*—but only when they design their houselots and streets around an open space framework that includes meadows, fields, and woodlands that would otherwise have been cleared, graded, and converted into houselots and streets.

This handbook is an outgrowth of two similar documents prepared by the author and the Natural Lands Trust. The first document, a technical report that focused on conserving wooded areas around the Inland Bays of Delaware, was prepared for the Sussex Conservation District in Sussex County in 1993 with funds from the U.S. Environmental Protection Agency. In its second incarnation, written the following year, this report was greatly expanded into a full-fledged handbook for conservation education, with funding support from the W. Alton Jones Foundation. As such, it has been used by the Natural Lands Trust in its Community Land Stewardship program, which was conceived and inaugurated by the Trust's president, Michael G. Clarke. Under the title *Designing Open Space Subdivisions,* that edition attracted national attention, with copies being requested by a wide variety of people and organizations involved in conservation and development in 35 different states and several Canadian provinces.

With the interest, support, and involvement of Island Press, the text of this handbook has been further modified to place greater emphasis on this technique's potential for protecting larger, community-wide networks of conservation land, with color plates added to illustrate the design concepts with greater clarity. Reflecting these improvements, the handbook has been retitled *Conservation Design for Subdivisions: A Practical Guide to Creating Open Space Networks,* and its publication has been cosponsored by both the American Planning Association and the American Society of Landscape Architects. It is anticipated that this handbook will be updated every few years to include further new ideas and innovations in the field.

Thoughts about "institutionalizing" the ideas contained in this handbook in the zoning ordinance and subdivision regulations in your community are included in Chapter 8. In addition, some "model" ordinance language is also provided in Appendix H, which contains design standards and regulatory procedures for creating conservation subdivisions that should ideally be viewed as "building blocks" in a community-wide network of protected open space. These networks will in many cases also contain areas protected by land conservation organizations; these open spaces can ultimately be buffered and connected through conservation areas in new subdivisions laid out according to the principles described and illustrated in this handbook.

Although a conscious effort has been made to write this handbook in a clear and friendly style that will engage the reader's interest, it is expected that many users will thumb to particular sections most relevant to their immediate needs. In fact, before delving into the other sections, many readers might flip to the illustrated examples in Chapter 7 first and then turn to Chapter 5 for a more detailed explanation of the planning steps that produced the open space designs in each case.

Whether you choose to read the chapters in sequence or skip around bit, the central message of the text and pictures should come through clearly: *that there are better ways of designing new residential developments than we have typically seen in our communities, and that the approach recommended in this handbook is really quite simple and straightforward.*

Introduction

If you live in a rural area or along the suburban fringe of a metropolitan region, chances are that you live not far from a stream valley, wildflower meadow, or a patch of woods. Chances are also good that none of these special places will be recognizable twenty or thirty years from now, unless they are in a public park, forest, or wildlife refuge, or unless they happen to be protected through a conservation easement held by a land trust or similar organization. That is because most townships and counties have adopted zoning ordinances whose principal purpose is to set rules for the orderly conversion of natural lands into developed properties. In these communities, every acre of buildable land is typically zoned to become houselots and streets, strip malls, or office parks. There is no "greener vision" of a different kind of future, because the land-use regulations in most communities are based on a very limited model that knows only how to produce more and more suburbia composed of endless subdivisions and shopping centers ultimately covering every bit of countryside with "improvements."

Fortunately, practical alternatives to conventional zoning do in fact exist, and one of the principal techniques for conserving natural lands is the subject of this handbook. The special places that give our rural and semi-rural communities their distinctive character need not all be cleared, graded, and paved over just because they contain flat, dry, buildable land, although that has been the fate of countless similar natural areas in virtually all suburbs built up to this time.

Every region of our country possesses its distinctive landscapes and habitats. The diversity is enormous not only *among* the different regions but also *within* small localized areas that typically support hundreds of species of plants, grasses, shrubs, trees, insects, amphibians, reptiles, birds, and mammals.

During the historic settlement of our country, vast areas were stripped of their original flora and fauna, with fields of corn and grain replacing native woodlands and prairie. Now, in the latter part of the twentieth century, we are witnessing a second wave of change, as suburban lawns and streets are carved out of the farmland that had previously been carved out of the forests, meadows, and plains that had existed for hundreds of thousands of years.

During these two revolutions—the first agricultural, the second post-industrial—the loser has been natural diversity. In every one of our major regions, fewer native plant and animal species exist than did 50, 100, or 150 years ago. It is true that some new species have been introduced, but usually to the detriment of the original habitats that occupied unique positions within a highly interconnected web of life. Nonnative plants such as phragmites and purple loosestrife have invaded our wetlands, pushing out other plants and with them many of the insects and birds that had depended on the food and cover provided by the indigenous wetland plant species. Forests in the Mid-Atlantic states are being choked by Oriental bittersweet and Japanese honeysuckle; New England pastures sprout vigorous stands of multiflora rose; and huge regions of the South are being engulfed by the creeping kudzu vine (imported from Japan by the federal government to help retard

soil erosion during the Dust Bowl era—something that seemed like a good idea at the time, no doubt).

Although in many parts of the country forests regenerate naturally from farmland left fallow for a decade or two (often with an unhealthy complement of nonnative invasives), suburban development is much more final. Put quite simply, this may well be our last chance. If we do not get it right this time it will be impossible, for all practical purposes, for our children or grandchildren to re-create any functional semblance of the natural world in our communities. Parcel by parcel, townships and counties that have relied on conventional zoning have found that they ultimately become blanketed with "wall-to-wall development."

In the community in which I spent the first half of my childhood, the township government adopted zoning without any comprehensive planning to protect natural areas, except the floodplain along the river which was inherently unbuildable. While I was growing up, a few local farmers continued to grow vegetables and other produce, selling directly to an increasing number of suburban customers who had moved in nearby. But by the time I enrolled in college every row of sweet corn had been replaced by a municipal sidewalk and a tidy lawn. The small woodland behind my house was cleared away for a clump of condominiums, and the bramble-filled vacant lot across from my grammar school (where the berries attracted birds and omnivorous children) was paved over for parking.

History continues to repeat itself as most communities still operate under conventional zoning ordinances without any clear idea whatsoever as to how the natural lands that make up their special places could possibly be preserved. The answer is disarmingly simple, so basic in fact that the average nontechnical person is able to grasp it and put it into practice just by reading this handbook. Stated simply, the trick is to rearrange density on each development parcel as it is being planned so that only half (or less) of the buildable land is consumed by houselots and streets. Without controversial "down zoning," the same number of homes can be built in a less land-consumptive manner, *allowing the balance of the property to be permanently protected and added to an interconnected network of green spaces and green corridors criss-crossing one's township or county.*

The *density-neutral* approach advocated in this handbook respects private property rights and the ability of developers to create new homes for an expanding human population, accommodating newcomers without unduly impacting the remaining natural areas that make our communities such special places in which to live, work, and recreate. In so doing, this approach provides a fair and equitable way to balance conservation and development objectives, and it offers an opportunity for developers and conservationists to meet in the middle, creating more livable communities in the process.

Conservation Design for Subdivisions

How This Handbook Can Help You

This handbook has been written and illustrated to make it relatively easy for readers to learn *the basic steps involved in designing residential developments that maximize open space conservation* without reducing overall building density.

In addition to working within the existing legal densities allowed under current zoning, this technique allows the land protected in new conservation subdivisions to remain under private ownership and control—preferably in an undivided manner and according to certain management standards—typically by a homeowners' association or a local land trust.[1]

This handbook also shows how communities can use this technique, through state-of-the-art zoning and subdivision standards, to *create an interconnected network of permanent open space using the conservation subdivision as the basic building block.*

In addition to those designated wetlands, floodplains, and steep slopes that are often already regulated under federal, state, or

---

[1]Because this technique does not require the dedication of any land for public access or use, it avoids the legal issues associated with the "takings" doctrine embodied in a long line of judicial decisions.

local law, the types of open space that can easily be protected through the simple design approaches illustrated in this handbook include upland woodlands, meadows, and fields, plus historic, cultural, or scenic features of local or greater significance.

Readers might wonder why they should bother learning how to design subdivision sites for both conservation and development, when more commonly practiced approaches seem to work adequately. Here are several reasons:

(1) *Simply put, conventional approaches to subdivision development ultimately produce nothing more than houselots and streets.* This process eventually "checkerboards" rural areas into a seamless blanket of "wall-to-wall subdivisions" with no open space, except for perhaps a few remnant areas that are too wet, steep, or floodprone to build on. Whether one is a landowner, developer, realtor, planner, engineer, surveyor, landscape architect, or local official, few people can take a great deal of professional pride in helping to create just another conventional subdivision, converting every acre of natural land within a site to lawns, driveways, and streets.

(2) *Alternative methods of designing for the same overall density while also preserving 50% or more of the site are not difficult to master, and they create more attractive and pleasing living environments that sell more easily and appreciate faster than conventional "houselot-and-street" developments* (see Appendix E, "Economic Benefits of Open Space upon Real Estate"). This is particularly true for three large and growing sectors of the housing market—young households, single-parent families, and "empty-nesters."

(3) *The significant land protection achievable through "conservation subdivision design" should help smooth the local review and approval process* by responding to many environmental concerns even before they are raised by officials or by members of the public interested in preserving wildlife habitat and protecting water quality in neighborhood streams, ponds, and aquifers.

(4) *Conservation subdivisions are simply better places to live.* When well designed, the majority of lots abut or face onto a variety of open spaces, from formal "greens" or "commons" to wildflower meadows,[2] farm fields, mature woodlands, tidal or freshwater wetlands, and/or active recreational facilities. At present, *only golf course developments offer comparable amounts of open space,* but those green areas are managed for only one kind of activity, and they typically convert all previously natural areas (except wetlands and steep slopes) into intensively managed lawns that are off limits to everyone but golfers and that are uninviting to most forms of wildlife (except the more tolerant animals, such as geese).

One measure of the demand for open space among homebuyers is the fact that *nearly 40% of people living in golf course developments do not even play the game.* One successful Florida golf course developer near Tampa has found that many non-golfers are attracted to those of his lots that back onto wetland areas, offering views of egrets and herons and of tree boughs laden with Spanish moss. In fact, in some of the new golf course developments in the Mid-Atlantic region, four out of five sales are to non-golfers. According to published reports, these people are buying "the parklike views of open space, views that can command a premium in a home's initial sale price and its resale value" (see Appendix G for a feature article on this subject from the *The Philadelphia Inquirer,* September 26, 1993).

This handbook will show how virtually anyone can adapt— and improve upon—the basic technique used for decades by the designers of golf course communities. *Briefly stated, that technique is to outline the open space first and to let its size and location become the*

---

[2]The section of this handbook entitled "Recommended Further Reading" contains several outstanding "how-to" publications for those interested in planting with indigenous species of trees, shrubs, and wildflowers. Of particular note are those by Laura Martin, Jeff Cox, Hal Bruce, and Elizabeth DuPont. Martin's book is perhaps the best resource for anyone thinking about planting wildflower meadows.

central organizing element driving the rest of the design. The next three steps are to locate the houses around the open space, to trace in access street alignments, and finally to set the lot lines (where applicable).

It is almost as simple as it sounds. Naturally, a number of resource base maps are required (typically pertaining to soils, slopes, wetlands, floodplains, existing vegetation, wildlife habitats, and historic resources), and several elemental principles relating to physical layout and neighborhood design should be observed. These are illustrated and described in later chapters.

Of course, this publication does not reduce the need to engage a team of professionals (including a landscape architect or physical planner, in addition to a surveyor and engineer). It can, however, make everyone's role clearer by articulating a "greener vision" for residential developments of nearly every size, shape, and variety. An added benefit stems from the fact that these design principles are applicable regardless of house type or sales price, meaning that they can be as easily used to provide starter homes for young people and other households with moderate incomes as they can for middle-aged folks and retirees with more ample means.

Conventional Layouts versus "Conservation Designs": Comparisons and Contrasts

CONVENTIONAL RESIDENTIAL DEVELOPMENTS

As used in this handbook, the term "conventionally designed subdivision" refers to residential developments where all the land is divided into houselots and streets, with the only open space typically being undevelopable wetlands, steep slopes, floodplains, and stormwater management areas.

In these types of developments there are no nice places to walk, such as a central green or a wooded grove, or a riverbank or lakeshore, because all the land has been cut up and parcelled out to individual lot owners. There are no open meadows for wildlife, or playing fields for children (of any age). Because there are no community areas in which to take an evening stroll, to throw a frisbee, or have a game of catch, there are often no sidewalks, nor any informal trails. All the land has been paved over, built upon, or converted into lawns or backyards. Except for wetlands and steep slopes, all the natural areas have been cleared, graded, and planted with grass and nonnative shrubs and trees, which offer little to any remaining wildlife. In addition to there being fewer species of plants and animals, there is typically little community life, for the public realm has been reduced to an asphalt street system, and even that lacks much visual appeal because in most cases no one has thought to plant shade trees at regular intervals on each side. Without any parks, commons, or community woodlands, there are no informal places where neighbors can easily meet, engage in casual conversation, and gradually become better acquainted with each other. As a result, residents of conventional subdivisions miss a lot of social opportunities, and they depend on their cars even more to bring them into contact with other people.

Although no one ever sets out consciously to create these deficiencies, they have come about because minimal thought has been given to the results produced by basic development design standards contained in local ordinances which ask little, if anything, with respect to conserving open space or providing neighborhood amenities. Consequently, in the vast majority of cases, little or nothing is offered along these lines, and the deficiencies are repeated time and again until, at some point, people begin to notice that they are living amidst a lot of lawns and asphalt and realize that there must be more to life than just houselots and streets.

About thirty years ago, professional planners around the country touted the idea of "planned residential developments" (PRDs) as an improved alternative to conventional subdivisions. In PRDs, greater design flexibility is permitted by reducing standards for lot width and area, but the absence of any comprehensive standards for the quantity, quality, and configuration of open space allowed many uninspired designs to be proposed and approved. In many PRDs minimal land is set aside as open space, and this land typically consists of unbuildable areas, stormwater basins, and relatively narrow and unusable strips of grass between parking lots, with an occasional tennis court sometimes thrown in, perhaps as an afterthought.

The most notable exceptions to this pattern have been the "golf course PRDs," where it is not unusual to find more than half the dry and otherwise buildable land now hosting fairways, sand traps, and putting greens. This specialized form of PRD offers a lot more than the opportunity to live near a golf course: to the creative observer it offers a general approach to development design that can transform ordinary PRDs and conventional subdivisions into "open space communities." Fortunately, the basic steps involved in designing golf course developments can be applied to almost any residential development situation, regardless of scale, location, housing type, or market value.

CONSERVATION SUBDIVISION DESIGN

In its purest form, the term "conservation subdivision design" refers to residential developments where, as in golf course communities, *half or more of the buildable land area is designated as undivided, permanent open space.* This result is typically achieved in a *density-neutral* manner[1] by designing residential neighborhoods more compactly, with smaller lots for narrower single-family homes, as are found in traditional villages and small towns throughout the United States. Alternatively, the objectives can be accomplished with semi-detached or attached dwellings or by combining these two approaches. (When market conditions are such that full economic return can be realized with fewer but more expensive homes, that method can also be used to preserve open space, although the smaller number of potential buyers for such upscale properties limits the applicability of that technique.)

Not surprisingly, *the most important step in designing a "conservation subdivision" is to identify the land that is to be preserved.* This should always be the first major design step that is taken, just as

---

[1]"Density-neutral" means that the overall number of dwellings allowed is the same as would be permitted in a conventional layout. Dwellings not constructed on buildable conservation land are erected in other more appropriate locations on the site.

in golf course developments, where the course itself is the first and foremost element to be planned. This process is described in detail in Chapter 5, but basically open space identification involves delineating both "Primary Conservation Areas" (such as unbuildable wetlands, waterbodies, floodplains, and steep slopes), and "Secondary Conservation Areas" (including mature woodlands, upland buffers around wetlands and waterbodies, prime farmland, natural meadows, critical wildlife habitat, and sites of historic, cultural, or archaeological significance).

After deducting unbuildable "Primary Conservation Areas" (PCAs) from the total parcel acreage, calculations are made to determine the number of dwellings allowed by zoning on the remaining parts of the site (including the "Secondary Conservation Areas," or SCAs).[2] That number of units is then located around—but not within—those Secondary Conservation Areas. The result is a density-neutral subdivision with significant upland open space that would normally be developed. In conservation subdivisions, up to half of the dry, buildable land may be used for houselots and streets, and the other half must remain as undivided open space. Of this open space, at least half should be retained as woodlands, meadows, or farm fields, while the balance may be converted to more formal, intensively managed open spaces, such as grassy commons and active recreation facilities (including ballfields, tennis courts, and fairways). In other words, looking at all the *buildable* land on a site, at least one-quarter must remain as relatively undisturbed open space, one-quarter may be modified for active

recreational purposes, and up to one-half may be developed (at twice the normal density, to preserve the owner's equity).

Because 18-hole golf courses typically consume more than a quarter of a site's developable area, and generally leave much less than a quarter of the buildable land in a relatively undisturbed state, developments featuring them are usually not considered to reflect "conservation design," where one of the primary objectives is the protection of natural areas. They are, instead, specialized forms of recreational developments, and they of course play an important role in meeting one kind of recreational need.

To the extent that many people who move into golf course communities have little or no interest in that game but are instead very interested in enjoying open space convenient to their homes, promoters of such facilities would be well advised to broaden the appeal of their developments by conserving more natural areas on their sites, such as woodland habitat and riverbanks where forest trails and waterside greenways would provide appealing opportunities for passive recreation and wildlife corridors.

It is not the purpose of this handbook to discourage further golf course developments, but rather to suggest ways in which these and other residential development forms could be significantly improved. It is obvious that there must be some limit to the number of new golf course developments that can be created before the total demand for this kind of community is satiated. Taking the best qualities of this development form, and leaving the rest behind, the following general recommendation may be stated: *Let us build many more "golf course developments," but for the most part without the golf courses themselves—substituting community greens for putting greens, and greenways for fairways.*

This conservation-minded approach offers a unique opportunity to developers of parcels that are too small to accommodate golf courses (under 350 or 400 acres), giving them an easy way to provide significant open space amenities attractive to many potential homebuyers. In many developing communities it is no

---

[2]Density can be determined either through calculations based on formulas in an ordinance, or by drawing "yield plans" showing the maximum "build-out" of a site, with houselots and streets covering the entire parcel. The latter approach is more visual and tangibly demonstrates a site's capacity. However, guidelines must be established to ensure that lots on these conceptual plans do not include less buildable land than would be required on actual lots meeting the standards of the ordinance. In other words, "yield plans" must be realistic. Examples are shown in Chapter 7. See model ordinance language in Appendix H.

longer possible for developers to acquire 350 contiguous acres of buildable land. For them, the conservation subdivision approach offers a highly attractive alternative to conventional layouts, as golf course developments are not even an option in those areas.

RELATIONSHIP WITH THE "NEW URBANISM" AND REGIONAL PLANNING

The ideas in this handbook essentially complement, rather than compete with, the more formal design approach typically seen in "neo-traditional" neighborhoods (also called the "New Urbanism"). Although both approaches involve more compact lot sizes, the conservation subdivision has as its central principle the preservation of natural lands as building blocks in community-wide open space networks. As such, it is an appropriate development approach in less developed areas on the metropolitan fringe. It is especially adaptable to situations in which central water or sewer is not available and where low-density, residential zoning is a given. These areas have sometimes been described as potentially *green wedges"* between the higher density corridors that typically radiate out from metropolitan centers.

In contrast, the more formal designs of most of the New Urbanists (as exemplified in Kentlands, Maryland, and Laguna West, California) are perhaps most appropriate in metropolitan *corridor locations,* as *new nodes* along the regional transportation network, or as extensions to the fabric of traditional historic towns. These are generally the kinds of locations that can gracefully accommodate both higher densities and beneficial mixtures of uses and thus offer the greatest opportunity for local officials, landowners, and developers to structure future regional growth in positive, land-saving, community-enhancing ways.

Looked at in this manner, conservation subdivision design and the New Urbanism are two sides of the same coin: that of more compact neighborhood development. Occupying different positions on the rural–urban continuum, they both provide fresh solutions to the challenge of dealing with change in areas subject to growth pressures. Taken together, these complementary approaches provide the range of tools many communities need if they are to avoid repeating the mistakes that have marked much of the post-war suburban development pattern in this country.

Planning at the county or regional level should provide the overall organizing structure and context for all community-level plans, whether they be for neo-traditional settlements or for smaller conservation subdivisions. In terms of defining a broad conservation network of interconnecting open spaces, the approach being taken by Orange County, North Carolina (described in Chapter 6), serves as one very noteworthy example. In more urbanized metropolitan regions, the Third Regional Plan produced by the Regional Plan Association in New York City (published as *A Region at Risk,* by Island Press, 1996) is perhaps the best document of its kind in decades, from which numerous constructive ideas may be extracted for application in other similar city-regions around the country.

Advantages of Conservation Design

ECONOMIC ADVANTAGES

Conservation subdivision designs offer distinct and measurable economic advantages over conventional layouts in at least five different ways, reflecting various stages or periods in the life of a project.

Smoother Review

The first advantage occurs during the review period, which is likely to proceed more smoothly because site designers have anticipated and taken into account many of the concerns that would otherwise become time-consuming and costly issues to resolve. While it might not be possible to avoid all potential problems or conflicts, the chances of confrontation and dispute can certainly be minimized by site planning that is sensitive to the conservation objectives of township or county officials and interested residents.

There is a growing awareness among local leaders, realtors, developers, and other business people that an area's quality of life is one of its chief economic assets, for few new businesses choose to locate or expand in locales that do not offer enjoyable places in which to live. Communities that have allowed all or most of their natural lands to be sliced into houselots or paved over for parking facilities often suffer a competitive disadvantage when trying to attract new employers. And rural areas that rely on outside dollars from retirees and tourists to stimulate their economies ultimately depend upon the natural beauty of their farms, woodlands, hills, or water features (as the case may be) for their continued prosperity, because few people choose to retire or vacation in communities that look as commonplace as the anonymous suburbs where they have spent most of their working lives.

Luckily there are practical ways to develop land without eradicating the natural features that give places their special character. Because this more creative design approach minimizes the visual and environmental impacts of new development on critical resources, and also provides crucial "building blocks" needed to create interconnected networks of open space throughout the community, it offers the potential for a mutually beneficial alliance between the development sector and conservation advocates.

Lower Costs

The second advantage of conservation subdivision design is the opportunity if offers to *reduce infrastructure engineering and construction costs.* To the extent that single-family houselots can be narrowed, or that multiple unit dwellings can be incorporated, street and utility runs can be shortened. This reduction becomes greater as the development pattern itself becomes more compact and village-like, but it is also measurable even when houses are interspersed with open space to provide good views from the maximum number of homes. Open space design can also reduce the number of costly or contentious wetland crossings needed by avoiding parts of a site where such conditions exist. And, to the extent that street pavement is reduced, the size and cost of stormwater management facilities can also be lessened. The shorter street

and utility systems that often result from more compact layouts can also reduce the public sector's long-term infrastructure maintenance costs.

Subdivisions designed in this conservation-minded manner are also much less expensive to create than another well-known kind of development that features a specialized type of recreation: golf course communities. The costs of transforming fields, meadows, and woodlands into regulation golf courses are extremely high for a number of reasons, chief among them being the typical need to move and shape two or three million cubic yards of soil. Added to this are the extra costs associated with meeting increasingly stringent environmental regulations designed to prevent degradation of the groundwater or downstream surface waters from the fertilizers, herbicides, and pesticides that are usually applied to the turf. Other concerns that applicants must address include erosion, sedimentation, habitat and species protection, thermal pollution (from removal of woodlands that shade ponds and streams), and the impact of heavy irrigation requirements upon local water supplies. All of these costs and concerns are substantially lessened by conservation subdivisions that leave 50 to 75 percent of a development site relatively unchanged or intact as natural areas.

Marketing and Sales Advantages

The third advantage occurs during the marketing and sales period, when developers and realtors can capitalize on the amenities that have been preserved or provided within the development. These positive features can form the basis for an *environmentally oriented marketing strategy* highlighting the benefits of living in a community where upland forest habitat and/or productive farmland have been preserved, along with riparian or wetland buffers and wildlife meadows. Sales brochures should be prepared to illustrate and describe neighborhood trails through protected greenways paralleling creeks or traversing ridgelines, and formal commons for passive recreation and specific facilities for certain active sports should also be mentioned.

This technique has been used successfully by an increasing number of developers, including Siepmann Realty in Brookfield, Wisconsin, whose sales agents point out to potential customers that *when they buy a one-acre lot in one of their conservation subdivisions, they are actually receiving the use of more than 80 acres:* their houselot plus 80 acres of woodland, meadows, ponds, trails, and active recreation facilities (tennis courts and ballfields). This has proven to be a successful counter to the comment that lots in Ron Siepmann's developments are not as large as those in competing subdivisions offering no special amenities. The logic and the experience have been similar despite differences in density in some of his developments, such as the quarter-acre lots in Pebble Valley (in a half-acre zone) or the one-acre lots in Hawksnest (instead of the three-acre lots prevailing in that area). With open space ranging from 50% to 65%, sales strategies focusing on this kind of amenity strike a responsive chord among many homebuyers, particularly when lots are laid out to maximize views of the conservation land.

Such has also been the case in the northern suburbs of Philadelphia, where development is consuming Bucks County farmland at a rapid rate. In this context, where the conventional wisdom had been that homebuyers would insist upon houselots of at least one acre in size, Realen Homes thought differently, and has been enjoying record sales based upon its open space layouts. In its "Farmview" development, which is the fastest selling subdivision in its price range in the county, large homes are located on lots one-third to one-half the normal size. But because more than half the land has been preserved, most homes command long views over the protected fields, which have been donated to a local land trust. *When given a choice, consumers have demonstrated their clear prefer-*

ence for buying homes that look out onto farmland or other open space, rather than houses where the only view is of their neighbor's picture window or backyard.

Homebuyers' general preference for houselots that abut or face onto protected land is illustrated in Figure 3-1, showing that the majority of the first lots sold in Realen's "Garnet Oaks" development were those that adjoined the woodland preserve or the cen-

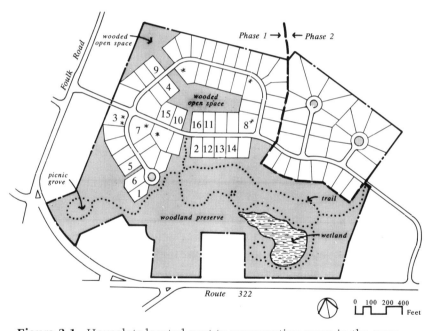

Figure 3-1. Houselots located next to conservation areas in the new "Garnet Oaks" subdivision in Bethel Township, Delaware County, Pennsylvania, generally sold more quickly than others, and at higher prices. Numbers refer to the order in which lots in the first phase had been sold as of December 31, 1993. Single asterisks indicate lots able to accommodate side-entry garages (a popular design feature), and the double asterisk marks the largest lot without a premium price.

tral open space (also wooded). These lots sold quickly, even though most commanded premium prices, based on their adjacency to the protected areas—which gave them more privacy and more of a rural feeling (see Fig. 3-2). Recognizing their customers' desire for a rural setting, the developers emphasized the neighborhood open space in their marketing approach, and they even published a nicely designed interpretive guide to the trail system that their landscape architect had laid out through the woodland preserve.

Copies of this guide were given to prospective buyers, who were encouraged to take a stroll along the trail before leaving to visit the

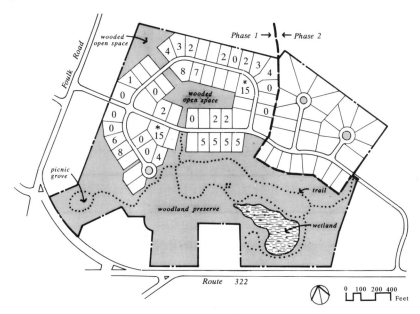

Figure 3-2. Lot premiums added to base price (in thousands of dollars), at the "Garnet Oaks" subdivision in Bethel Township, Pennsylvania. Most of these premium lots adjoin the open space. Asterisks indicate sloping lots that could accommodate houses with walk-out basements.

next subdivision on their lists. The relatively rapid sales rate in this subdivision is attributed, in part, to the unique parkland experience that these buyers encountered at Garnet Oaks.

Confirming this information, a national survey of people who shopped for or bought a home during 1994 has revealed that, of 39 features critical to their choice, consumers ranked "lots of natural open space" and plenty of "walking and biking paths" as the second- and third-highest rated aspects affecting their decisions (Harney 1995). According to the survey director, Brooke Warwick of *American Lives,* these results demonstrate that consumers are becoming more selective and are looking more and more for the kinds of features that encourage informal social interaction among neighborhood residents in relaxed parkland settings. Perhaps significantly, golf courses within developments ranked 29th on the list, just below tennis courts. (See *The Washington Post* article in Appendix G.)

Value Appreciation

A fourth advantage is that homes in conservation subdivisions tend to appreciate faster than their counterparts in conventional developments. (This fact can also be used as part of one's marketing approach when selling or reselling homes where open space has been thoughtfully conserved in the original layout.) One of the more widely known studies of this type compared two subdivisions in Amherst, Massachusetts, built at about the same time, with very similar houses that originally sold for almost the same price, at the same overall density (two dwellings per acre). The only real difference between the two developments is that homes in the first were located on half-acre lots with little community open space, while those in the second were built on quarter-acre lots with 36 acres of open space, including mature woodlands, trails, a large meadow, a swimming pond and beach, a picnic grove, a baseball diamond, and tennis courts that also serve for basketball use. After twenty years the homes in the second development sold, on average, for $17,000 more than their counterparts in the other subdivision, where lots were actually twice as large. This 13% price differential is attributable to the neighborhood open space amenities, with all other aspects being nearly equal (Lacy 1991, also quoted in Arendt 1994).

A dozen other examples of the positive influence of open space upon residential property values have been documented by the National Park Service in its publication *Economic Impacts of Protecting Rivers, Trails, and Greenway Corridors,* excerpts of which appear in Appendix E of this handbook.

Reduced Demand for New Public Parkland

A fifth advantage of conservation subdivision design, from the local governmental perspective, is that the natural areas that are preserved and the recreational amenities that are provided in such communities help to reduce the demand for public open space, parkland, playing fields, and other areas for active and passive recreation. Current deficiencies with regard to such public amenities will inevitably grow larger as population continues to rise. To the extent that each new development meets some of its own needs for these amenities, pressure on local governments will be lessened in this regard, a factor that may make such designs more attractive to local reviewing bodies (at least when this is pointed out).

As mentioned earlier, communities also benefit economically from the environmental advantages associated with conservation designs: cleaner water, greater wildlife habitat, and more attractive natural surroundings are vitally important to the communities' quality of life, their economic competitiveness, and their recreation and tourism opportunities. In Spotsylvania County, Virginia, where heritage tourism associated with Civil War battlefields adds millions of dollars to the local economy every year, the new County Comprehensive Plan identifies conservation subdivision design as a recommended tool to help conserve public viewsheds of the cultural landscapes along scenic highways (as illustrated in Chapter 7, Site F).

ENVIRONMENTAL AND ECOLOGICAL ADVANTAGES

In addition to preventing intrusions into Primary Conservation Areas such as wetlands and floodplains, *conservation subdivision design also protects upland buffers* alongside wetlands, waterbodies, and watercourses—*areas that would ordinarily be cleared, graded, and covered with houses, lawns, and driveways in a conventional development.* Important terrestrial habitat in these "Secondary Conservation Areas" is thereby preserved for wildlife to dwell in and travel through. The greenways that are one of the hallmarks of conservation subdivision design provide cover and naturally sheltered corridors for various species to move through as they travel from their nests and burrows to their feeding places or hunting grounds.

Conservation subdivisions shed less stormwater than conventional developments and also provide larger areas of natural vegetation that act as buffers to help filter stormwater flowing into lakes, ponds, rivers, and streams. This traps pollutants and excessive nutrients dissolved or suspended in storm runoff. Leaf litter and groundcover can also slow stormwater velocity, thereby reducing soil erosion and stream sedimentation. Reducing runoff velocity allows stormwater to be more readily absorbed into the soil and taken up by the vegetation. Buffers also offer important infiltration and "recharge" benefits because they help maintain adequate flows of filtered water to underground aquifers (upon which local wells depend). Tree canopies provide shade that is especially important in maintaining cooler water temperatures needed by certain aquatic species during the hot summer months.

The minimum effective greenway width for water quality buffering therefore depends on factors such as the permeability of the soils, the steepness of the slopes, and the amount and type of plant material growing there, in addition to the volume and character of the pollutants likely to be found in the runoff. *To filter runoff from residential developments where a moderate amount of lawn fertilizer is used, wooded buffers 100 feet deep on slopes not exceeding 8% should be adequate* (compared with buffer requirements of 165 to 256 feet that have been recommended to filter nutrient-rich agricultural runoff in Maryland and North Carolina).

While no such buffers are typically required in conventional developments, true conservation subdivisions are designed with buffers at least 100 feet wide because the preponderant opinion in the scientific and planning communities is that this is the minimum width that is necessary if basic environmental goals are to be met. However, for development design purposes, it should be noted that *full density credit is allowed for all otherwise buildable land located within the recommended greenway buffer.*

Where these buffer areas are not currently wooded they should be planted with a variety of native-specie trees and shrubs and allowed to revegetate naturally through a general "no-cut" policy (except for creating informal walking trails; removing invasive alien plants, vines, and trees; and selectively pruning lower limbs to allow water views from the developed areas). Providing such buffers should also significantly reduce the size and number of stormwater detention basins needed on the development site, thereby lowering some infrastructure costs and freeing that land for other uses. (Those basins could also be reduced by directing roof runoff to lawns and into "French drains" in backyards or open space areas, as 30 to 50 percent of stormwater runoff in cluster developments typically comes from roofs.)

Conservation biologists tell us that riparian woodlands along rivers, creeks, and streams offer our "best hope for creating a system of interconnecting corridors" for a variety of wildlife at all lev-els of the food chain—from aquatic organisms and fish to amphibians and small terrestrial mammals (such as raccoons, muskrats, and otters) that link the aquatic system to the adjoining upland.

In addition, conservation subdivisions can include areas managed as wildlife or wildflower meadows, cut once a year at the end of the summer after flowers have bloomed and seeds have been set—and after the young from ground-nesting species have fledged and departed. These areas provide food and cover for birds, insects, and small mammals and require the barest minimum of maintenance in terms of mowing, irrigation, and fertilization. Such areas also help to slow storm runoff velocity, trap sediments, and absorb stormwater and the nutrients (and other pollutants) contained in it. On the aesthetic side, they add visual interest for residents who enjoy observing seasonal changes in the landscape and seeing wildlife at relatively close range.

Conservation subdivisions also offer greater opportunities to implement environmentally sensitive sewage treatment and disposal systems known alternatively as "land treatment," "spray irrigation," and "wastewater reclamation and reuse." These terms describe variations of a well-documented technology that are superior to conventional mechanical sewage treatment systems in many ways because they produce only very small amounts of sludge by-products and because they help to replenish local aquifers (rather than diverting the treated water into rivers, bays, or oceans where it flows into different systems, often carrying heavy nutrient loads that degrade the receiving waters and aquatic habitats downstream).

With spray irrigation, wastewater is heavily aerated in deep lagoons where it receives a "secondary" level of treatment, similar to that provided by conventional sewage plants. It is then applied to the land surface at rates consistent with the soil's natural absorption capacity. Nutrients in the treated wastewater are taken up by the vegetation (which may consist of forest trees, meadow grass, cropland, or lawns). This approach has a long and successful track record in twenty different states; those with the largest number of operating systems are Pennsylvania, Illinois, Florida, and Delaware.

In New Castle County, Delaware, the Public Works Department has published a 15-page booklet describing this technology in simple layperson's terms. Some of that region's more environmentally sensitive golf courses, such as the one at Hershey's Mill in East Goshen Township, Chester County, Pennsylvania, are irrigated and fertilized with community wastewater treated with this technology. This practice is well-accepted by residents and golfers in this upscale development because it is cost-effective, safe, odorless, and environmentally sound. Woodlands are irrigated with treated wastewater in the Kennett at Longwood retirement development near Longwood Gardens in East Marlborough Township, Pennsylvania, and wildflower meadows and farmland are sprayed with similarly treated effluent in The Fields, an expensive suburban development in Long Grove, Illinois (where 75% of the site has been preserved as open space, including 45 acres of restored prairie). In all these cases the treated wastewater is sprayed within a few hundred feet of homes, without problems or complaints.

Although conservation design approaches allow for land treatment systems to be implemented, they may of course also be served by conventional sewage plants, by individual septic systems, or by a variety of in-ground community septic systems. The key point here is that *the layout flexibility allowed with conservation subdivisions makes it easier for site designers to locate subsurface septic systems on those parts of the property that are best suited for such facilities.* In conventional developments built without central sewers, septic systems are located on each lot, regardless of whether soils are excellent, good, moderate, fair, or just marginally approvable for such purposes. However, in subdivisions laid out according to the principles in this handbook, houselots can be located on the deepest, driest, or best-drained soils available on the parcel. Alternatively, if the area of superior soil is not very extensive, the development can be laid out so that *either individual or community*

septic systems are located "off-lot" on the best soils within the community open space (which may also function as a village green, playing field, or wildlife meadow).

In Wayne County, Ohio, where the local Board of Health initially did not allow lots smaller than one acre to be served by individual septic systems, exceptions are now being made to permit separate drainfields serving different homes to be located within conservation areas designated on the Final Plan for such purposes, typically underneath wildflower meadows, playing fields, and neighborhood parks adjacent to the more compact houselots. Concerns about system failure can often be met by requiring individual septic tanks to be pumped every three years by the homeowners' associations so that sludge levels will never accumulate to the point where they will flow into and clog the drainage fields.

Because of their favorable texture for filtration, these same soil types—where they occur in other parts of the subdivision—could also be "designed around" to function as groundwater "recharge areas" and as sites for stormwater retention ponds. Other areas with coarser, sandy to gravelly soils should, if possible, be left in their natural state due to their poor filtering qualities.

SOCIAL AND RECREATIONAL ADVANTAGES

As mentioned earlier, the formal greens and commons typically featured in conservation subdivisions present *opportunities for neighbors to meet casually and to get to know each other a little better.* Whether they are walking the dog, enjoying a game of catch with their children or grandchildren, or just out on a stroll to see spring flowers, autumnal foliage, or local wildlife, neighbors have more opportunities to become better acquainted with one another when they are outside and on foot. In conventional developments most people spend nearly all their time indoors or in their private backyards (where there is little possibility for neighborly contact) largely because there is nowhere else to go, except by stepping into the car and driving away. Another advantage is that in conservation subdivisions the more compact yards typically require less maintenance, allowing people more free time to spend enjoying the greens, trails, and other features in these well-designed "natural neighborhoods."

When one Wisconsin developer of conservation subdivisions revisited one of his earlier projects, he was told by one of the residents that she had moved there a few years ago from a lakefront house several miles away. Since her new home had no water views, nor really any long distance views of any kind, he was puzzled and asked her why she had relocated. Her reply was that her lakefront house, while very nice, was essentially "one-dimensional"—if she tired of the lake there was not much else to interest her. On the other hand, she continued, her new home in the 160-acre Woodfield Village subdivision abutted 75 acres of protected open space including woodlands, meadows, a creek for canoeing, several miles of trails for walking and riding, courts for tennis and paddle tennis, a stable, a ballfield, and several children's play areas. She added that she felt there was also much more of a "sense of community" in her new neighborhood and that she frequently met people from other parts of the development when she used the trails or other recreational facilities, adding to her enjoyment and conviction that this type of subdivision provides "a better place to live."

Since numerous national recreational surveys have documented that short walks are one of the most frequent and popular forms of recreation enjoyed by Americans, it is not surprising that many people do in fact take advantage of opportunities to walk around their neighborhoods when that choice exists. *The basic elements of pedestrian-friendly neighborhoods are inviting places to walk and interesting destinations.* Under the first category one may list sidewalks (preferably along shady streets scaled for slow-moving traffic) and trails (preferably through woods or alongside water features). Under the second category one might include natural areas such as woodlands, meadows, beaches, and viewing points over ponds, lakes, tidal marshes, creeks, and bays, as well as human-made elements such as greens, commons, playing fields, landscaped gardens, orchards, and arboreta.

Community activities occur in a surprising number of conservation subdivisions, from annual picnics to summer sports events and races, to garden tours and winter skating parties. This is not to suggest that such development forms always produce a great deal of social activity, but they do seem to foster more neighborly interaction and a stronger sense of community pride than often exists in conventional developments, especially when the site designers have provided attractive footpath systems connecting their homes with interesting places to visit.

Conservation subdivisions also make it easier for municipalities to implement community-wide greenway network plans, which may depend on developers to provide critical links along particular stream valleys or hilltop ridges. Developers can generally be persuaded to dedicate a portion of their subdivision open space to the local government for active or passive recreation. This may take the form of a "green ribbon" of public trails through the otherwise private homeowner association open space. In Worcester Township, Montgomery County, Pennsylvania, Natural Lands Trust staff redesigned a proposed subdivision, which was bordered on two sides by township and state parkland, to include a greenway connection along the course of a brook that flows between the two parks.

Some jurisdictions are beginning to look at conservation subdivision design as their principal tool for *buffering existing public parkland* from the incursions of development on adjoining parcels. To achieve this objective, municipal zoning and subdivision ordinances should specify parkland buffers as one of the required design elements of open space systems proposed in new conservation subdivisions. Among many park professionals, this approach is known as the "adjoining lands strategy."

Roles and Responsibilities of Various Parties

The responsibility for encouraging superior conservation subdivision designs in rural townships and counties is shared by a number of different individuals and groups. This chapter looks at seven of these groups—landowners, developers, realtors, site designers, technical planning staff, planning commissioners, and conservation organizations.

LANDOWNERS

The decision to convert land from its natural state to some form of development is a personal and private one. Usually local officials are the last to know, after the landowner has made the decision and sold or optioned a parcel to a developer, who in turn has engaged a surveyor or engineer to prepare a preliminary plan meeting the community's adopted standards. Such decisions are made individually and generally in isolation from larger considerations such as those relating to habitat loss and fragmentation, water quality degradation downstream, or long-term community objectives for creating an interconnected greenway network. When the plans are eventually unveiled, landowners and developers are frequently surprised by the lack of a more enthusiastic response from community officials and nearby residents, because their plans are generally very consistent with the minimum standards established under local zoning and/or subdivision regulations. This situation could be avoided through a new submission requirement for conceptual sketch plans (or at least for simple, conceptual preliminary plans), a recommendation that will be further discussed later in this chapter, as well as in Chapter 8.

The best approach is one that involves the landowner from the very first moment. In most cases, no one knows a property as well as the person who has owned it for a long while, who has walked the land many times in different seasons or plowed the fields every year for decades. Even better than the soil scientist, the landowner knows where the fields dry out most slowly in the spring, and where foxes have dug their burrows—a sure sign of deep dry soil. The landowner will often know the woodlands and be familiar with the locations of the larger trees or the nesting places of certain birds. Most of all, the landowner will frequently have a personal feeling for both the land and the natural landscape and, if asked, will be able to tell you about its special places, those features he or she will miss most deeply after the land is developed.

Because of this knowledge, the landowner is one of the key information resources available to developers and their site designers, and should always be consulted. (Amazingly, this seldom happens, perhaps because in most instances the land is developed conventionally and insensitively into a standard checkerboard of houselots and streets, in which case such consultation would only pain the landowner and frustrate the engineer.)

With the layout flexibility inherent in conservation subdivisions, there is often ample opportunity to design streets and houselots in areas that will not directly impact a site's special features. In fact, landowners should be encouraged to draw up their own rough concept plans, at least to the extent that potential open spaces and possible development areas are identified in a general

way. Those interested in participating actively in shaping the future pattern of conservation and development on their land could even sketch out possible street alignments, lot lines, preservation areas, and trails. Landowners could use such plans as the basis for selecting a developer or declining option offers from those who do not agree to submit detailed plans consistent with their conservation-based sketch plan. Landowners who would like to take this course, but who are unsure of their ability to prepare such a sketch plan, should engage a qualified landscape architect or physical planner who has had experience with this kind of approach.

DEVELOPERS

In most cases landowners leave all design decisions—even the most fundamental ones—to the developers. As their preferences often determine whether conventional or more creative design approaches are selected, developers are usually the single most influential group involved in the land conversion process. And in the vast majority of cases they tend to continue with layouts with which they have had previous success in terms of gaining approval and selling their products.

As a whole, developers tend to be a rather conservative lot, hesitant to make major changes in the way they do business. This is largely because so much is at stake: if they misjudge the market, they can lose huge sums with a single unpopular development. (Bankers and others who lend them the capital to undertake those developments tend to be even more conservative with regard to innovation and change.)

The most effective approach in such situations is for advocates of conservation-minded design to put factual material into the hands of local developers and bankers, describing financially successful examples of creative development containing significant open space. (Two sources for such information are the "Project Reference File" series published by the Urban Land Institute, and the several dozen "case examples" of creative development described in *Rural by Design,* published by the American Planning Association.)

Because each market area is potentially different, the relevance of examples from outside one's immediate locale could be discounted by skeptical developers. But every group contains some innovators, and those who have demonstrated *any* flexibility in their thinking should be encouraged to consider at least sketching out a conservation subdivision design on one of their properties. Conservation groups or governmental units interested in promoting this approach could offer to pay the relatively modest fees involved in sketching an alternative concept plan showing how conservation principles could be applied to a developer's property. In order for this approach to be at all effective, it should be done not only with the developer's support but also at an early stage in the design process, before heavy engineering costs have been incurred in preparing a conventional layout (unless the local government is willing to grant a density bonus to help the applicant recover those engineering expenses).

REALTORS

As realtors deal with both the sellers and buyers of land, they have two opportunities to mention the advantages of conservation subdivision design each time land is sold. Sellers might become interested in this kind of approach if they were told how it could help preserve some of their property's special features. And developer–buyers could be informed of the creative possibilities and marketing advantages offered by layouts that increase the number of dwellings that could enjoy views of natural areas (such as wetlands, waterbodies, meadows, and woodlands), formal open spaces (such as community greens or commons), and recreational facilities (such as playing fields).

Of all the participants in the land development process, realtors are the only group for which there are continuing education requirements. The mini-courses offered as part of professional accreditation present a unique opportunity for realtors to learn about better ways to design subdivisions. For example, in Sussex County, Delaware, the Association of Realtors has sponsored several mini-courses explaining how creative design techniques can help to preserve more of the county's diminishing open space, especially around its critical natural areas, while maintaining full "lot yield" and also helping to create neighborhoods with an enhanced sense of place and community feeling.

As realtors are essentially intermediaries and advisors, they cannot do more than offer their observations and professional recommendations. However, because they are often involved at one of the most critical stages in the land conversion process—before concept plans have been formulated—they are well-positioned to sow the seeds of creative thinking in the minds of both the seller and the buyer at a time when the slate is often absolutely clean. In addition, their credibility in the eyes of developers might be higher than those of some of the other players because realtors typically have a good sense of what would sell well in their community. To the extent that they can help developers recognize that conservation design offers some distinct marketing advantages, they could be effective advocates for this type of approach.

SITE DESIGNERS

Residential developments should always be designed by a professional *team* that includes a landscape architect and/or a physical planner with demonstrated experience in designing conservation subdivisions, a civil engineer, and a land surveyor. Consulting members should include a soil scientist, a wildlife biologist, a forester, and the original landowner, among others. Of these professionals, landscape architects are typically the only ones specifically trained and examined in the aesthetics of site design, and therefore they should generally lead the team. Surveyors and engineers bring different but equally critical skills to the process and thus should always play significant roles.

After the hard data (relating to property boundaries, soils, slopes, wetlands, drainage, vegetative cover, wildlife habitat, easements or rights-of-way, etc.) have been collected and mapped, the landscape architect or physical planner should work closely with the civil engineer to prepare a concept plan. The recommended process is described in a step-by-step manner in the next chapter, but the initial steps—where both Primary and Secondary Conservation Areas are identified and the conceptual layout is sketched—should be the principal responsibility of the landscape architect or physical planner, in consultation with other members of the team. The engineer's and surveyor's roles increase as the plan becomes more detailed, and they would typically assume major responsibility for the final plan, having been involved to a greater or lesser extent in all previous design phases.

The above scenario assumes that the developer has asked these professionals to prepare a conservation-based design. If that is not the case, they should offer to show examples of such development types, both on paper and on the ground. Few consultants can afford to turn down a project because the client's preconceived ideas are very conventional and unimaginative, but I believe they do owe some responsibility to their profession to at least inform each client of the special opportunities presented by the property for retaining open space, enhancing community life, and marketing new homes. Part of their approach might include an informal roundtable discussion with the developer, a few local realtors, and a member of the township or county planning staff who might actively support the idea of a more creative layout. Another developer who has had positive experiences with conservation design might also be invited. Ultimately, however, the decision is the client's (unless the previous landowner has stipulated conservation design as a condition of sale). Again, as with the realtor, the site designer essentially serves as an advisor. But because the die

has usually not yet been cast when the site designer is first approached, the time is ripe for pointing out alternative ways of dealing with the land in question.

In rural areas where the only local site designers are land surveyors and civil engineers, officials should conduct information sessions where these professionals are introduced to the principles of conservation subdivision design (as distinct from standard "clustering"), possibly with assistance from the state chapters of the American Planning Association, the American Society of Landscape Architects, or the American Institute of Architects. Chances are that many surveyors and engineers would be interested in hearing more about alternative design approaches, particularly when local reviewing bodies publicly express a preference for more creative layouts.

From my own experience in presenting slide lectures to rural surveyors in Pennsylvania, in which the four-step process for designing conservation subdivisions has been described and illustrated, I know that some of these individuals can be extremely receptive to the idea of designing homes and streets to avoid impacting certain special site features, such as hedgerows, stands of large trees, unusual rock formations, stone walls or cellar holes, prominent knolls, wildflower meadows, vernal ponds, and forest glades. One of the reasons some people are attracted to the surveying profession is that this type of job enables them to spend a fair number of their working hours outdoors, walking across farm fields and through the woods.

Some surveyors have told me that they would like to learn more about conservation subdivision design because it would enable them to protect many of the special site features they enjoy seeing in the field, by providing the flexibility they need to design around them. They have also said they would welcome the opportunity to do more interesting designs, rather than continuing to produce look-alike "cookie-cutter" layouts on every piece of property they are given to work with. With some real ordinance flexibility and a few pointers on conservation subdivision design, many surveyors would create much finer developments, with substantial green spaces connecting nicely into community-wide open space networks. In Fauquier County, Virginia, consideration is being given to sponsoring instructional workshops for local surveyors and engineers, offering certification in the four-step approach to conservation subdivision design. It is proposed that such certification be required for all those submitting subdivision proposals within the county's rural zoning districts.

TECHNICAL PLANNING STAFF

By the time the local planning staff becomes involved, a concept plan has typically been prepared, and considerable thought may have already gone into its preparation. Hopefully the design process has not proceeded further than the concept plan stage, because the engineering costs involved in producing standard "preliminary plans" are so great that most applicants are completely unwilling to discuss alternative approaches to developing their properties once that work has been performed.

For this reason it is critically important that the planning staff meet with applicants while many design options are still open. A *pre-application sketch plan stage* should become standard operating procedure, either formally or informally. Informal arrangements are difficult to enforce, but it could become common knowledge around the town hall or county courthouse that development reviews will proceed much more smoothly, and proposals will generally be much better received, if applicants bring in conceptual sketch plans before basic layout decisions are firmly made. These sketch plans should be lightly drawn and accompanied by several resource maps illustrating the constraining factors and opportunity areas that have shaped the design.

Discussions at this stage should be informal, and planning staff should have the financial means to offer a constructive review by a consulting site designer, who would be asked to offer his or her insights and suggestions. This is generally not a costly exercise and can often be covered through the review fees paid to the local government by each applicant. Typically such fees defray the costs incurred by the planning, public works and legal staffs, and engineering or other professional consultants who are asked to render opinions. The practice of engaging design consultants early in the review process is becoming more widespread as officials in many areas recognize the critical importance of additional input of this kind at this stage, which usually requires a somewhat specialized background typically not found among permanent staff.

Ultimately, the planning staff should work toward a more formalized sketch plan review, suggesting to the planning board or commission that zoning and subdivision regulations be amended to include this as a basic requirement. To the extent that state enabling legislation specifies a maximum review period, from first submission of a complete application to final approval, the sketch plan stage may have to be folded into the preliminary plan review periods, as was done in the Model Ordinance language in Appendix H. Relatively little time should be needed for final plan reviews, as plans at that stage are typically not much more than modified "re-runs" of the very detailed preliminary plan—with certain revisions and adjustments specified by the planning commission.

Whether formal or informal, *the sketch plan stage is the community's last best hope for influencing the pattern of conservation and development within new subdivisions.* To be most effective, recommendations should be based upon official policies regarding the location and character of conservation lands within new residential developments. Ideally the local government will adopt an "open space element" in its comprehensive plan, describing the desirability of creating a network of greenspaces connecting stream valleys, shorelines, and remnant woodlands with meadows, community commons, and outdoor recreation facilities in new developments. Such a policy statement should be accompanied by a generalized *Map of Conservation and Development* encompassing the entire town, township, or county. The Orange

County (North Carolina) Planning Department through its geographical information system (GIS) has prepared computerized maps that show the approximate locations of Primary and Secondary Conservation Areas throughout the county, based on the procedures described in the next chapter. (See Fig. 6-1.)

Finally, planning staff should promote the idea of ultimately incorporating the recommended four-step procedure for designing conservation subdivisions (as detailed in Chapter 5) into new *requirements* for all subdivisions so that this approach will be routinely followed by every applicant (except those with parcels below a certain acreage). This would require that applicants at least evaluate and consider the conservation design approach. Without actually requiring developers to follow those principles, the ground would be prepared (figuratively speaking) for serious talks about the ways that conservation planning could be accomplished on each new development site.

In addition to improving the quality of the ultimate product, revised procedures for designing and reviewing residential development proposals should also help expedite this entire process, enabling developers to control the costs of holding land or renewing their options to purchase while approvals are pending. Relatively few people in the public sector seem to realize how much the ability of developers to provide extra amenities and quality touches is diminished when their project costs are escalated by protracted reviews.

PLANNING BOARD AND COMMISSION MEMBERS

Members of planning boards or commissions are uniquely positioned to play a key leadership role in encouraging the concept of conservation subdivisions. Alone among local officials, they deal with land-use issues on an intensive basis, examining all subdivision proposals at every stage, visiting the sites, studying the plans,

asking questions at public meetings, wrestling with the issues, and making numerous and sometimes detailed recommendations to the governing body for its consideration and final determination.

After serving a few years on a planning board or commission, these lay planners gain considerable experience and acquire a deeper perspective on the future of their communities. Their opinions therefore carry a fair amount of weight, giving them some influence over various decisions and actions taken by others. Because of the way their responsibilities are defined, these boards and commissions usually do not possess a great deal of power, but they can provide encouragement and direction to their technical planning staffs to continue working on ways to promote the idea of conservation subdivision design. As mentioned in the preceding section, this can occur through informal discussions at the sketch plan or conceptual preliminary plan stage, or through regulatory refinements requiring sketch plans to be submitted and further requiring that they be prepared according to the procedures described in the next chapter.

Board or commission members play a pivotal role, recommending for and against proposed developments and proposed regulatory changes. The stage is set for them to help their community move from rather conventional approaches to land-use regulation and development design to more creative and beneficial techniques that will ultimately produce a greener future for coming generations. Because such a proactive stance could be misunderstood by some of their constituents, they should also be prepared to repeatedly explain why code revisions are essential if their township or county is to retain much of its special character in the decades to come.

CONSERVATION ORGANIZATIONS

The term "conservation organization" is used broadly in this handbook to include voluntary nonprofit groups as well as governmental bodies. Such groups and organizations are not only comple-mentary to each other but also complement the efforts of the other parties described in this chapter by providing pertinent in-formation, offering constructive comment, and sometimes help-ing in the long-term management of protected open space.

All too often conservation organizations allow themselves to be cast in an opposition role, leading to negative perceptions of their objectives and purposes. Such groups must become more proac-tive, perhaps initiating and leading public discussions that explore positive alternatives to land-consumptive conventional develop-ment and broadening the understanding of participants in the land conversion process. A growing number of local and regional land trusts, for example, have been sponsoring workshop presen-tations at which conservation subdivision design techniques are described and illustrated. Such efforts tend to be most effective when also cosponsored by local builders, developers, or realtors, and when they provide illustrated examples of financially suc-cessful conservation subdivisions demonstrating the feasibility of this concept.

There is a wealth of existing information on the location and im-portance of environmentally sensitive areas in many communi-ties, and landowners need to become better acquainted with the ecological significance of such places on their own properties and in their immediate neighborhoods. It is one thing to know where the land is wet or where wildlife is abundant, but it is quite an-other to know how significant these places might be, either indi-vidually or as part of larger ecological systems.

Since it is probably true that nearly everybody's land is for sale, sooner or later (often as a result of death or taxes, both of which are inevitable), it would be prudent for conservation groups to en-sure that landowners are aware of the existence and significance of certain kinds of natural areas on their properties, and that they are also aware of practical alternatives to conventional develop-ment design.

At the same time that landowners are informed about environ-mentally sensitive features on their lands, as listed in various state and federal inventories, they should be told about the differ-ent techniques available to help them preserve their equity while still conserving most or part of their property. Many landowners either have or can anticipate heavy federal tax payments, which can be substantially reduced by wise planning. These people in-clude not only the relatively few who enjoy large incomes but also those facing sizable inheritance taxes and those who will have to pay large capital gains taxes when they sell the land they inher-ited or purchased years ago when its value was much lower. For all of these landowners, land donations or "bargain sales" to land trusts could help to reduce their federal tax burden substantially. (The best information source for such people is Stephen Small's definitive and exceptionally readable booklet, *Preserving Family Lands,* available through the Land Trust Alliance in Washington, D.C.)

For landowners without such tax problems, who need to receive the full economic value of their land, two other alternatives exist: "limited development" and "conservation subdivision design." The first option involves dividing the land into a smaller number of higher priced lots, which are typically much larger than the stan-dard development lot (often ranging from 10 to 30 acres), with per-manent conservation restrictions in areas outside designated "building envelopes" on each lot. This approach requires an afflu-ent clientele and is viable in very special areas such as those with high landscape value, attractive views, and access to water. These lots typically market best in upscale suburbs and in vacation areas.

The second approach, which also involves the conservation sub-division concept that is the main focus of this handbook, is ap-plicable virtually everywhere. Because it is "density-neutral" and offers homebuyers an attractive park-like setting with a variety of recreational and natural areas, while also reducing certain infrastructure costs, it represents a four-way winning situation for developers, conservationists, local officials, and residents.

To increase their overall effectiveness, conservation groups should proactively encourage and support proposed developments that preserve natural lands that would ordinarily be cleared, graded, and built upon (in addition to environmentally sensitive areas where development is prohibited anyway, such as wetlands). The fact that developers receive density credit for avoiding those otherwise buildable natural areas—manifested through somewhat higher densities on other parts of their sites—might be displeasing to a few staunch preservationists who may argue that these developers give up nothing and receive free support and public commendation for simply doing the right thing. But the beauty of this approach is that developers need give nothing up in order to create residential developments that preserve many acres of otherwise unprotected land.

Natural areas within such subdivisions should be permanently protected by conservation easements, and conservation organizations can help facilitate this process by accepting these easements. Holding easements does not entail ownership, liability, or maintenance responsibilities; in essence it gives such groups legal control to prohibit further development or other changes that would be inconsistent with preservation objectives stated in the easement (such as converting a wildlife meadow into a parking lot or tennis court). Holding an easement obligates a conservation organization to monitor the land annually, and to take appropriate enforcement action to deal with any encroachments or violations. For this reason, land trusts typically request (and receive) "endowment contributions" from developers, the interest on which would cover the organization's annual monitoring costs. Another excellent rule that land trusts should studiously observe is to accept easements on subdivision open space only when it is *undivided* (i.e., specifically *not* the "backyard" open space at the ends of individual subdivision lots, which can lead to unbelieveably com-

plicated and time-consuming situations with regard to monitoring and enforcement).

Occasionally, title to land within an open space subdivision may be offered to a conservation organization. This happened at Farmview in Bucks County, Pennsylvania, where the developer—Realen Homes—gave 137 acres of flat, dry, buildable farmland to the Lower Makefield Township Farmland Preservation Corporation to hold in perpetuity (it is currently being leased to a local farmer who is cropping the land under a long-term arrangement). Although such offers are infrequent (most developers being inclined to transfer conservation land ownership to homeowners' associations instead, through which residents retain control of their neighborhood open space), local land trusts should be prepared to accept such donations when they involve relatively undisturbed natural areas requiring little ongoing maintenance (as distinguished from commons, greens, or playing fields). Although lands within developments are not always ideal places for conservation organizations to own, they can offer special opportunities for building neighborhood support to conserve other nearby natural areas that the land trust might want to protect as well. And to the extent that they are suitable for informal walking trails open to the surrounding community, they can be a visible demonstration of the trust's interest in providing convenient public access to places where people can freely observe wildlife and seasonal changes in the natural landscape.

Whether land within conservation subdivisions is owned by a homeowners' association, a local land trust, or another entity, its very existence provides more opportunities for people to enjoy the beauty of natural areas. Whether one enjoys hearing birdsong or bullfrogs, identifying warblers or butterflies, or sighting deer or foxes, chances are that these interests have grown out of personal experiences in natural areas—spending time in the woods or out on the marshes, standing in a meadow, or sitting beside a tidal creek.

Conservation organizations that would like to increase the number of people who share their interests might look to this development design approach as a way of introducing nature to a larger number of individuals. Some of these residents are bound to notice the wildlife in the woodlands, wetlands, or upland meadows around their homes, and to take evening strolls or weekend walks along the trails connecting their neighborhoods with nearby conservation areas. Some of the children growing up in such developments might well acquire a lifelong interest in protecting natural areas. Distinguished leaders in land conservation and wildlife biology, such as John Muir, Aldo Leopold, Jane Goodall, and E.O. Wilson, have cited enjoyable childhood experiences in natural areas close to their homes as having influenced their career decisions and their continuing commitment to conservation efforts (Orr 1994). I can trace my own interest in conservation planning to having lived in an open space development during my teen years. And Wisconsin's leading developer of conservation subdivisions grew up in a planned neighborhood featuring parks and greenways—which he took for granted at the time, and which he decided to include in all of his developments.

One can never predict the many positive results attributable to the protection of natural areas, and conservation subdivisions offer one of the best opportunities to build wider public support, over the long term, for a greener future in your community.

Steps Involved in Designing Conservation Subdivisions: A Straightforward Approach

It is best to divide the process of development planning into two broad phases, one dealing with basic information collection and analysis and the second organizing this information and making judgments about the shape of the development itself. While the first is more objective, the second clearly involves more subjective decisions, which should usually be based upon certain design principles that provide a defensible rationale.

BACKGROUND STAGE

The first phase, the "background stage," involves four distinct steps: understanding the locational context, mapping special features, prioritizing objectives, and integrating the information layers.

Understanding the Locational Context

Within most townships or counties there are a variety of different locational contexts, some of which are more significant than others in terms of their relevance to the design process. Perhaps the

Figure 5-1. Site plan for the proposed expansion of Romansville, an historic hamlet within the rural/suburban township of West Bradford, Chester County, Pennsylvania. The author's design (at right) retains the entire density of the developer's original "cookie-cutter" plan (shown on the left) but arranges the development in a more compact village-like manner that preserves a substantial greenbelt of woodlands and farm fields around its perimeter. Due to their very compact nature, neo-traditional village layouts do not have the same high proportion of "view lots" that are commonly found in well-designed "conservation subdivisions." To compensate for this, the Romansville design includes five internal greens or commons (plus two ballfields), a relatively high number for a development of approximately 150 houselots.

most important is the site's proximity to traditional small towns or villages. New development within or adjoining such settlements should reflect and extend the historic streetscape and street pattern, especially in terms of their regularity and interconnectedness. Relationships between dwellings and streets are also important, in terms of modest, land-conserving front setbacks, sidewalks, and continuous rows of shade trees lining both sides. Special opportunities also exist here to avoid large off-street parking lots in higher density developments by designing streets with parallel parking spaces on both sides.

An interesting example of neo-traditional village design is the one prepared for Romansville, a hamlet within West Bradford Township, Chester County, Pennsylvania, where 150 dwelling units are proposed to occupy approximately 60 acres of a 160-acre site adjacent to this country crossroads settlement (a density consistent with local zoning standards). Dwellings are predominantly single-family detached, with about a dozen semi-detached homes and several apartments above shops or offices. The design is notable for its variety of lot sizes (5,000 to 30,000 square feet); its numerous commons, greens, and playing fields; and its extensive greenbelt of fields, woods, and trails (see Fig. 5-1).

The way neighborhood streetscapes would actually look in new developments that are patterned upon traditional small towns is perhaps better illustrated by the perspective sketch in Figure 5-2, from a conservation subdivision proposed in Dutchess County, New York.

In other more rural locations it is not imperative that the "traditional neighborhood" principles described above be observed, although it would be difficult to imagine a situation where they would *not* be appropriate (except in the midst of several conventional suburban subdivisions). On outlying parcels it is often equally fitting to follow more informal, irregular, or "organic" layouts, such as the one shown on the schematic plan in Figure 5-3,

depicting the recent "River's End" subdivision on land bordering Deep Creek, near its confluence with the Nanticoke River, just outside the town of Seaford, Sussex County, Delaware. River's End is the county's premier example of an "open space subdivision" modeled on the principles of golf course development design, but without the course (which would be expensive to build and maintain). As with its conceptual prototype, the great majority of lots abut or face onto protected open space, including greens, meadows, ponds, wetlands, and woods. Altogether the 142 lots occupy a little less than half of the 245-acre property.

Although this particular development features commodious ³/₄-acre houselots, this approach is particularly appropriate when smaller lots are involved, because *the adjoining open space psychologically enlarges their actual dimensions to include some of those meadows, woodlands, or wetlands that are within direct view of the houses. In addition, the open space creates a welcome buffer on at least one boundary of each of these lots, which is preferable to being closed in on all sides by other people's yards.* Interestingly, this successful subdivision was not laid out by a landscape architect or developed by a professional developer. Rather, it is the creation of a retired economist who returned to his native Sussex with a vision for building a better place to live. As an observant layman who had thought quite a lot about the subject but who had never studied it formally, Ron Hastings concluded that the most pleasant kind of rural neighborhood he could create would be one in which about half the land remained in its natural state. And, as he says succinctly, *"Open space sells."* Having established a successful start at River's End with its upscale homes, Hastings has recently begun planning a second open space development. This development will be for Sussex County residents with moderate incomes, demonstrating that this design approach meets the needs of a wide variety of people, not just golfers and retirees with comfortable pensions.

Figure 5-2. Perspective sketch of streetscape featuring simple vernacular homes in Squire Green, a new conservation subdivision in the town of Pawling, Dutchess County, New York. Note the shade trees, front porches, modest front yards, and familiar feel of this new subdivision designed along the lines of traditional neighborhoods in the classic American small town. (Courtesy SCI Real Estate Development, and Do Chung Architects of Stamford, Connecticut.)

Figure 5-4 shows a perspective sketch of a typical scene from a "conservation subdivision" designed in a more open and less formal fashion for a rural site out in the countryside (as contrasted with a "neo-traditional" village or an extension to a preexisting settlement).

Mapping Natural, Cultural, and Historic Features

Every new development should be based upon a fairly thorough (but not necessarily costly) analysis of the site's special features, both those offering opportunities and those involving constraints. All too often such efforts are limited to identifying legally un-

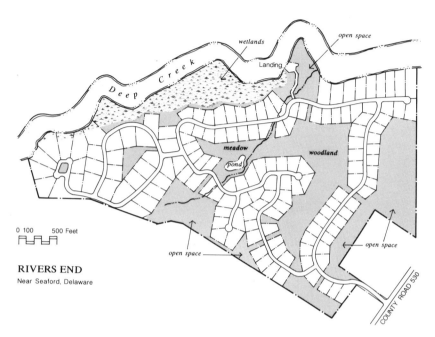

0 100   500 Feet

RIVERS END
Near Seaford, Delaware

Figure 5-3. The site plan for River's End, near Seaford, Delaware, shows the relationship of its 142 lots to the 100 acres of open space preserved in this layout, including woodlands, meadows, ponds, streams, wetlands, riverbanks, and a neighborhood boat landing. Very few non–golf course developments in Delaware contain significant open space features such as these.

buildable areas to avoid, and moving as many units as possible onto the remaining land. That type of "short-circuit planning" could be discouraged through a new design standard for residential development, one that requires "Existing Features and Site Analysis Plans" to be submitted for review and that requires applicants to be prepared to demonstrate how they have followed the four-step design process described in the second half of this chapter.

Many of the special features of interest to site designers will be known to the landowner, who should always be consulted. A coun-

try landowner will know the fields that remain damp until late spring, places where the waterfowl nest, and the hollow trees where raccoons make their homes. After walking the site several times, from end to end in different directions (preferably in early morning or late evening, when wildlife is apt to be more visible), or in the early spring when groundwater levels are highest and vernal pools might still be present, the site designer is ready to relate to the published or readily available data. To this material he or she will then bring a personal familiarity with the land in question, including an appreciation of the visually most significant aspects of the property in terms of views into the site from existing public roads, and outward prospects toward external landscape features (such as meadows, marshes, and hills).

Listed below are the factors that development designers should include in their site analyses. An asterisk (*) denotes that the particular resource should be considered to constitute part of the site's "Primary Conservation Area" described in Chapter 2. Other resources fall into the category of "Secondary Conservation Areas." If your local government or land trust has completed a community-wide natural resources inventory, that set of documents would be the best place to start. If such information has not already been compiled for your area, individuals or groups interested in eliminating that deficiency should consult *Where We Live: A Citizen's Guide to Conducting a Community Environmental Inventory* (Harker and Natter, 1994, Island Press).

1. Soils

When on-site sewage disposal is proposed, the most suitable soils for filtering effluent (whether from individual or community filter beds, or from "spray irrigation" systems) are one of the most significant resources around which development should be organized. These locations should be identified and targeted for such purposes, including "reserve areas" for use if primary areas even-

Figure 5-4. View across a protected meadow toward a group of new homes built at the edge of the woods. This view, from a township road, typifies the pattern of conservation and development represented by the examples illustrated in Chapter 7.

tually become saturated. The most favorable soils for septic disposal are those where the seasonal high water table or the impervious layer are four feet or more from the surface and which possess a medium texture, not being either too fine and silty (impeding drainage) or too coarse and gravelly (providing little filtration).

Other typical limiting conditions involve steepness or stoniness. *Medium-intensity soil survey maps* are available from local county agents of the USDA Natural Resource Conservation Service (NRCS), formerly the Soil Conservation Service (SCS). These maps

are usually quite accurate down to about two acres, meaning that areas smaller than this can differ from the mapped category by being either less favorable or more suitable for the intended purpose than the map portrays. This level of mapping is generally quite adequate for identifying, in a broad-brush manner, the "Potential Development Areas" shown on the drawings for the case-study sites in Chapter 7. For purposes of identifying soils that would be suitable for subsurface sewage disposal, the accuracy of the SCS maps can be either greater or lesser than the two-acre standard, depending on the internal consistency of individual soil types, which can vary from region to region. When dealing with soil types that are highly variable over short distances (such as the shallow-to-bedrock soils of northern New England, for example), special site-specific "high-intensity" soil surveys, accurate down to one-tenth of an acre, are strongly recommended at this stage in the design. (As this kind of detailed information will eventually be needed during the review process, when individual house sites and lot lines are proposed, such a requirement would not add to total project costs.)

On-site testing would also be desirable when the soil types occurring on a property are borderline in their suitability for sewage treatment. For example, in areas where septic system regulations require a minimum depth of 24 inches of *natural* soil above the impervious layer or the seasonal high water table, NRCS soil survey categories that include soils ranging from 18 to 36 inches in this vertical dimension will not be sufficiently detailed for the site designer, who will need the results of some on-site testing before he or she can do a good job of identifying viable house sites and lot boundaries. (This is true even when the septic systems are proposed to be situated within the undivided open space, because the locations of the best soils for such facilities play a role in determining where homes can or should be sited.)

Even when sewage will be discharged off site, the medium-intensity maps are a valuable resource, as they will show locations where basements can be built without flooding, and where *wetlands* can be expected. While they are not a substitute for a detailed wetlands analysis, these NRCS maps will show approximate locations of wetlands through their "very poorly drained" classification (which means that the land is occupied by standing water for at least several months every year). The next wettest soil class, "poorly drained," is a similarly good indicator of the presence of hydric soils where seasonal water tables close to the surface make cellars impractical and road construction somewhat more costly.

2. Wetlands*

Both tidal and freshwater wetlands should be identified, together with dry, upland buffer areas around them. To the extent that land in such buffer areas would be buildable under federal, state, or local regulations, full density credit would be granted for applicants to use in other locations on their sites. As noted in several other parts of this handbook, these buffers perform a number of significant functions—filtering stormwater runoff, providing critical habitat at the land–water interface, and offering opportunities for wildlife travel corridors and informal walking trails for the immediate neighborhood.

Although a good general idea of their location can be determined by consulting the medium-intensity soil survey maps described above, the National Wetlands Inventory maps published by the U.S. Fish and Wildlife Service of the Department of the Interior, and/or wetlands maps published by state planning or environmental agencies, an on-site delineation by a wetlands specialist will be necessary at some point in the process to provide greater detail. If the applicant simply wants to sketch a rough layout first, to get an approximate idea of the site's potential for open space design, these materials will probably be sufficient. However, if he or she wishes to submit a concept plan on which more detailed layouts will be closely based, on-site investigations by appropriate specialists are advisable. Since these investigations will eventually be required, they might as well be done as early in the design process as possible, to improve the accuracy of every planning step along the way.

3. Floodplains*

Although there is a long-standing tradition in some coastal areas and river valleys of permitting new structures elevated on specially engineered piers in areas prone to slow-moving floodwaters (but not in high-velocity floodways), this handbook recommends against continuation of that practice because it is inherently unsafe and is contrary to broadly accepted principles of sound planning. Because such areas are sometimes deemed to be buildable in those communities, a density bonus—in addition to full density credit—should be offered to encourage developers in those areas to set their buildings, whenever practicable, beyond the 100-year floodplain, as shown on maps published by the Federal Emergency Management Agency (FEMA). On unwooded sites, views to the water will remain essentially the same, while on parcels with intervening woodlands, views can be substantially opened by removing lower tree limbs, an accommodation to developers that strikes a better balance than would otherwise be achievable. Unless wetlands are also present, construction could begin fairly close to the edge of these floodplains. A more effective measure would be to amend zoning to require that new buildings be set back 50 to 100 feet from the edge of floodplains wherever feasible, with appropriate, internally transferable density credits to avoid the "takings" issue.

4. Slopes*

Due to their high potential for erosion and consequent sedimentation of watercourses and waterbodies, slopes over 25% should be avoided for clearing, regrading, or construction. Slopes of between 15 and 25% require special site planning and should also be avoided whenever practicable. Although slope maps are not published, they can be easily prepared by an engineer, planner, or landscape architect working from readily available topographic sheets printed by the U.S. Geological Survey.

5. Significant Wildlife Habitats

Habitats of threatened or endangered wildlife species form part of the "Primary Conservation Area" of any site and should be designed around and buffered. Likely travel corridors linking the areas used as food sources, homes, and breeding grounds should likewise be protected by including them in the conservation areas designated within the development. Locations that have been officially documented by state or county agencies should be identified on the development plan and buffered with additional open space for added protection whenever feasible. One of the greater challenges facing wildlife managers today involves minimizing the continued fragmentation of natural areas caused by new development, which at best often safeguards only isolated "islands" of habitat, without maintaining essential land and water connections needed on a regular basis by native animals. The importance of creating continuous greenways along waterbodies and watercourses lies primarily in their habitat conservation benefits (in addition to water quality protection and recreational trail opportunities). When isolated wildlife populations dwindle below a certain number (because their habitat has been fragmented and diminished to the point where it is unable to provide adequate food, water, and shelter), there is great danger that they will fall below their "minimum viable population" level and will disappear entirely from the locality.

Habitats of lesser significance should be placed in "Secondary Conservation Areas" to whatever extent is feasible, so that most of them will be safeguarded as well, reinforcing the "web of life" in the area's natural ecosystem. In both cases, of course, full density credit is allowed for all otherwise buildable land designated for conservation uses.

6. Woodlands

In areas where the majority of original forest has long been cleared away for commercial agriculture, woodlands may be described as remnants, often located in lower lying areas with relatively damp soils or on the steeper slopes. Despite—and perhaps because of—their small areal extent, these small woodlands play a particularly pivotal role for wildlife. Those woodlands growing on wetland soils or on steep slopes are addressed in items #2 and #3 above and should be designated as "Primary Conservation Areas" on the Site Analysis map. Those on higher, flatter terrain often consist of mature upland forest where the land is easily buildable. To the maximum extent practicable, such areas should become "Secondary Conservation Areas" to be designed around and spared the chainsaw and bulldozer blade. In other parts of the country where woodlands constitute the primary land cover, Secondary Conservation Areas might include the most mature stands, or places where unusual species or special habitats occur. In recent years concern has risen among conservation biologists and others who point out that decreases in the number of some species of "neo-tropical" songbirds (that summer in this country and migrate to Central and South America every fall) have been caused in part by both the reduction and the fragmentation of our temperate woodland habitat. Because of rising costs of woodland clearing and stump disposal—estimated to be $9,000 per acre by one Pennsylvania developer—and due to a growing preference among many homebuyers for wooded houselots offering greater privacy and requiring less maintenance, the goal of minimizing woodland clearing is likely to be abetted by market forces in the future.

The best sources for defining the extent of woodlands, hedgerows, or tree-lines are the vertical aerial photographs that are commonly available through county offices of the USDA Natural Resource Conservation Service. These may be ordered as enlargements at working scales (such as 1 inch = 100 feet) and are indispensable in accurately locating not only tree stands but even individual trees (in meadows or fields, or alongside roads). This kind of detail enables site designers to take maximum advantage of these landscape elements, which can add immense value and enjoyment to new neighborhoods. Even a simple line of trees between abandoned fields is a feature worth designing around—for its value in privacy screening, the welcome shade it casts in summer, and the limited habitat it provides. Aerial photos can also be helpful in locating the relative positions of coniferous and deciduous trees, even when the latter are in leaf, due to the darker coloration of the conifers as registered on black-and-white film.

7. Farmland

According to many environmental officials, commercial agriculture frequently contributes to water quality problems in the groundwater and surface waters of many farming counties. There are a variety of techniques that could be made better known to farmers about ways in which they could operate their farms for high crop yields in an environmentally sensitive manner. Spreading manure in appropriate amounts and at the right time, and allowing untilled filter strips to grow along streambanks and drainage channels, are a few such ways. Some would argue that conversion of farmland to residential development is environmentally preferable because it is relatively easy to control nutrients in runoff from new subdivisions. Apart from the debate on the environmental impact of commercial farming upon surface water and groundwater, it is relatively difficult to maintain viable agriculture on the relatively small parcels spared through conservation subdivision design, especially if the land continues in traditional low-value pursuits such as field corn, soybeans, or dairying operations. For this reason, farmland preservation is not one of the principal goals of this handbook.

Environmentalists in farming areas also point out that it is usually preferable to develop farmland rather than woodland because the latter provides a much richer and diverse habitat for wildlife. Also, most of the original forest in farmland areas has already been cleared away for commercial agriculture, creating hot, dry, well-drained monocultural fields in place of shady woodlands, wetlands, and natural meadows that support a wider variety of wildlife.

However, former fields that were managed in an environmentally unfriendly manner, with heavy doses of agrichemicals to boost monocultural crop yields, can be easily converted to wildlife meadows where many species of native grasses, wildflowers, and shrubs can provide cover, food, and habitat for birds and small mammals (as has been done at the Gwynedd Wildlife Preserve of the Natural Lands Trust in Upper and Lower Gwynedd Townships, Montgomery County, Pennsylvania). In metropolitan fringe areas it is also possible to retain some of this land in specialized high-value crops (such as vegetables, fruit, and nursery stock). Such arrangements seem to work best on larger sites when overall building densities are relatively low, in the range of one acre or more per dwelling. One example is the highly successful "Farm-view" development in Bucks County, Pennsylvania, where Realen Homes built on half-acre lots (half the size usually required under existing zoning), leaving 137 of its 300 tillable acres in crops (and donating that conservation area to a local land trust). This is the fastest-selling development in its price range in the county, largely because people are buying permanent views of open space when they purchase lots in this subdivision. Because they can offer relatively attractive terms (low rents just to cover property taxes, and long leases), land trusts are often in a better position than most rural landowners to set conditions regarding the use of pesticides, manure, and so on, and to be more selective about whom they lease to.

However, in areas with serious, viable commercial agriculture, scattered large-scale residential development of any kind (including "open space designs") should be discouraged, and prime farmland should be comprehensively preserved through mechanisms such as urban growth boundaries, the purchase of development rights, the transfer of development rights, and combinations and variations of these approaches (such as the "density exchange option," as practiced in Howard County, Maryland).

8. Historic, Archaeological, and Cultural Features

Published documentation on the location of buildings or other resources with historic, archaeological, or cultural significance is far from complete. Therefore, after reviewing official lists such as the National Register of Historic Places and the historic or archaeological site inventories compiled by state and county offices of historic preservation and cultural resources, landowners and local historians or historical groups should always be consulted. In most cases, old buildings, ruins, cellar holes, earthworks, stone walls, burial grounds, or other resources will be of local rather than county-wide or regional importance. Nevertheless, as with small tree groups or nesting areas of relatively common waterfowl, it is worthwhile to steer roads, houses, and lawns to other parts of the development site to avoid impacting them when other, more suitable, locations exist for these new uses.

Because even outstanding structures listed on the National Register are not protected from demolition (unless federal funds would be involved, or unless they are also governed by a strict local historic district ordinance), these resources possess none of the legal status accorded to environmentally sensitive wetlands or floodplains and therefore should be considered as part of the "Secondary Conservation Areas." Features such as stone walls marking old field patterns and sites of known battles would be classified in the same way—placed within the open space so that they may remain intact and buffered wherever appropriate.

As no building density value is lost through this approach, it makes good sense even from a business point of view. On a wooded tract in Spotsylvania County, Virginia, one developer located his lot lines and houses to avoid disturbing or too closely encroaching upon an old mill site and lengthy earthen trenches used during the Civil War. He later capitalized on these features by erecting large cast-iron historic marker signs describing their significance and by incorporating the historic theme into his marketing strategy. In the absence of any land-use regulations prohibiting development on top of these resources, staff at the Fredericksburg–Spotsylvania National Military Park have applauded his initiative. They are also supporting proposals to incorporate "conservation subdivision design standards" into new county regulations governing development of sites containing battle-related resources.

Similar steps are being taken in Currituck County, North Carolina, where the owner of a development parcel bordering Currituck Sound has expressed interest in utilizing these creative design techniques to avoid impacting a significant Woodland Era Native American site, while also increasing the number of new homes that would face onto the water across a waterside conservation area. County officials have expressed similar interest in incorporating these design principles into their new land-use codes, based upon a demonstration design for the above site prepared by the Natural Lands Trust as part of the Albemarle–Pamlico Estuarine Study (see Site G in Chapter 7).

9. Views Into and Out from the Site

This aspect of site design is often one of the most important from the perspectives of both the developer and the general public, who tend to see properties from different directions. Developers usually wish to maximize attractive views outward from potential homesites, while the public typically desires that new development be as visually inconspicuous as possible. Although these two objectives can easily conflict, it is often possible for development to be sited or buffered in such a way that everybody's principal interests are accommodated.

From a developer's point of view, it is desirable for sales purposes to maximize the number of homes with attractive views. This can often be achieved in creative ways that are less disruptive than the results produced through conventional platting. In areas with visually prominent ridges on which homes may be perched, Secondary Conservation Areas might include the ridgetops, requiring that new development be located sufficiently below the crest so that the horizon will continue to be defined by the ridgeline, rather than by rooflines. In situations where this is not feasible due to steeply sloping hillsides or parcel configura-

tions, houses should be designed with a low profile, and sufficient woodlands should be retained (or planted) around and behind them to soften their visual impact. Large clear-cuts to open up panoramic views should also be prohibited, and cutting should be limited to "view tunnels" from principal rooms and/or thinning of lower limbs to create "view holes" through the foliage.

In lakefront, riparian, or coastal locations offering views of waterbodies or wetlands, the design procedures recommended in this handbook would generally allow a greater number of such lots, with views through a wooded greenway where lower limbs may be removed so that the water (or wetlands) would be visible from living room windows. In addition to these "view lots," a very large proportion of the remaining lots in a well-designed conservation subdivision will abut or face onto other types of open space, such as commons, greens, ponds, meadows, and woodlands. Given the options of a conventional development, where one-third of the lots have immediate views of the water and the other two-thirds have immediate views of their neighbors' picture windows or backyards, and a conservation subdivision, where the vast majority of lots enjoy views of water, meadows, greens, woods, or other natural features, the choice seems clear. The larger total number of "view lots" in a conservation subdivision outweighs the somewhat filtered and less immediate water views available through greenway buffers. Also, the high proportion of interior lots with views of other kinds of open space makes those lots much more desirable than they would otherwise be—if simply facing other houselots.

This design approach benefits not only developers and realtors but also future residents and the general public. Greenway buffers provide the best of both worlds, helping to screen new waterfront development while not obstructing important views. One of the best examples of this is Woodlake in Midlothian, Virginia, 18 miles southwest of Richmond. Home sales have been brisk in both waterfront and interior locations in this award-winning development. It uses a 75-foot deep greenway running along the edge of the water, between Woodlake's most expensive homes ($650,000 to

$700,000) and the Swift Creek Reservoir, to provide a delightful walking or bicycling experience for both abuttors and residents of interior lots (where single-family homes sell for as little as $80,000). The water is clearly visible through the wooded buffer from all abutting homes, while habitat and water quality are protected to a much higher degree than would have been the case with conventional development.

Recognizing the economic value of maintaining clean, clear water in the Inland Bays (in terms of tourism, recreation, fisheries, and real estate), a growing number of realtors have joined conservationists in advocating greenway buffers for subdivisions as well as for PRDs in Sussex County, Delaware. The highly successful Woodlake example demonstrates that providing water views and greenway buffers are not mutually exclusive, and it suggests a new planning principle for waterside development: each site should be laid out with greenway buffers, *as if the adjacent waterbody were a reservoir.*

As pointed out in item #7 above, views of preserved farmland can also add value to new houselots. And to the extent that home sites are located away from existing public roads, at the far edges of fields as seen from those thoroughfares, some rural character can be maintained with each new development.

10. Aquifers and Their Recharge Areas

The term "aquifer" refers to underground water reserves occupying billions of tiny spaces between sand grains and other soil particles, including gravel. They are "recharged" with surface water seeping downward through coarse sandy or gravelly deposits, and/or at low points in the landscape where wetlands frequently occur. Present groundwater levels in many farming areas are several feet lower than they were before drainage ditches and tiles were installed to make formerly wet ground suitable for commercial agriculture. These areas are buildable today for structures without basements and where sewage is disposed of through public sewers or with central sewerage linked with a private disposal facility (such as spray irrigation) located on higher, drier ground on other parts of the site (or on a neighboring property). Since stormwater retention ponds often dip into areas of high groundwater, runoff entering them can recharge the underlying aquifer with dissolved pollutants (typically excess nutrients from agricultural or lawn fertilizers), requiring special buffering along drainage swales to remove as much of these substances as possible.

Although many aquifer recharge areas consist of soils that are not inherently unbuildable (such as excessively drained sands and gravels, and certain of the less severe hydric soils), they should be avoided for construction when other parts of the property are available and are less constrained by environmental factors. As with all other kinds of buildable land that are placed into natural open space in a creative development plan, full density credit should generally be allowed for these soils (when their buildability is not in question, and typically when wastewater is proposed to be treated in a central location or off site). When it is not feasible to rearrange the development pattern within the site to minimize such impacts, density transfers to neighboring properties (under a "landowner compact" agreement between two or more adjoining landowners, or under a TDR plan involving nonadjacent parcels) should be thoroughly explored. Sometimes these strategies can be combined, each playing a partial role in the process of creative development and land conservation.

Integrating the Information Layers

Once all the pertinent features have been identified, located, and evaluated in terms of their significance, they need to be drawn onto overlay sheets (typically tracing paper) and looked at together. Because ten sheets of even the lightest tracing paper would be too dense to show all the underlying information, even if they were placed on a light table (or taped to a large window on a sunny day), it is recommended that several types of features be drawn onto the same sheet—preferably features that do not coincide in terms of their location on the site. A composite map can eventually be prepared by looking at all the information layers together to see the overall pattern of potential conservation areas.

This is essentially the same basic technique used by generations of geographers and planners; it is sometimes referred to as "sieve mapping" because all the most suitable land for development becomes apparent as those areas that drop through the "sieve" of information layers. All *buildable* land will be in those areas *not* limited by the basic constraints posed by the "Primary Conservation Areas" (wetlands, floodplains, and steep slopes), and these will emerge clearly as the appropriate sheets are placed together. (This technique was substantially expanded and refined in the 1960s by Ian McHarg and given the name "ecological planning" in his widely acclaimed book *Design With Nature.* See also *The Living Landscape* by Frederick Steiner.)

After integrating those information layers, which typically comprise only a small fraction of any site, the remaining land is examined with regard to the other layers. Because two of these layers include farmland and woodland, it is obvious that all the remaining land to be considered for development will usually be entirely covered by one or more resource types. This is not a problem because these are simply information layers at this point, and *there is a basic commitment in this design approach to accommodate the entire amount of development that would otherwise be legally possible under conventional design.* As will be discussed in the next section, these other resource types must be prioritized to determine which are the most critical, significant, or irreplaceable. Those that meet such tests are placed into "Secondary Conservation Areas." This typically consumes no more than half the buildable land on the site, leaving the other half for homes, yards, and streets.

Therefore, the two steps of "integrating information layers" and "prioritizing objectives" are not entirely separate and sequential. It makes sense to look at the information layers first, then begin thinking about priorities for conservation, and then revisit the information layers to prepare a composite map showing the location of both Primary and Secondary Conservation Areas.

Prioritizing Objectives

As a rule of thumb, those features listed above with an asterisk—wetlands, floodplains, and slopes—take first priority for inclusion in the designated open space, as they represent highly sensitive environmental resources that are generally considered to be unbuildable in a legal sense, in a practical sense, or for reasons of common sense. As mentioned above, because of their limitations or inherent unsuitability for development, they should be placed in "Primary Conservation Areas," the first type of open space to be drawn on any site plan.

Within the second broad category of open space, called "Secondary Conservation Areas," resources vary more widely in importance, vulnerability, or fragility. Within each type of resource there are examples of *greater and lesser significance,* whether one is looking at woodlands (from large and/or mature stands or unusual species, to woods that are young, diseased, already thinned out, or degraded by invasive vines, for example), farmland (soils rated from "prime" to "of local significance"), or sites of historic, archaeological, or cultural interest (from inclusion on a federal list, to a typical pristine example of local vernacular building traditions, to a much altered older house missing many original features).

Within the elements or features listed above that are not marked with an asterisk, those ranking among the top of their category (such as *mature* woodland or *prime* farmland) should always be included in the open space protected as "Secondary Conservation Areas." When decisions must be made regarding the sacrifice of one resource to preserve another (such as developing fields to save woodlands, or vice versa), they should be based upon broad township-wide or county-wide considerations. For example, if one resource type is scarcer or more unusual than another, or if it contributes to biodiversity or water quality in a more compelling way, that could provide the basis for deciding which is to be spared.

In short, *priorities for conserving or developing certain kinds of resources should be based upon an understanding of what is more special, unique, irreplaceable, environmentally valuable, historic, scenic, etc., compared with other similar features, or compared to different kinds of resources altogether.* Although this process will always contain some subjectivity, a ratings approach can help to reduce inconsistent and arbitrary choices. Within each category it is often fairly obvious which features are the most worthy of preservation. The harder decisions usually involve comparisons between different categories, such as whether a small isolated woodland or a historic house should be designed around, when it is impossible to save both.

It is the overall recommendation of this handbook that natural areas generally take precedence over human artifacts, except in situations where the latter are clearly more exceptional, such as most archaeological sites. The reason is that buildings can often be reconstructed or moved, and they can certainly be photographed and documented with measured drawings. On the other hand, it is more difficult to re-create a wetland or a mature forest because of the interrelationships among plants, animals, soil, and water that comprise each natural site. There is also a growing body of evidence that it may be nearly impossible, without intensive management, to regenerate a mature deciduous woodland in the mid-Atlantic region, due to invasive vines and alien species of shrubs and trees (such as Oriental bittersweet, rosa multiflora, Japanese honeysuckle, wild grape, Tartarian honeysuckle, and Norway maple,) that seed themselves and infest newly afforesting areas. Of course, in other areas with more numerous and significant historic locations, such as pastures and ridges that once witnessed major Civil War conflicts, battle-related resources could take precedence for conservation over other types of buildable land, such as prime farmland or mature woodlands.

There will generally be special reasons in each township or county for favoring one resource type over another. In New England where forests cover most of the land, and fields are relatively uncommon, the most widely favored approach is to locate new development among the trees and to leave farmland intact. In much of the Mid-Atlantic region between southern New Jersey and the Chesapeake Bay, the reverse landscape pattern exists, providing a logical rationale for a policy preference that is exactly opposite of the one which New Englanders typically choose. Taken in its own context, each policy makes sense for the area in which it is applied.

To sum up, in the Mid-Atlantic states where the Natural Lands Trust is active, it is recommended that preference generally be given to natural areas over human-made features in the landscape, and that within the natural world, buildable woodlands be afforded greater protection than buildable farmland when one must decide which to favor. (In addition to their greater wildlife habitat value and stormwater filtering capacity, woodlands typically do not pollute watercourses and waterbodies as do farm fields with their greater nutrient loads, pesticides, and erosion–sedimentation problems.) This recommendation should not be interpreted as favoring natural areas, especially woodlands, in any situation, for there may be occasions on specific sites where cropland conservation and historic preservation could assume relatively greater importance than woodland habitat protection.

DESIGN STAGE

After completing the somewhat tedious but essential steps involved in the "background stage" described above, it is time to start *the four-step design process,* which is where the fun begins. Since the quality of the design result depends in large measure upon the accuracy and completeness of the information layers prepared previously, the findings on those sheets are critically important, and the majority of time and effort is typically spent on that background stage. Once this information is in place, it is a relatively easy process to create a conservation subdivision design, because the overall pattern of open space and development appropriate for each site is frequently rather obvious when the various layers are collated.

At this point, readers are encouraged to jump ahead to examine the site plans in Chapter 7, where the recommended approach to designing conservation subdivisions is graphically illustrated in a step-by-step manner. It is generally advisable to look at those drawings in conjunction with the textual description of the steps that makes up the remainder of this chapter.

If the maximum legal development density has not yet been calculated (on the basis of wording in the zoning ordinance relating to areas that must be excluded), or through the "yield plan" approach (in which a realistic conventional layout has been drawn), this should be done at this time. Of particular relevance here is the unbuildable land shown on the "Primary Conservation Areas" map. These areas (e.g., wetlands) should be excluded from the yield plan houselots to the extent that zoning restrictions normally prohibit them from being considered for density. The number of dwellings that would ordinarily be buildable on the property is then adopted as the number to be accommodated in the conservation design. Examples of yield plans can be seen in Chapter 7.

The following four subsections describe the basic steps involved in designing conservation subdivisions. They are applicable to both major schools of thinking current in rural planning discussions today: proponents of "rural clustering" and advocates of "neo-traditional" hamlets and villages. Whether one's design preference is for more organic layouts and loosely configured groups of houses, or for the more formal streetscapes and street patterns associated with traditional neighborhood development (based closely upon local historic precedents), the "four-step approach" described on the following pages makes good sense. However, in the case of neo-traditional village or town design, Steps Two and Three are generally reversed since the design of streetscapes and squares is of greater significance than the location of house sites (which predominate more in lower density rural conservation subdivisions, where lots tend to be larger than those in village layouts).

The following descriptions are relatively brief for two reasons. First, their brevity reflects the fact that the conceptual design stage is typically much less time-consuming than the information collection and analysis stage. Second, the text is supplemented with explanatory illustrations in Chapter 7, where seven different sites are evaluated for their conservation and development potential, culminating in broad concept plans showing proposed locations of houselots, streets, greens, commons, meadows, woodlands, and other types of open space.

Step One: Identifying All Potential Conservation Areas

The heart of the design process can be summarized as *four sequential steps* beginning with the all-important first one: identifying the conservation land that should potentially be protected.

These features of the property, as mentioned above, consist of the unbuildable wetlands, floodplains, and steep slopes (the "Primary Conservation Areas"), to which are added that part of the buildable uplands that are most sensitive environmentally, most significant historically or culturally, most scenic, or which possess unusual attributes that cause them to stand out from the rest of the property as areas that the average observer would miss most if they disappeared under new houselots and streets.

As mentioned earlier in this handbook, this is the general approach used by designers of highly successful golf course developments, with the basic distinction that here we are advocating preservation of natural areas as fields, meadows, and woodlands and the creation of informal public open space in the form of neighborhood commons instead of fairways, sand traps, and putting greens. Whether one is interested in building homes around a facility for a single sport or arranging them in a parklike setting full of natural features that all can enjoy (including wildlife), the only practical way is to begin by mentally defining the open space first.

When the site plan is first sketched, the site designer should not be reluctant to include more land than he or she thinks will eventually be designated as open space, so that no potentially desirable area is prematurely left out, excluding it from consideration in the design process. If zoning provisions allow one to save about half the site by reducing lot sizes from two acres to one acre (or from one acre to 20,000 square feet), for exploratory design purposes it is recommended that two-thirds of the parcel be tentatively sketched as conservation land, at least initially. If zoning allows houselot reductions of only 25%, one should aim for 35% to 40% conservation in the first "rough cut" on sketch paper.

This exercise will quickly identify where the core areas of future development are likely to lie on the property. One should then work outward from those cores, being careful to recommend for development only those other areas that appear to be least important to conserve, looking at the site as a whole (including its relationship to neighboring parcels, as described in the next chapter). This analysis may suggest to the site designer a creative way to reduce the "development footprint" through a more compact layout than the community's clustering regulations would ordinarily allow, while saving additional land that most people would appreciate being protected and at the same time securing full legal

density for the client. If so, that possibility should be further discussed, first with the client, then possibly with a realtor, and then the planning staff, all on a tentative basis before presenting it as an option at a public meeting. (There are some fairly easy ways to reduce the extent of the developed area without sacrificing any marketability, livability, or safety. These concern building setbacks and lot depth, which are discussed below in the subsection on Step Four.)

Step Two: Locating the House Sites

As with golf course developments, the next design step is to identify potential house site locations. Since a developer's fundamental motivation is to make money by selling either houselots or lots with houses newly built on them, and since it is well known that most people prefer (and are often willing to pay extra) to see open space from their windows, it makes economic sense to create as many "view lots" as possible and to ensure that usable open space is located within convenient walking distance from other houses in the subdivision.

One obvious way to maximize the number of view lots is to minimize their width and to maximize the livability of the homes built on them through creative modifications (such as designing houses with a windowless side wall virtually abutting one side lot line, and another sidewall containing windows facing onto a wider side yard—and the "blind" side of the next house). Such arrangements enable the development portion of the site to be utilized nearly as efficiently as if semi-detached ("twin") houses were involved, while offering buyers genuinely detached homes. Where market conditions are favorable, however, semi-detached and multi-family dwellings should be considered. Those containing just two or three units can often be designed to resemble large single-family homes, through careful attention to their bulk, massing, window arrangement, and "front" doorway locations (which can sometimes be internalized inside common entry vestibules, or situated on the sidewalls).

Another way to increase the number of houses with views is to design several flag-shaped lots (sometimes called "pork chop lots" or "pipestem lots" because of the long narrow strip of land connecting them with the street). These lots are especially useful as a design tool in odd corners of a neighborhood, such as at the end of a cul-de-sac or where a road takes a sharp turn. This kind of lot is essentially a variation on the triangular or wedge-shaped "pie lots" common in these situations, but because they need to be only wide enough to accommodate a driveway, they can have minimal street frontage (usually 20 to 25 feet is sufficient). And since their shape in the area where the house is situated tends to be more or less rectangular, they often provide more usable yard space than does the less efficient "pie lot" alternative.

Although flag-shaped lots are most appropriate in relatively low-density subdivisions where the overall density is one acre or more per dwelling, they can be useful at higher densities and should generally be permitted in all developments, with certain restrictions. To curb potential abuses, they should be limited to no more than 15 or 20 percent of the total number of lots (for instance), and when the "flag" portion is less than 10,000 or 15,000 square feet the planning board or commission should be authorized to require adequate visual screening between adjoining lots (particularly those that share a front/back boundary).

Although it is rarely possible to design layouts so that every house has a view over major open space, it is often feasible to give nearly every house a view of at least a minor open space, such as a small neighborhood common or village green, or several acres of trees and grass around a small pond doubling as a stormwater retention facility, attractively landscaped with native species such as red-twig dogwood shrubs. To the extent that residents of these homes live only a short walk away from a larger open space, hopefully including a network of informal trails through woodlands or around wildflower meadows, the neighborhood will offer much more than standard subdivisions (and also more to the non-golfing majority than do golf course developments).

According to research conducted at the University of Washington by zoologist Gordon Orians, most people's ideal dwelling location consists of a home set on a rise of ground offering long views over parklike terrain dotted with large trees with broad crowns (not unlike many golf courses). As Harvard biologist E.O. Wilson has observed,

> It happens that this archetype fits a tropical savanna of the kind prevailing in Africa, where humanity evolved for several million years. Primitive people living there are thought to have been most secure in open terrain, where the wide vista allowed them to search for food while watching for enemies. Possessing relatively frail bodies, early humans also needed cover for retreat, with trees to climb if pursued (Wilson 1994).

These possibly innate landscape preferences provide yet another reason supporting the appropriateness of the conservation subdivision approach, which enables development to be designed around site features that people generally like to see and be around.

It is clear that identifying house sites before lot lines and streets allows building locations to be carefully selected so that natural features worth preserving can be avoided, including large trees and prominent rock outcrops, as well as historic or cultural features such as stone walls, cellar holes, battle trenches, and archaeological remains. Because it is not always possible to draw the Secondary Conservation Areas sufficiently large to include all these features, some of them will probably fall into those parts of the site slated for development. However, the flexibility of this design approach enables the majority of such features to be "designed around."

Step Three: Designing Street Alignments and Trails

After the conservation land has been at least tentatively identified and potential homesites sketched in, the third logical step is to determine the best way to access every residence with a street system.

Areas with relatively level or rolling topography pose few street design challenges from an engineering standpoint, the major considerations being to avoid crossing wetlands and to minimize the length (and cost) of new access streets. There are further considerations from an environmental perspective, such as avoiding large trees, mature tree stands, or wildlife habitats that might happen to be within the proposed development area, or which could be in part of the open space that must be traversed to access the proposed house sites. Sometimes it is possible to split the travel lanes so that they curve apart forming an elongated, boulevard-style island between them, where a certain large tree or other natural or historic feature may be preserved and given visual prominence. (When the preservation of large trees is involved, it is essential that the entire area under the canopy's outer "drip line" be kept undisturbed from heavy construction equipment, which can easily cause permanent damage to root systems. To achieve this, temporary construction fences should be erected along such drip lines until all construction activity has been finished in the tree's immediate location.)

From an aesthetic and speed control perspective, it is important to avoid long straight street segments. Curving roads in an informal rural cluster layout, or shorter straight segments connected by 90-degree and 135-degree bends in a more formal or traditional town-like arrangement, are preferable. (Variations that combine elements of these approaches are also possible, such as short curvilinear segments terminating in frequent intersections where the choices are to turn left or right, thereby making it more difficult for motorists to travel at excessive speeds. Such practices, also including use of Y-shaped intersections, are a hallmark of many late nineteenth century subdivisions designed by Frederick Law Olmsted, such as in Brookline, Massachusetts, and Riverside, Illinois.)

Whenever possible, street systems should be designed so that their curvature or alignment produces *"terminal vistas"* of open space elements, such as village greens, water features, meadows, or playing fields. This technique will maximize the visual impact of such areas so that residents and visitors will correctly perceive the conservation emphasis that has guided the development design and recognize the subdivision as contributing positively to the community's open space goals (see Fig. 5-1, as well as the conservation development designs appearing in the case studies in Chapter 7).

The use of *"reverse curves"*[1] in street design is advised because of their grace and beauty. However, they should be employed in conjunction with relatively long horizontal curve radii (at least 250 feet) and on streets where traffic speed will not generally exceed 30 mph. The common prohibition against reverse curves in municipal street standards is a carryover from the highway design manuals on which many such ordinances were based. While reverse curves without intervening straight sections (or tangents) can be unsafe for high-speed traffic, a completely different situation exists for local access streets in residential subdivisions.

---

[1]*Reverse curves* are consecutive left and right curves of a street in a serpentine fashion without a straight segment separating them.

Hardly anything destroys the grace of a street curving through a rural "conservation subdivision" more than the introduction of long, straight tangents between curves.

Another design approach that has proven to be of value in both land conservation and real estate marketing is the use of *"single-loaded" streets.* This is a technical term describing streets having houses on only one side. When lots are trimmed down in width (with homes designed more compactly to fit onto them easily, as illustrated in Appendix D), developers can easily reserve certain street lengths for single-loading—such as alongside conservation areas or around village greens or commons—without increasing their average houselot to street length ratios. In other words, the street savings gained by reducing lot widths can be used to create single-loaded situations in other parts of the subdivision, where homes can be allowed to face onto open space.

Single-loading provides homebuyers with views that are more uplifting than their neighbors' garage doors staring back at them. It also provides all subdivision residents with welcome views of their conservation land as they drive, bike, jog, or walk through their neighborhood on a daily basis, increasing everyone's quality of life as well as their property values. Such designs can be seen in most of the case studies illustrated in Chapter 7. Sales records in subdivisions featuring single-loaded streets show that homes located there sell faster and for premium prices compared with similar houses elsewhere in the development. Not surprisingly, when all the streets in a subdivision are double-loaded (as is often the case in many unimaginatively designed "cluster" developments), conservation areas are essentially hidden behind continuous rows of houselots and the streetscape takes on a very ordinary appearance, much like those found in conventional "checkerboard" subdivisions.

One of my favorite ways to employ single-loaded streets in open-field situations is to use them in creating *"foreground mead-ows"* bordering the public road that serves the development. Upon entering a conservation subdivision laid out in this manner, one's first view would be of a wildflower meadow (or horse pasture) with homes located at its far end and facing this landscape feature (see Figures 5-4 and 5-5). If such a meadow or pasture were bordered instead by a double-loaded street curving around behind it, the view from the public road, the subdivision street, and the meadow would be of house-backs, typically dominated by sliding glass doors, pressure-treated wood decks, and asymmetrical arrangements of windows (perhaps further graced by swing sets and tool sheds as well). Not only do most new houses look far better from the front (where builders spend extra money creating "curb appeal") but residents also prefer the backyard privacy provided by not turning their rear walls toward the public road in this far-too-typical manner.

Whatever layout approach is taken, every effort should be made to *connect each street with another* so that dead ends will be minimized. Interconnected streets provide easier and safer access for fire engines, ambulances, school buses, and garbage trucks, while distributing traffic more evenly and helping to avoid conditions where certain residential streets become "collectors" with everyone in the entire development funnelling through them. In circumstances where cul-de-sacs are unavoidable (typically for topographic reasons), they should always be provided with pedestrian and bike linkages to other nearby streets or to a neighborhood trail system. Where space permits they should also be designed with a central island where existing trees have been preserved or where native specie trees, shrubs, and wildflowers can be planted. Where additional off-street parking is needed, these cul-de-sacs can also function as well-treed "parking courts."

Streets serving new developments should, whenever possible, be designed to *connect with adjoining properties* that are potentially developable in the future. Although many developers strongly re-

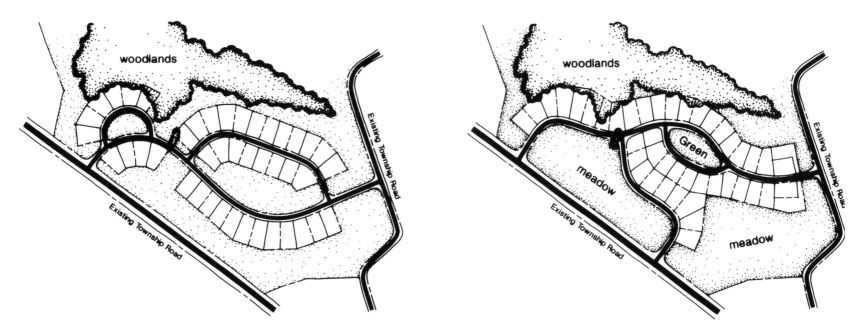

Figure 5-5. *Foreground meadows* offer special opportunities to provide attractive buffers between new homes and existing thoroughfares bordering the subdivision. Following this approach, homes located along a single-loaded street typically look out over a meadow, so that the view from the township road (or rural highway) is one of a large grassy area and house fronts, which are always visually more appealing than rear elevations. This arrangement also ensures that backyard privacy will not be compromised by house backs facing onto busy thoroughfares, and it avoids the suburban artifice of the landscaped berm (which usually symbolizes a design failure). In the above two examples, where a typical "suburban cluster" approach on the left is contrasted with a "rural conservation design" with the same number of houselots, it is worth noting that the preferred approach on the right does not require any additional street length, nor does it utilize lots that are narrower. Another unusual feature, not central to the concept of foreground meadows, is the use of two flag lots, on the extreme right, paired with two frontage lots, so that all four homes would face the existing township road across a smaller grassy expanse. This provides a slightly more formal and attractive secondary entrance to the subdivision than would a view of side yards. (See also Fig. 5-4 for a perspective sketch of a foreground meadow.)

sist such connections, preferring to market their houses as being in self-contained neighborhoods, the lack of connecting streets between developments ultimately frustrates normal travel between neighborhoods, forcing everyone back out onto the township's or county's principal road system to travel to their friends' homes in adjacent subdivisions. In most of the examples shown in Chapter 7, cul-de-sacs have been provided with "stub-street" extensions to the adjoining properties to facilitate future connections.

Step Four: **Drawing in the Lot Lines**

The fourth and final step is the easiest—once the conservation areas have been delineated, the house sites located, and the road alignments determined. At this point in the design process, drawing in the lot lines is usually little more than a formality (one that is unnecessary in condominium developments where all land is jointly owned). Clearly the most significant aspects of a development, from the viewpoint of future residents, are how their houses relate to the open space, to each other, and to the street. Lot lines are the least important element in the development design process, yet they and the street pattern are typically the first items to be set down on paper.

Maintaining livability on the somewhat smaller lots needed in conservation subdivisions does not pose much of a design problem in zoning districts where the normal required lot size is one or two acres. The challenge increases as density rises and lot sizes become more compact. As mentioned above in the subsection describing Step Two, lot lines in high-density single-family developments can be drawn fairly close to side walls with few or no windows, enabling larger and more usable side yards to be provided on the opposite side of the house. This approach can be taken further by building on one of the side lot lines ("zero-lot line" construction), and these lot lines can follow zig-zag patterns (so-called "Z-lots").

The issue of appropriate lot depth is related directly to the presence or absence of open space along rear lot lines. When conservation land is located immediately behind them, there is good justification for shortening proposed houselots since the open space visually extends the perceived depth of backyards.

Therefore, a logical argument can be made to reduce both the width and depth of lots where houses are located off-center (i.e., closer to one side line, thereby maximizing one side yard) and where lots abut conservation areas behind them. In developments with public sewerage or with private central treatment facilities (such as "spray irrigation"), where zoning densities allow one dwelling per 20,000 square feet of land, 75% open space can be achieved by designing houselots of 5,000 square feet. These smaller, village-scale lots are often deemed to be more desirable than conventional half-acre lots by several distinct groups of potential homebuyers—such as empty-nesters, young couples, and single parents with a child or two—who want some private outdoor living space but who also wish to minimize their yard maintenance responsibilities. These lots are especially popular when they back up to protected open space, which psychologically enlarges the dimensions of the actual lot.

Architects, landscape architects, and site designers have for many years recognized that the most efficient use of a houselot occurs when the house is located "off-center and up front." Equal side yards generally produce two functionally useless areas on lots narrower than 80 feet, and front yards are practically useless in any case because they are almost always within the public view. Unless homes are located along heavily travelled streets with considerable traffic noise, there is little need for deep front setbacks to provide buffering. Placing homes where front porches or stoops are within conversational distance of sidewalks helps create conditions for friendlier neighborhoods, where passersby can exchange pleasantries with porch-sitters on weekend afternoons or summer evenings. The illustrations in Appendix C, "Detailed Houselot Designs at Higher Net Densities," show how houses, driveways, garages, and livable backyards could be accommodated even on the smallest lot size recommended in this handbook for single-family detached houses (in Site C, where base zoning is two dwellings per acre and where lots of between 5,000 and 6,000 square feet could be utilized to conserve three-quarters of the site as open space).

Note: The above sequence of steps may be modified in situations where a more formal, "neo-traditional," or village-type layout is desired. In such cases Step Two becomes the location of streets and squares, followed by the location of house sites. Whereas the relationship between homes and open space is of the greatest importance in conservation subdivisions, the relationship between buildings, streets, and squares is the dominant design consideration in the neo-traditional approach to site design. Both design approaches place more emphasis on the designation of public open space and on the provision of sidewalks, footpaths, and trails—in an effort to foster a pedestrian-friendly community atmosphere—compared with conventional suburban "cookie-cutter" layouts offering just houselots and streets.

Linking Conservation Lands in Future Subdivisions to Create an Interconnected Open Space Network: A Greener Vision

AREA-WIDE MAPS FOR CONSERVATION AND DEVELOPMENT

From the standpoint of people who are interested in how their township or county will look and feel in 10 or 20 years—as a place in which to live, raise families, and conduct business or vacation—*possibly the most important aspect of the development approach known as conservation subdivision design is the opportunity it offers to create an interconnected network of protected lands.*

Rather than simply preserving isolated pockets of greenery here and there, which do little to protect water quality and which are of relatively little use to wildlife, people in your community have within their reach the chance *to create a true fabric of open space that flows among any number of new subdivisions, as more and more properties are converted from fields and woodlands to residential developments.*

Without such a comprehensive approach, wildlife habitat will continue to dwindle and become increasingly fragmented and nonfunctional, opportunities to connect informal neighborhood trails into an area-wide greenway system will be lost forever, and water quality could be jeopardized over the longer term.

Open space connections will not be automatically preserved

simply by following the general design approach described and illustrated in this handbook, on such a site-by-site basis.

The *critical unifying element,* one that can be readily created by paid professional planning staff working together with landowners, developers, conservationists, and state agency officials, *is a tool called an area-wide map of conservation and development.* This tool is essentially a composite map that brings together all the published information and the data, which are readily available from state and federal agencies, pertaining to natural features and other limiting factors that should be avoided when first sketching the broad "footprint" of future development on individual properties. Although all this information is on the public record and is freely available to those who are interested, the task of "designing around" such elements would be made considerably easier if these data were collected and charted on a series of area-wide maps that together would ultimately cover one's entire township or corner of the county. Whether the appropriate geographical divisions for these maps should be based upon watershed "divides," the convenient grid that is the basis for U.S. Geological Survey maps, or some other factors is not important to decide here.

The information that should be recorded on these area-wide maps includes the following items:

1. Wetlands (tidal and fresh)

2. The 100-year floodplains (high velocity zones and areas with only slow-moving shallow water)

3. Steep slopes (25 percent or greater)

4. Habitats of species that are endangered, threatened, or considered by state or federal agencies to be significant at the state or county level, and other ecologically unique or special areas

5. Historic, archaeological, or cultural sites listed on the National Register of Historic Places, and on state or county inventories

6. Active farmland with soil rated as prime or of "state-wide importance" by the USDA Natural Resource Conservation Service

7. High-yielding aquifers and their recharge areas

8. Woodlands of a size that makes them locally significant, and mature woodlands of one acre or more in extent

All these items should be mapped separately (including related resources grouped together above, such as fresh and tidal wetlands, which are typically regulated in different ways).

The usefulness of this tool to site designers would be greatly increased if these maps also showed *existing tax parcels,* so that potential development sites could be easily located with respect to the natural features and other constraints mapped on them. *Although area-wide maps cannot show all the features that are important for site designers, they would provide a basic understanding of the most critical elements existing on each site, especially as they relate to similar elements on adjoining parcels that may also become developed with open space designs in the future.*

In addition to these elements, others that should be considered by site designers—but which cannot be incorporated into area-wide maps—include (as mentioned in earlier chapters) views into and out from the subject property and the landowner's own knowledge of the land, including the location of areas that are special to him or her on a local or personal level, even though they might not show up on county, state, or federal maps and inventories.

After the ten data layers listed in Chapter 5 have been compiled, the broad outlines of an *open space network* should begin to emerge. Since 50% of the buildable land on any development site can often be conserved simply by grouping new development in a more compact, efficient, and neighborly manner—without reducing overall density or profitability—at least half of each potential development parcel could be shaded green on the new Area-wide Maps of Conservation and Development without adversely affecting landowners or developers.

The great advantage of taking a broader view of future patterns of development and conservation is the opportunity it offers to pre-identify the most logical and fruitful ways of connecting conservation lands

in new subdivisions. From the perspective of maintaining *functional habitats*—which include travel corridors for native wildlife as they move from nests or burrows to areas where they hunt, feed, or breed—it is essential that natural areas be linked together to the greatest extent feasible. The resulting greenways frequently offer an additional benefit that is potentially very useful to realtors and residents alike: the creation of informal walking trails through woodlands, or alongside meadows, creeks, or other natural features. The demonstrated sales advantage of homes that are located adjacent to or near open space—including greenways—constitutes convincing evidence that this is a development pattern that is sound economically as well as environmentally. (Please see Appendix F, "Sample of Real Estate Ads Mentioning Proximity of Homes to Greenways.")

Inspired by the first edition of this handbook, planners in Orange County, North Carolina (the Chapel Hill area), prepared county-wide computerized maps showing the location of lands that they have classified as possessing the characteristics of either "Primary Conservation Areas" or "Secondary Conservation Areas," using a variation on the criteria offered in Chapter 5. These maps, which are a recent product of the county's geographical information system (GIS), are intended to serve as guidelines to developers using the new "flexible development" zoning and subdivision regulations (which were based on the model language contained in the handbook's appendix). Their county-wide network of potential conservation lands is illustrated in Figure 6-1. Figure 6-2 provides a visual impression of the way that various elements of the rural landscape could be protected in one neighborhood if several adjacent parcels were developed according to the conservation design principles described in this handbook.

On a more local level, officials in West Manchester Township, York County, Pennsylvania, have prepared overlay maps showing the preferred location of conservation areas with respect to existing tax parcel boundaries. By adding this information layer to its land ownership maps, the township is effectively showing each

property owner where the conservation land should ideally be located in any new subdivision subject to its new open space zoning provisions. This map represents a "rebuttable presumption" that the conservation areas should be laid out in this manner. Subdivision applicants may propose other configurations, but variations

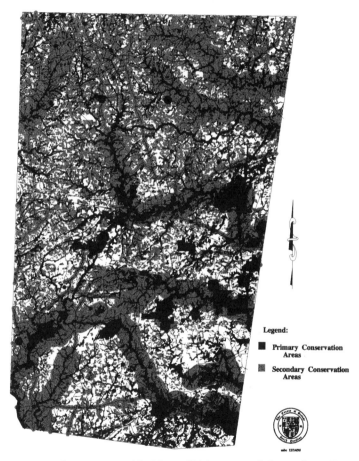

Legend:
■ Primary Conservation Areas
▨ Secondary Conservation Areas

Figure 6-1. The county-wide Map of Primary and Secondary Conservation Areas prepared by the Orange County (North Carolina) Planning Department, using its computer mapping capability, provides developers and their site designers with the information they need to lay out conservation subdivisions that will ultimately produce an interconnected network of open space.

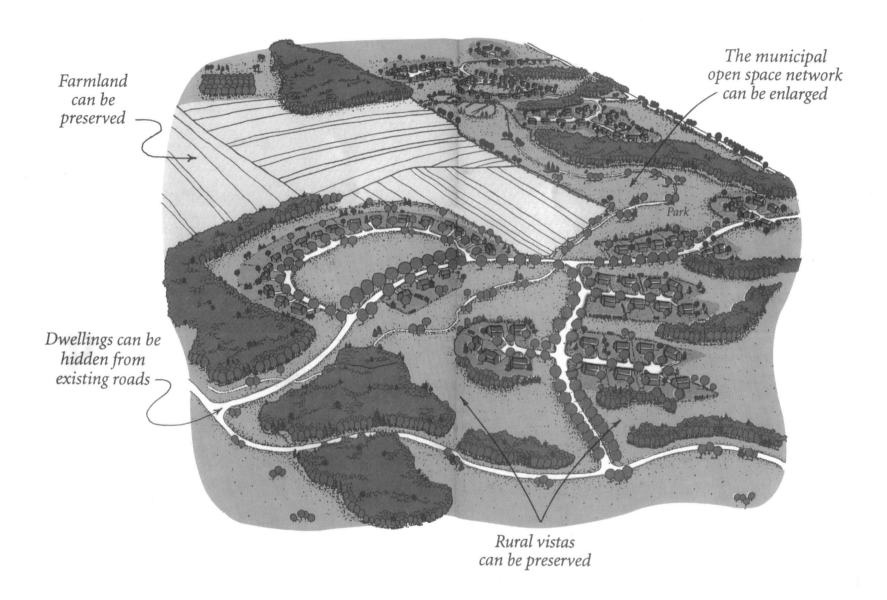

Farmland
can be
preserved

The municipal
open space network
can be enlarged

Park

Dwellings can be
hidden from
existing roads

Rural vistas
can be preserved

Figure 6-2. This aerial perspective sketch illustrates the multiple benefits that can be achieved when conservation design is used in laying out new subdivisions on several adjoining properties. Prepared by the Montgomery County Planning Commission in southeastern Pennsylvania, this drawing shows how a conservation fabric of protected lands could be woven together to form an interconnected network of open space meeting a number of related community objectives, including the protection of woodlands, fields, scenic vistas, cultural landscapes, and additions to the municipal open space system of parks and trails.

from the official map must be approved by the township supervisors. In the largely agrarian landscape of West Manchester, the remaining woodland areas are deemed to be of critical conservation value, and the township's map of preferred open space areas reflects a desire to preserve and enlarge existing tree groups, especially along the Little Conewango Creek, a tributary of the Susquehanna River and ultimately the Chesapeake Bay (see Fig. 6-3).

In Figure 6-4, the potential for a stream corridor greenway is illustrated in a conservation subdivision design, along with a previous conventional development where that linkage has been interrupted (and where access agreements would have to be negotiated

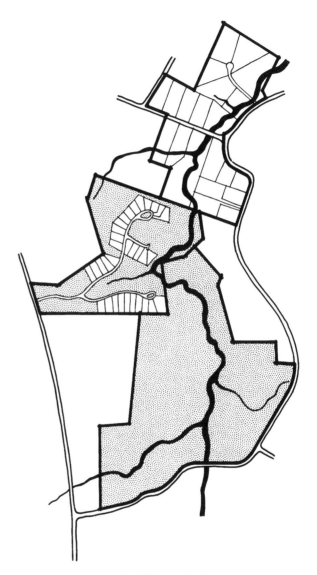

Figure 6-3. Tax parcel maps form the base onto which officials in West Manchester Township, York County, Pennsylvania, identified those parts of each property that should ideally become designated as undivided open space in new conservation subdivisions, to protect and enhance existing woodland habitats and buffers, in this largely open agricultural landscape.

Figure 6-4. Three parcels of land located along a stream illustrate how opportunities to conserve open space networks are typically lost when developments are conventionally laid out, and how such connections can be incorporated into the design of conservation subdivisions. This illustration also shows the role of a land trust preserve (or of a public park) in protecting additional segments of the stream corridor.

after the fact with all riparian lot owners—a daunting prospect). The third property shows a land trust preserve that serves as a conservation node along the greenway.

While the creation of such area-wide maps would benefit both developers and conservationists, the site design principles of this handbook can certainly be implemented before they are compiled. Site designers and township or county staff members should both look at the larger picture of what is happening ecologically in the vicinity of each development as the conservation lands within it are being determined.

EIGHT SELF-DIAGNOSTIC QUESTIONS

Each of the following questions has been framed to help municipal officials examine a different aspect of their community's abilities to manage growth in a way that fosters land conservation. For many people, simply posing these questions will help them obtain a clearer understanding of some of the critical activities their township or county needs to undertake if they are to increase the effectiveness of their land conservation efforts. These questions, which have been posed by Michael Clarke of the Natural Lands Trust for use in the Trust's Community Land Stewardship program, are aimed at helping local leaders discover and identify areas that their community needs to work on.

1. *The Community Resource Inventory.* Has the community adequately inventoried its resources, and does the public have a sufficient understanding and appreciation of them?

2. *The "Community Audit."* Is the community monitoring and assessing its likely future under its current growth management practices, and is it taking steps to change what it does not like?

3. *Policies for Conservation and Development.* Has the community established appropriate and realistic policies for land conservation and development, and do these policies produce a clear vision of lands to be conserved?

4. *The Regulatory Framework.* Do the community's zoning and subdivision regulations reflect and encourage its policies for land conservation and development?

5. *Designing Conservation Subdivisions.* Does the community know how to work cooperatively and effectively with subdivision applicants?

6. *Working Relationships with Landowners.* Does the community have a good understanding of working relationships with its major landowners?

7. *Stewardship of Conservation Lands.* Does the community have in place the arrangements required for successfully owning, managing, and using lands set aside for conservation purposes?

8. *Ongoing Education and Communications.* How are local officials and the general public maintaining their knowledge of the state-of-the-art in managing growth to conserve land?

Simply asking these questions, quietly and to oneself, is likely to stimulate considerable thought about subjects that are typically not in the forefront of issues on the minds of many local officials, who are generally too busy dealing with day-to-day affairs to keep one eye on the horizon. Part of the usefulness of these questions is that they enable people to see important areas that are generally not focused upon by anyone in the community. They can help residents and officials take stock of where they are heading as a town, township, or county and to propose a mid-course correction, if necessary. It is my observation that many communities are essentially drifting, without a clear sense of direction or an established means of getting there. As the saying goes, "If you don't care where you end up, any road will take you there."

However, it is the rare community that cares little about its ultimate future situation. The usual problem is that, before such a list of questions is posed, most people living in areas with moderate to high growth rates often do not realize that their communities are drifting steadily in the direction of haphazard suburbanization produced by conventional zoning and subdivision codes.

Each year this process permanently forecloses more and more opportunities to conserve special areas and natural lands and to create interconnected networks of open space throughout the community. That is why this list, or one similar to it, should be considered and discussed by members of local planning boards and governing bodies at least once each year.

Creating Conservation Subdivision Designs on Seven Different Sites

This chapter shows how the principles of conservation subdivision design could be applied to seven different kinds of rural property. In the order of their appearance, they are:

- a predominantly open site on sloping terrain in the Piedmont region;

- a mostly wooded site at the base of a small range of foothills;

- an equal mix of farmland and estuarine forest bordering a saltwater bay and two tidal creeks on the coastal plain;

- an upland pasture and water meadows bordering a small creek;

- a waterfront property alongside a small northern lake;

- fields and woodlands containing historic resources pertaining to Civil War battle actions; and

- a mixture of old fields, swamp forest, and a Native American archaeological site located at the edge of a sound.

All but one of these sites are actual places, although certain aspects of several have been modified to present a more challenging set of resource constraints and more interesting opportunities for both conservation and development. These modifications were made so that the sites might serve as better examples of what could be accomplished under a variety of circumstances, and it is hoped that many aspects of these sites will reflect local conditions in areas where the readers of this handbook reside or do business.

Site A: GENTLY SLOPING SITE IN THE PIEDMONT REGION

The first site in this series is located in the Piedmont region of southeastern Pennsylvania where farmland still predominates in the local landscape, with woodland found mostly in stream valleys, on the steeper slopes, and in hedgerows between the open fields. Over the last twenty years most of the local farming families have come to rely more and more upon off-farm income to sustain themselves financially, and as the older generation retires few young family members have opted to continue the traditional lifestyle. As the number of farming operations has steadily declined, so have the locally available agricultural support services, such as large animal veterinaries, seed and feed merchants, and equipment dealers. In the context of this downward spiral, the subject property was offered for sale, at full development value, to neighboring farmers.

Not surprisingly, little interest was shown in the land except by real estate developers, most of whom saw this parcel in terms of the township subdivision code that contains standards allowing the land to be sliced into simple two-acre parcels, a pattern illustrated in the "yield plan" shown in Figures 7A-2 and 7A-3. The formula in the zoning ordinance for calculating density produced the same yield (32 lots) as the drawing, which took wetlands, floodplains, and steep slopes into account. Although the site contains 82 acres in total, 17 are either too wet or steep to develop under the ordinance, leaving 65 buildable acres. From that figure, 6.5 more acres (10% of the buildable area) are subtracted for street circulation, leaving 58.5 acres to use for net density purposes. Round-

ing that number up to 59 (the nearest whole number) and dividing by the 80,000 square feet for minimum lot size yields 32 lots.

The more creative approach to developing this property—one that is based upon the central organizing principle of open space conservation—involves a slightly deeper site analysis. In addition to identifying the inherently unbuildable soils and slopes (which are classified as Primary Conservation Areas, shown in Fig. 7A-4), half or more of the remaining land is initially "greenlined" as potential "Secondary Conservation Areas" (Fig. 7A-5). The balance— 25 to 30 acres—is then identified as "potential development areas" (Fig. 7A-6). *It is in the selection of the Secondary Conservation Areas that the special features and the natural beauty of the site are preserved, and this part of the first step is arguably the most critical part of the entire four-step development design process.*

After identifying the wetlands and associated hydric soils, and the steep slopes leading down to Hager's Run (shown in Fig. 7A-4), the site designer looked for the property's most notable natural and cultural characteristics. As depicted in Figure 7A-5, these special features consist of the public views into the site from Powelton Falls Road (a vista that is dominated by a huge white oak, 28 inches in diameter, towering above a grassy knoll rising from the surrounding fields), outward views down to the Swift Creek Reservoir, a wildflower meadow, several hedgerows, two small woodlands, a fieldstone spring house dating from the mid-18th century, and a stand of mature tulip poplars marking the site of a former farmstead.

Although the hedgerows are not visually spectacular, they are capable of providing instant buffering between backyards and possess some limited intrinsic habitat value. Tree species found there along a typical 300-foot length include white ash, cockspur hawthorn, wild crabapple, black cherry, shadbush, hackberry, sourwood, and white oak. These trees provide many perching, feeding, and nesting opportunities for a variety of arboreal birds

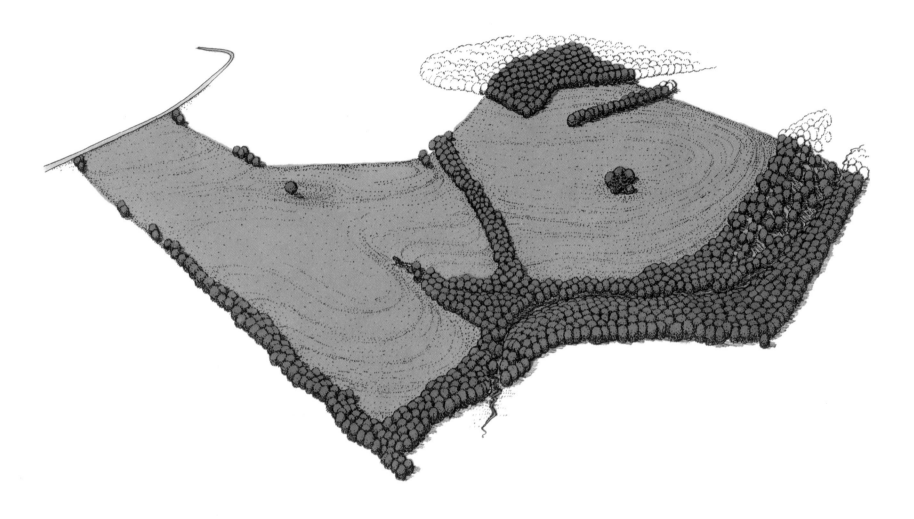

Figure 7A-1. Site A: Before Development

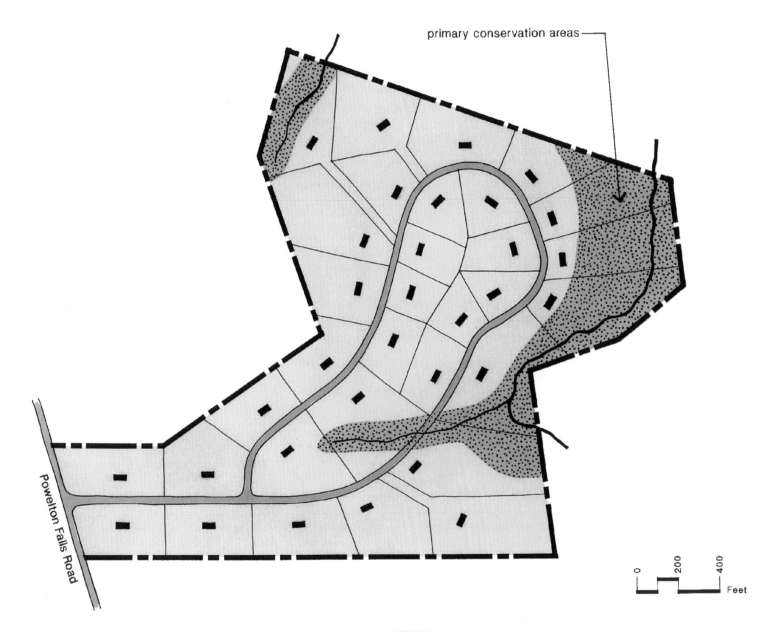

primary conservation areas

Powelton Falls Road

0   200   400
Feet

Figure 7A-2. Site A: Yield Plan

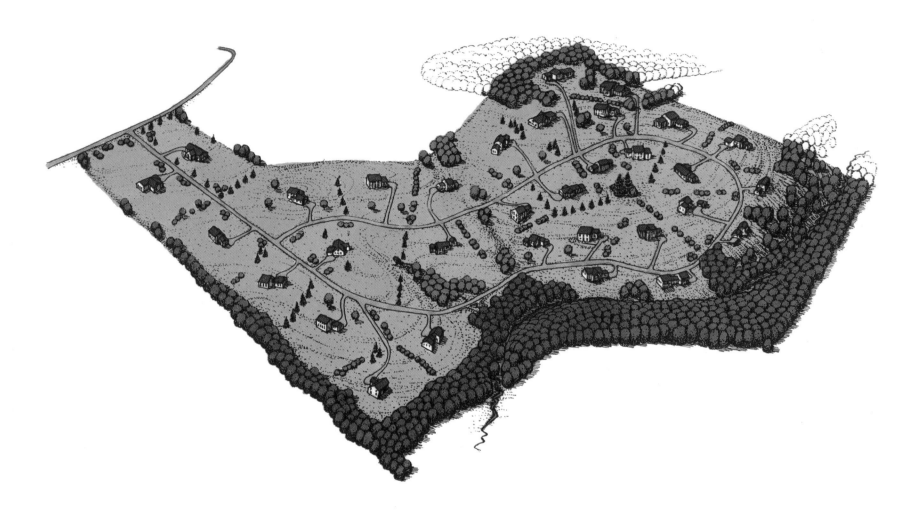

Figure 7A-3. Site A: With Conventional Development

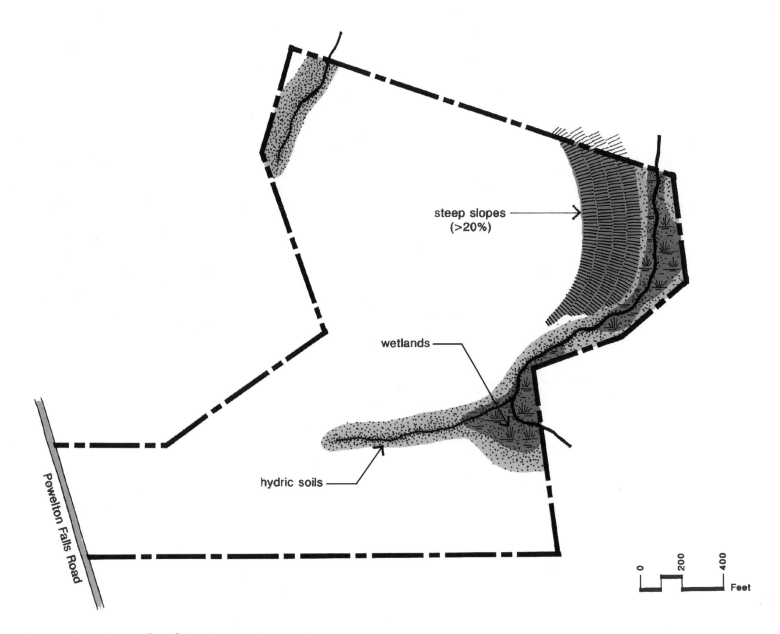

steep slopes
(>20%)

wetlands

hydric soils

Powelton Falls Road

0   200   400
Feet

Figure 7A-4. Site A: Identifying Primary Conservation Areas

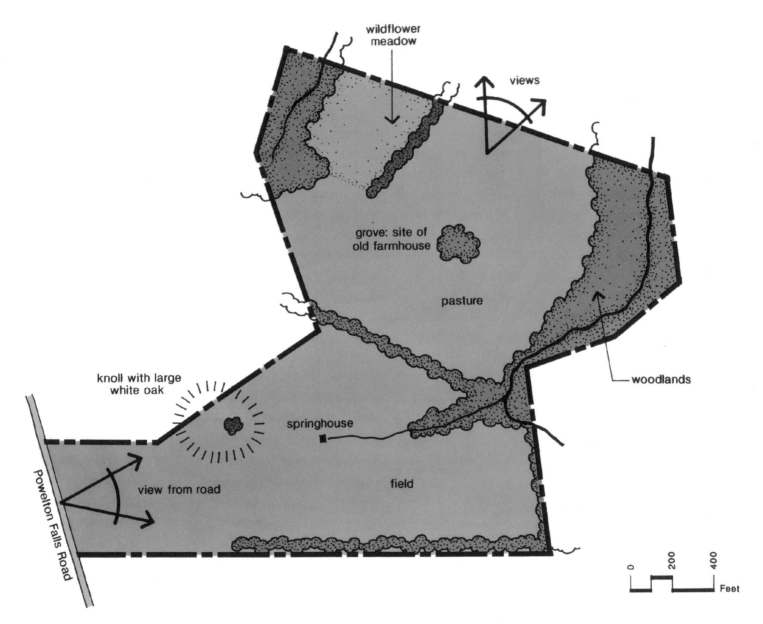

wildflower
meadow

views

grove: site of
old farmhouse

pasture

woodlands

knoll with large
white oak

springhouse

view from road

field

Powelton Falls Road

0   200   400   Feet

Figure 7A-5. Site A: Identifying Secondary Conservation Areas

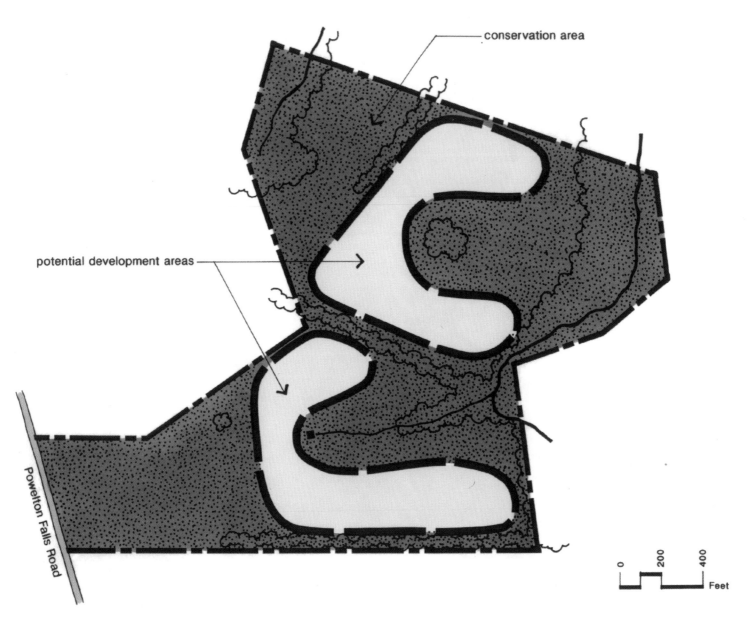

conservation area

potential development areas

Powelton Falls Road

0   200   400
Feet

Figure 7A-6. Site A: Identifying Potential Development Areas

such as indigo buntings, tree swallows, and bluebirds. Below them grows a dense thicket of shrubs (including black chokeberry, box huckleberry, pin cherry, American hazelnut, viburnum, elderberry and blackberry bramble) that, together with a variety of thick meadow grasses, offers excellent cover for meadow voles and other small rodents, providing abundant food sources for foxes and other carnivores.

The little hollow sheltering the spring house where Hager's Run rises is filled with rue anemone, sweet flag, marsh bellflowers, turtlehead, spearmint, milkweed, silky dogwood, and summersweet or sweet pepperbush, and the wildflower meadow in the northwest corner of the property is noted for its wild strawberry, sleepy catchfly, tall anemone thimbleweed, and broomsedge.

Under normal development circumstances, not one of these features would rate highly enough for it to be designed around and saved, or even noticed by most engineers, surveyors, developers, and realtors, who typically have little or no background in this kind of site analysis. However, taken together, they comprise the very fabric of the low-key elements that define the essential character of rural areas such as this one. More importantly, they provide food and shelter for a myriad of birds, small mammals, amphibians, and insects. (For example, milkweed is an absolutely critical plant in the life cycle of the Monarch butterfly, a species that is currently suffering markedly from the careless destruction of this kind of habitat, which is almost universally being replaced by tidy suburban lawns and conventional herbaceous borders in standard cookie-cutter subdivisions.)

After greenlining both the Primary and Secondary Conservation Areas (which together constitute the first design step), the next task is to identify potential house locations with regard to that open space. This *second step* recognizes the importance, from the standpoints of real estate marketing and homeowner enjoyment, of siting new homes carefully and deliberately to maximize the

number having interesting views of the conservation land at the bottom of the hill. For those lots that directly abut or face onto the open space, area dimensions can often be significantly reduced, as they are psychologically extended in depth by their views and vistas. The average lot size assumed in sketching Figure 7A-7 is 30,000 square feet, which allows sufficient room for wells and septic systems (provided that soils in the designated development areas are suitable for such facilities). Location of individual wells and/or septic systems within the undivided open space would be another option, as discussed in the description of alternative layouts for this site, at the end of this section.

The *last two steps* simply involve defining logical routes for new streets accessing the proposed lots (plus locations for a looped footpath system), and drawing lot lines midway between the houses. In the final layout, each and every one of the 32 lots abuts or is provided with direct views of permanently protected open space, including the informal common at the entranceway, the wetland vegetation in Spring Hollow, the wildflower meadow in the northwest corner, and the rough hillside pasture. Several homes enjoy double exposure, with front and rear views of the conservation land.

Although agriculture will probably never be resumed on the property, the green matrix of conservation land and walking trails preserves much valuable habitat and provides a neighborhood focus to help foster a sense of community, a spirit that is sadly lacking in most "checkerboard" subdivisions where all the land is converted to houselots and streets. The preferred plan also reduces development costs and simplifies the regulatory review process by eliminating the need for an expensive wetland crossing. Although the total street length would be virtually the same in both layouts, the entire street system in this land-conserving alternative is "single-loaded," meaning that practically every house faces open space from its front windows, and that walking or driv-

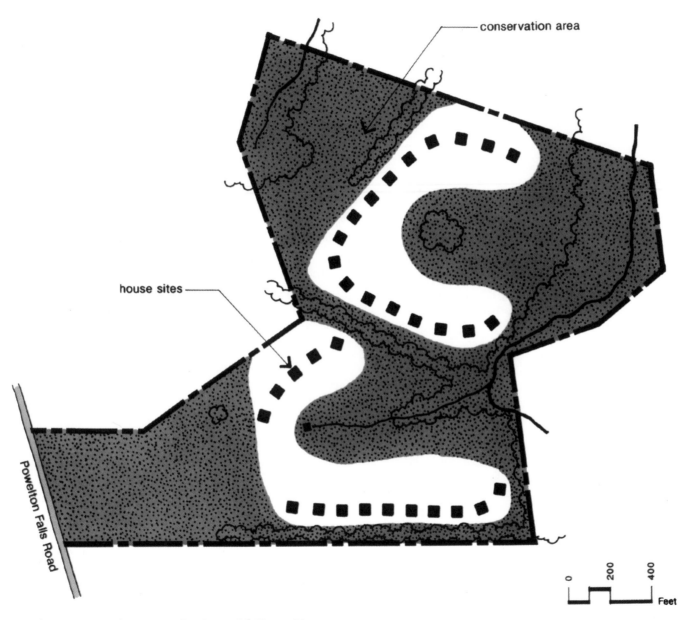

conservation area

house sites

Powelton Falls Road

0 200 400 Feet

Figure 7A-7. Site A: Locating Potential House Sites

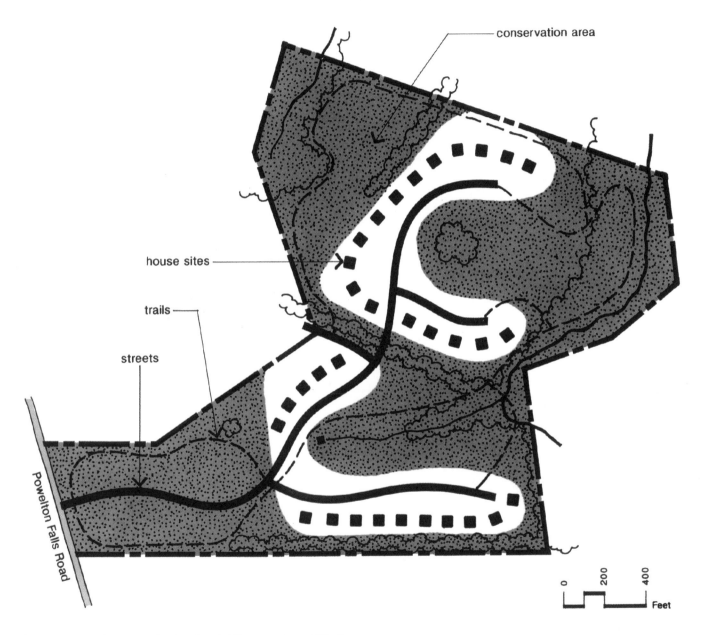

conservation area

house sites

trails

streets

Powelton Falls Road

0 200 400 Feet

Figure 7A-8. Site A: Designing Road Alignments and Trails

67

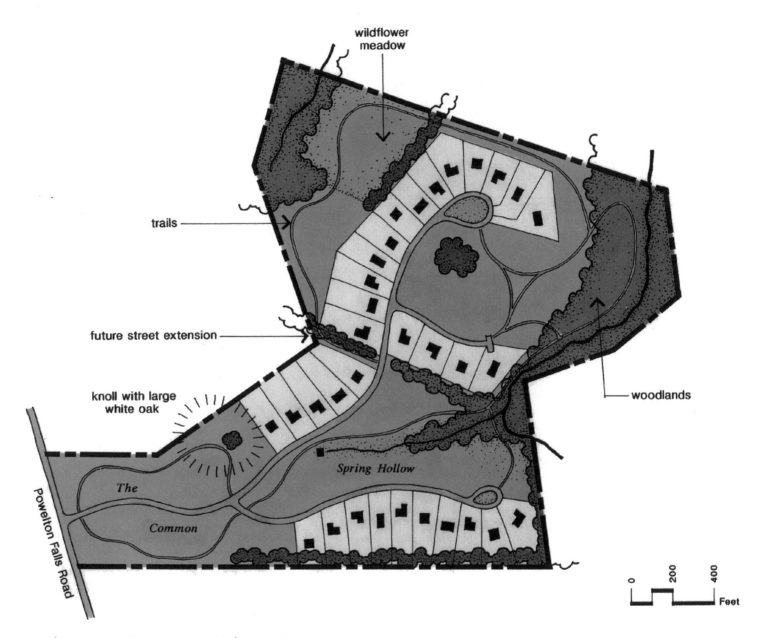

wildflower
meadow

trails

future street extension

knoll with large
white oak

woodlands

Powelton Falls Road

The

Common

Spring Hollow

0   200   400
Feet

Figure 7A-9. Site A: Drawing in the Lot Lines

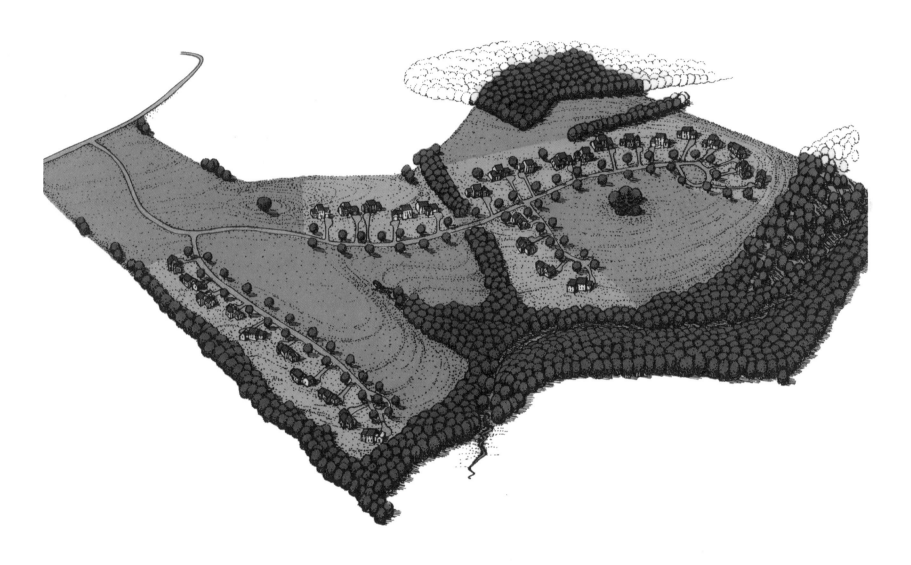

Figure 7A-10. Site A: With Conservation Design

ing through the neighborhood provides both residents and visitors with a rewarding park-like experience.

Alternative Example: Increasing the Density by Changing the Scale of Site A

It should be pointed out that this "conservation subdivision" approach is also viable at higher—and perhaps more common—densities in other unserviced rural or suburban areas that might lie closer to urban centers. For example, if the illustrations for Site A had been drawn at the scale of 1 inch = 300 feet instead of 1 inch = 400 feet, the gross area of the property would have been approximately half the size (about 46 acres instead of 82, with 10 of them being constrained by wetlands, etc., and 36 considered "buildable"). If Site A had also been located in another township and zoned for a higher one-acre net density, the same number of conventional houselots (32) could have been created, with lots containing 40,000 square feet of net buildable land per dwelling (instead of two net acres per dwelling unit). Under this set of circumstances, a practical approach to "conservation subdivision design" would have been to propose half-acre lots with individual wells located in the undivided conservation areas (such as meadows, greens, or ballfields), close to but outside the lots they would serve. It should be noted that these smaller lots could be shaped and arranged in very much the same manner as the lots shown in Figure 7A-9, enabling the advantages and integrity of this layout to be maintained, with every lot facing or backing onto permanent open space. (See also Fig. 7A-10 for a bird's-eye view of the property after conservation development.)

Other alternatives would include:

- locating individual septic systems in the undivided open space instead, with individual wells on each lot (assuming of course that the conservation land adjacent to each lot contains soils suitable for septic systems);

- serving lots from a central well-field in the conservation areas; and

- establishing a central sewage disposal facility (such as a community disposal field, or "spray irrigation") on the conservation land.

These alternatives have been listed in ascending order of complexity, with the simplest and most straightforward arrangement being individual septic systems on each lot and individual wells within the conservation areas.

When individual wells or septic disposal fields are located within the undivided conservation land, the final plan must clearly show the specific areas that are being designated for such use by each houselot. These individual systems would normally be owned and maintained by each homeowner and would not, in this arrangement, belong to the homeowners' association that owns the open space. This is not to suggest that wells or septic disposal facilities should not be owned and maintained by homeowners' associations, but rather to point out that such community arrangements would not be necessary for the "conservation subdivision design" approach to work in unserviced areas with one-acre zoning, where half-acre houselots in a "conservation subdivision" would not be large enough to accommodate both wells and septic systems.

Site B: MOSTLY WOODED SITE AT THE BASE OF THE FOOTHILLS

The second site in this series consists of a 70-acre parcel situated in the foothills of the Berkshire Mountains in western Massachusetts. It is located in a formerly rural area that is steadily suburbanizing, with small subdivisions being built primarily for commuters to Amherst and Northampton to the south, Greenfield to the north, and Pittsfield to the west. Typical of much of the rural

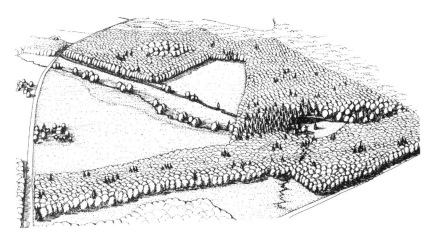

Figure 7B-1. Site B: Before Development

primary conservation area

Figure 7B-2. Site B: Yield Plan

New England landscape, this site is predominantly wooded, as is the majority of land in this part of the region. A twelve-acre field visible from Windsor Jambs Road and a five-acre field on the other side of a slough are all that remains of this pre-Revolutionary hill farm, which had been cropped intensively until the 1830s when many New England farmers migrated to western New York and beyond in search of more productive soils. A rough stone wall still marks the apparent division between a former pasture and a field.

The site contains gradual to moderate slopes, the only areas of notable topography being a small knoll toward the northwest corner and some steep hillsides on both banks of Moulton Brook where it enters the property from the east. This brook flows through an old ice pond near a small grassy glade and a majestic grove of tall hemlocks, and meanders slowly through the slough where it is bordered by sunny wetlands filled with marsh marigolds, peppermint, coltsfoot, forget-me-nots, joe-pye weed, swamp candles, and red-twig dogwood. Along the upland margins are a variety of meadow flowers including brown-eyed susan, Queen Anne's lace, purple coneflower, violets, ox-eye daisy, and

coreopsis. Except for the hemlock grove and the knoll with tall oaks, the woodland is relatively undistinguished second- or third-growth, of mixed hardwoods and white pine.

During a pre-submission walking tour of the site conducted by the applicant for the benefit of local officials, one planning board member (who was also an amateur lepidopterist) pointed out several great spangled fritillaries sipping nectar from joe-pye weed in the meadow, and a female viceroy laying eggs on the leaves of a cottonwood sapling along the brook. On their way back from the woods he also spotted a pale green monarch chrysalis dangling from the limb of a young white pine. Although none of the natural

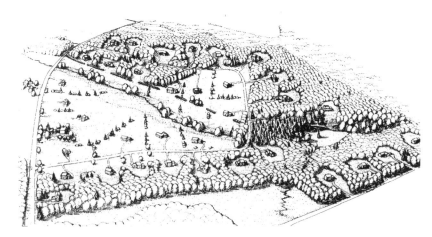

Figure 7B-3. Site B: With Conventional Development

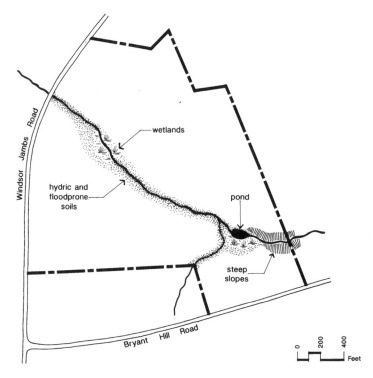

Figure 7B-4. Site B: Identifying Primary Conservation Areas

features or elements described in this or the preceding paragraph are normally protected from development, they can usually be "designed around" in such a way that they end up in future conservation areas, rather than within future houselots or street alignments.

The first step in the design process involves a site analysis to identify Primary and Secondary Conservation Areas. In this case the analysis is reasonably straightforward, with wetlands limited to the stream corridor, bordered by a low-lying floodplain, and steep embankments north of the ice pond. These unbuildable features comprise the Primary Conservation Areas shown in Figure 7B-4. To these are added the Secondary Conservation Areas, including the two fields (one which affords long views into the property from Windsor Jambs Road), the knoll with tall oaks, the hemlock grove, a small gently sloping glade overlooking the pond, the old fieldstone wall, and the original farmhouse (Fig. 7B-5). From a legal standpoint, all these features could be totally disregarded (and often are) by surveyors and engineers hired by developers to

lay out subdivisions according to most zoning and subdivision ordinances in rural areas, because they are completely unprotected by existing regulations. Because they consist of or occupy legally buildable land, full density credit is given to Secondary Conservation Areas, and the total number of houselots that could be created on the property are accommodated on the remaining acreage, called "potential development areas" (Fig. 7B-6).

In order to determine the maximum number of houselots that could realistically be created on this 70-acre site, a "yield plan" can be prepared, or the density could be calculated arithmetically, based on a "net-out" formula provided in the zoning ordinance.

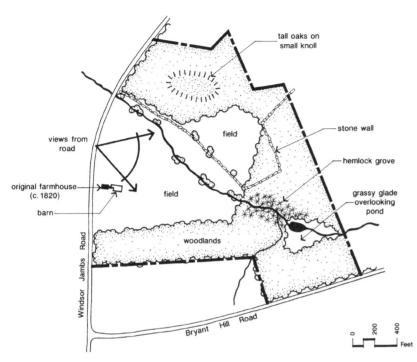

Figure 7B-5. Site B: Identifying Secondary Conservation Areas

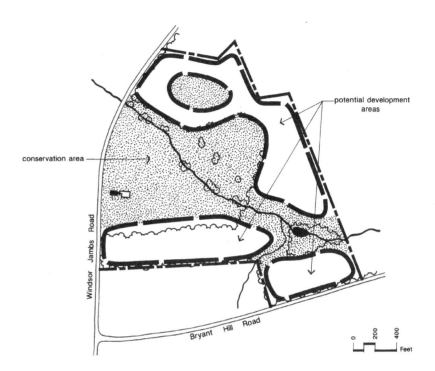

Figure 7B-6. Site B: Identifying Potential Development Areas

The "yield plan" for this site shows 36 houselots varying in size from 1 acre to 3.5 acres, which is consistent with the yield produced by the formula[1] (Fig. 7B-2). In its road alignment and placement of houses it recognizes the location of the unbuildable fea-

tures (wetlands, floodplains, and steep slopes). The only "creative" aspect of the zoning, as applied in this instance, is the provision for lot averaging, which frees the developer from having to maintain a two-acre minimum lot size as long as he does not increase the total number of lots created. However, the result produced by this provision is extremely disappointing, and it can be seen that this zoning flexibility has simply made it easier for the developer to divide the whole parcel into a checkerboard of large lots with homes more or less evenly spaced across the entire site, irrespective of its special features as identified in the Secondary Conservation Areas.

Returning to the preferred approach for designing rural subdi-

---

[1] The zoning formula for determining density without drawing a yield plan in this New England town requires that all land classified as inherently unbuildable (wetlands, floodplains, and slopes exceeding 25%) be deducted from the site area, and that a further 10% be deducted from that net area to allow for land required for new streets. On this 70-acre site, 15 acres were identified as unbuildable, leaving 55 acres, and 5.5 acres were subtracted from that figure to allow for new streets, producing a new net area of 49.5 acres, which is rounded up to the next whole number, or 50 acres. These 50 acres are then divided by the minimum lot size of 60,000 square feet to produce a yield of 36 lots.

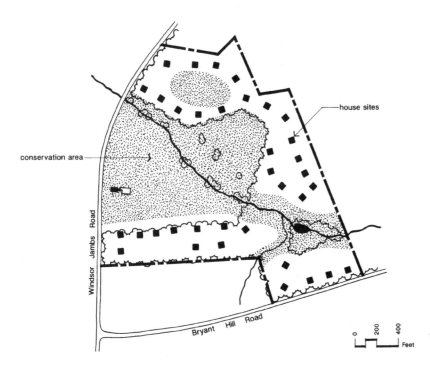

Figure 7B-7. Site B: Locating Potential House Sites

visions, the second step (after "greenlining" the open space that is to be "designed around") is to locate sites for the 36 houses that the formula and the yield plan inform us are the maximum legal density on this parcel (Fig. 7B-7). These house sites have been carefully located in order to avoid impacting the resources, but also in a manner that provides them with reasonable proximity to the special places on this site, thereby increasing both lot marketability and homeowner enjoyment.

The third step involves selecting a sensible street alignment to access all the proposed lots in a reasonable fashion (Fig. 7B-8).

Owing to a desire to avoid a wetland crossing and disturbance of the special site features in that part of the property, the preferred route consists of two cul-de-sacs off Windsor Jambs Road, plus a common driveway serving three houses off Bryant Hill Road. Both cul-de-sacs terminate with large asymmetrical loops within which existing trees have been preserved. The western cul-de-sac divides into two one-way lanes to provide access to lots on both sides of the oak knoll that has been "circumnavigated" and protected. In addition, an extensive network of footpaths and woodland trails connect residents living in all parts of the development.

All that remains to be done in the fourth and final step is to place the lot lines in a sensible manner between the 36 house sites. To a large extent, lot boundaries have been located to follow the edges of various site features such as the woodland, the hemlock grove, the grassy glade, the steep embankments, and the old fieldstone walls. Another aspect of the lot layout is that it contains two "flag lots," a shape that is often specifically prohibited by ordinance restrictions. If properly regulated, this design technique can benefit all parties by enabling site designers to locate a few homes in odd corners of a site where they can enjoy greater privacy without encroaching further into other parts of the property (Secondary Conservation Areas, for example), or requiring additional street length for lot frontage. On wooded lots nearly an acre in size there is usually sufficient vegetative screening to afford privacy between homes, especially when they have been sited with this consideration in mind.

The final layout contains 36 houses on lots of about 35,000 square feet (0.8 acres), all but six of which directly abut or face onto nearly 40 acres of protected open space. Twenty homes enjoy views of the open fields uncluttered with suburban development, two abut the majestic hemlock grove, two adjoin the preserved glade overlooking the ice pond, and eight are arranged around the two-acre knoll with tall oak trees. The two fields, to-

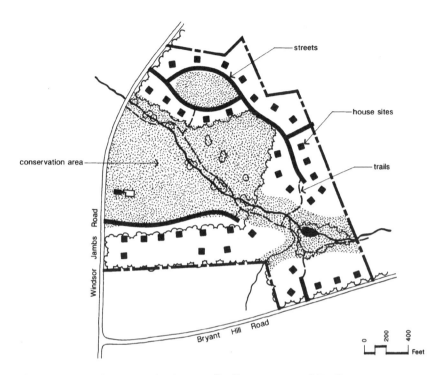

Figure 7B-8. Site B: Designing Road Alignments and Trails

times and physically connected in the venerable New England tradition of "big house, little house, back house, barn.")

Thus the ultimate development design has preserved the cultural landscape of a farmstead with old fields and rustic stone walls in addition to protecting several natural areas worthy of special treatment. For example, the simple act of drawing conservation areas to include the many small patches of violets helps provide essential habitat for the great spangled fritillary, a butterfly species that deposits its eggs only on that type of plant. Residents have the sense of living in the countryside rather than in a standard tract development, and opportunities to enjoy the outdoors and meet informally with neighbors are provided by the newly established trails connecting each street with the site's special features. The open space layout possesses many unique advantages over the alternative large-lot, cookie-cutter design, and it offers its residents a truly better place to live.

Postscript

Appendix B contains three alternative layouts for Site B generated by three groups of citizen participants who attended a workshop on the "four-step" method of designing conservation subdivisions conducted by the author in January 1994. These designs were generated by applying the methodology in this handbook to the information contained on the maps of Primary and Secondary Conservation Areas for Site B (Figs. 7B-4 and 7B-5). Although none of the participants had previously seen any of the other drawings in this chapter for that site, their design solutions all strongly resembled the general pattern of houselots and conservation land shown in Figure 7B-9. Interestingly, the three solutions contained different street systems and different lot configurations, but they all exhibited similar conservation features and they all maximized the number of houses directly abutting the protected open space, affording rural views to the majority of homeowners.

talling just 17 acres, are leased on a long-term basis by the homeowners' association to the proud new owner of the original farmhouse, a local attorney who enjoys being a gentleman farmer evenings and weekends, tending two horses, a few Belted Galloway cows, and a small flock of Dorset sheep. Unlike the yield plan, where the old farmstead becomes just another house lining the existing town road, the preferred approach treats this fine vernacular building with the dignity it deserves, by preserving much of its rural context. (In actuality the farmstead is not simply a building but rather a complex of buildings constructed at different

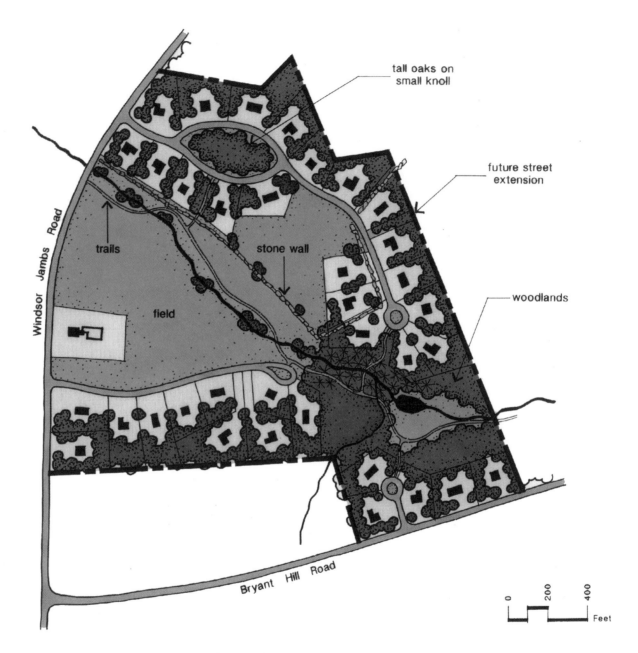

Figure 7B-9. Site B: Drawing in the Lot Lines

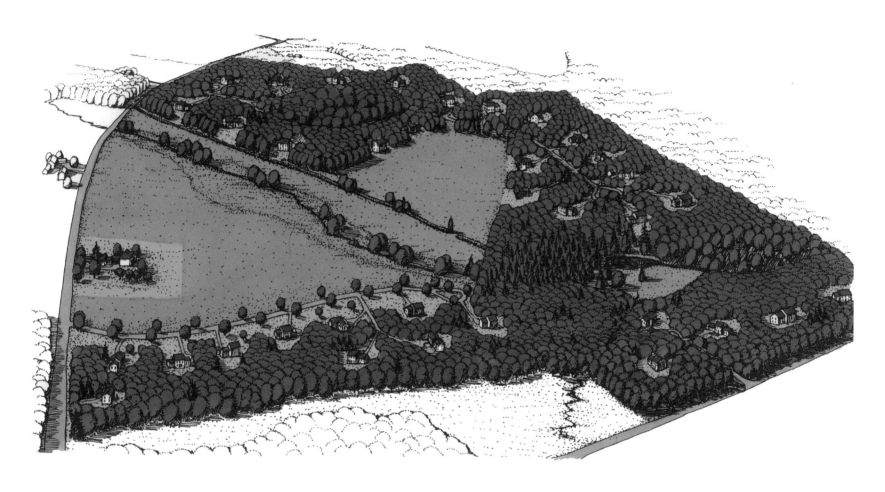

Figure 7B-10. Site B: With Conservation Design

Site C: ADJACENT TO A SHALLOW BAY AND TWO TIDAL CREEKS

This 58-acre site is located in the Lewes and Rehoboth Hundred[2] of Sussex County, Delaware, and is bordered on three sides by wetlands, floodplains, tidal creeks, and bayshore. The bay is one of the three "Inland Bays" of southern Delaware that are noted for their extremely shallow depth (averaging three feet) and their single outlet to the sea, which greatly limits the natural "flushing action" they receive. As a result, these bays are highly vulnerable to water quality degradation, and their habitat is considered to be quite fragile.

The central portion of the site, which is relatively high and dry, is about equally divided between woodland and farmland (see Fig. 7C-1). The property is served by public water and sewer, but if sewer were not available, "land treatment" (or "spray irrigation") would be the preferred alternative to scores of individual septic systems in this progressive county. This part of the Delmarva peninsula attracts large numbers of retirees, who choose to settle here because of its tranquility, access to the water, and mild winter temperatures (which permit year-round golfing, a favorite pastime in these parts).

The background stage begins with a site analysis and an understanding of the local context. Locationally, the site is notable for

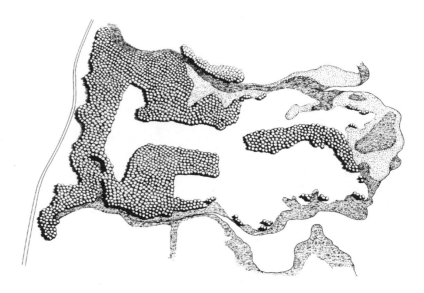

Figure 7C-1. Site C: Before Development

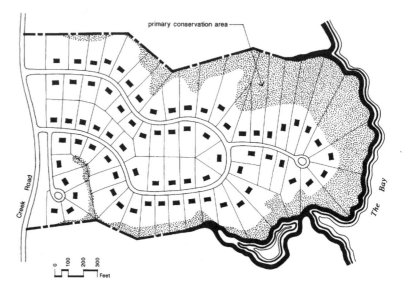

Figure 7C-2. Site C: Yield Plan

---

[2]The ancient sub-county system of "hundreds" still survives in Delaware and parts of Virginia. Hundreds were originally the intermediate unit of government between village and shire in medieval England and were so called because they initially contained 100 free families, their dependents, and the land needed to support them—typically about 120 acres each (or nearly 20 square miles altogether). Monthly meetings were held in the open air in each hundred from the 10th century until the end of the Middle Ages, and at these "moots" or assemblies, justice was administered to cattle thieves, millers who took excessive toll of the flour they ground, and freemen who failed their community obligations in maintaining essential infrastructure such as public roads, sea dikes, and drainage ditches.

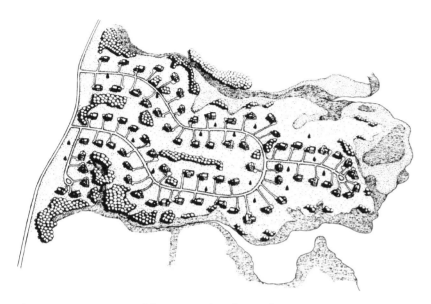

Figure 7C-3. Site C: With Conventional Development

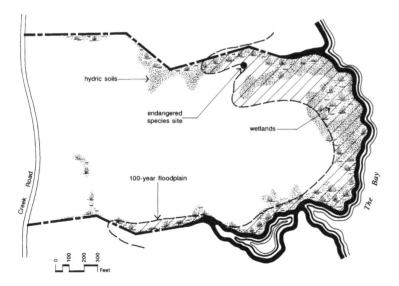

Figure 7C-4. Site C: Identifying Primary Conservation Areas

the high proportion of its perimeter that abuts environmentally sensitive land, where dry upland habitat meets low-lying wetland habitats. Even without a detailed wildlife study by a conservation biologist, there is a strong presumption of high wildlife value in these areas between the upland edge and the water. Such locations are typically used as travel corridors and nesting areas by local wildlife. Among the "Primary Conservation Areas" identified in Fig. 7C-4 are tidal wetlands, the 100-year floodplain, and three endangered species areas. This information, all from published or readily available sources (described in Chapter 5), is confirmed in conversations with the landowner and through a field check. The site analysis is completed with a second overlay sketch outlining "Secondary Conservation Areas," in this case an archaeological site (of Lenni-Lenape origin) and the upland woods that are a higher priority for conservation than the farmland because of their greater natural diversity and relative scarcity in this largely agricultural county. The exact location of these woodlands is determined by tracing enlargements of recent vertical aerial photographs. An informal vegetation survey has documented the presence of a rich variety of native trees, shrubs, and plants in these woodlands, including loblolly pine, pignut hickory, sweet gum, Southern red oak, tulip poplar, sassafras, sweetbay magnolia, American holly, evergreen bayberry, wax myrtle, winterberry, and red chokeberry. Among the meadow plants found along the field margins are chicory, goldenrod, milkweed, ox-eye daisy, bachelor's button, corpeopsis, and a strikingly beautiful reddish grass known as broomsedge or andropogon.

Areas deemed most suitable for development are the agricultural fields that occupy the remaining sections of the property. In addition to the fact that they do not provide critical habitat for the county's dwindling wildlife population, another environmental reason for favoring this part of the site for development is that commercial farming, as practiced in this area, unquestionably contributes to water quality problems in both the groundwater and

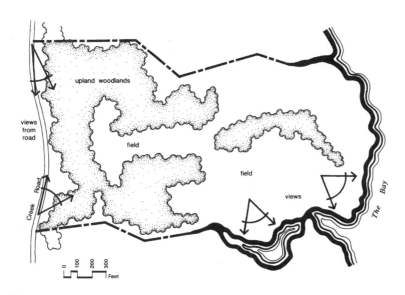

Figure 7C-5. Site C: Identifying Secondary Conservation Areas

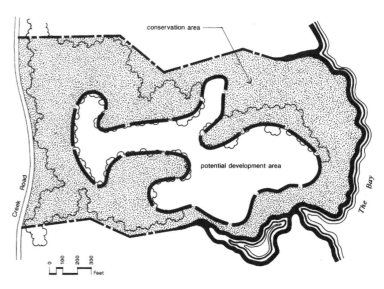

Figure 7C-6. Site C: Identifying Potential Development Areas

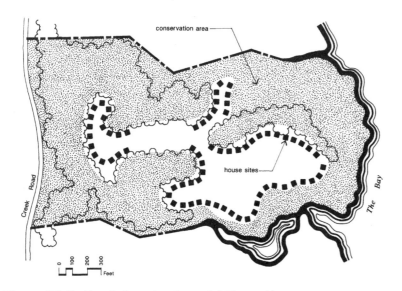

Figure 7C-7. Site C: Locating Potential House Sites

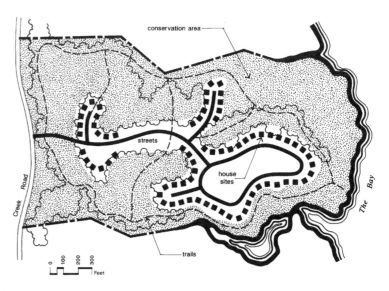

Figure 7C-8. Site C: Designing Road Alignments and Trails

surface waters. Conversion of such fields to residential development is preferable in the view of many observers because it is relatively easy to control stormwater runoff from new subdivisions, and because homeowners typically use fewer pesticides, herbicides, insecticides, and fertilizers than do most commercial farmers.

Outlining potential areas for conservation and construction constitutes the first step in the four-step design process for open space development. The second step consists of locating house sites within the proposed development areas. As in golf course communities, a principal consideration is maximizing the number of homes that will have pleasant views of the water, wetlands or interior open spaces. From a real estate perspective, homes without views should, whenever possible, at least abut wooded open space at the ends of their backyards for screening, privacy, and rural feeling. The total number of homes permitted is determined by a "yield plan" executed in a conventional "cookie-cutter" design. The conceptual "yield plan" for this site shows such a sketch, with 72 lots. (Of the 58 acres, only 40 were found to be buildable, and after deducting 10% for streets, 36 remained available for development. With Sussex County's half-acre zoning for fully serviced land, the yield would be 72 lots, as shown in Figs. 7C-2 and 7C-3.)

In place of standard 100 ft × 200 ft half-acre lots shown on the checkerboard "yield plan," the conservation subdivision approach in this case employs lots that are 50 to 60 feet wide and about 100 feet deep (5,000 to 6,000 square feet). At the present time Sussex does not allow cluster lots smaller than 7,500 square feet, but these drawings were prepared to illustrate the benefits of allowing more lot size flexibility, based on zoning recommendations made pursuant to the Recreation and Open Space Element of the *Coastal Sussex Land Use Plan*. These are substantially larger than townhouse lots in golf course communities in similar areas (which are extremely popular in the county), and are in fact large enough to permit single-family detached homes (as illustrated in Appendix

C). As discussed at the end of Chapter 5, to maximize livability such lots should be developed with the following principles in mind:

- To compensate for the lesser lot width, *houses should be located off-center* (zero to five foot setbacks on one side, with all or most of the side yard space provided on the other side).

- To compensate for the shorter lot depth and smaller back yards, *houses should be situated closer to local streets*—with modest 12-foot front setbacks from the sidewalk or right-of-way line—and should back up to open space or vegetative buffers wherever possible. (This last point is particularly significant because adjacent open space psychologically extends one's sense of boundaries, so that homeowners do not feel "closed in.")

After identifying potential conservation and development areas and locating proposed house sites, the third step in this creative design process is to access the homes with a street system (Fig. 7C-8), and the final step is to draw in the lot lines (Fig. 7C-9)—except in the case of condominiums.

Comparing the two broad alternatives (conventional and conservation design), 17 homes on the conservation plan (Figs. 7C-9 and 7C-10) enjoy direct views to the southern creek or westward to the bay, compared with 12 homes on the conventional layout. The northern creek is only a short inlet, just 300 or so feet in length, and is not a large factor in either layout. The greatest difference lies in the fact that *all but two of the houselots on the conservation plan face onto or abut the large six-acre central green, the long meadow, or the upland woods*, whereas 25 (more than a third) of the houselots on the conventional design are completely surrounded by other houselots, with no views of anything more uplifting than the street in front and neighbors' yards on the other three sides.

The fact that more than 70% of the site has been retained as open space on the recommended plan (with much of it visible from the street and from one's windows) offers a special market-

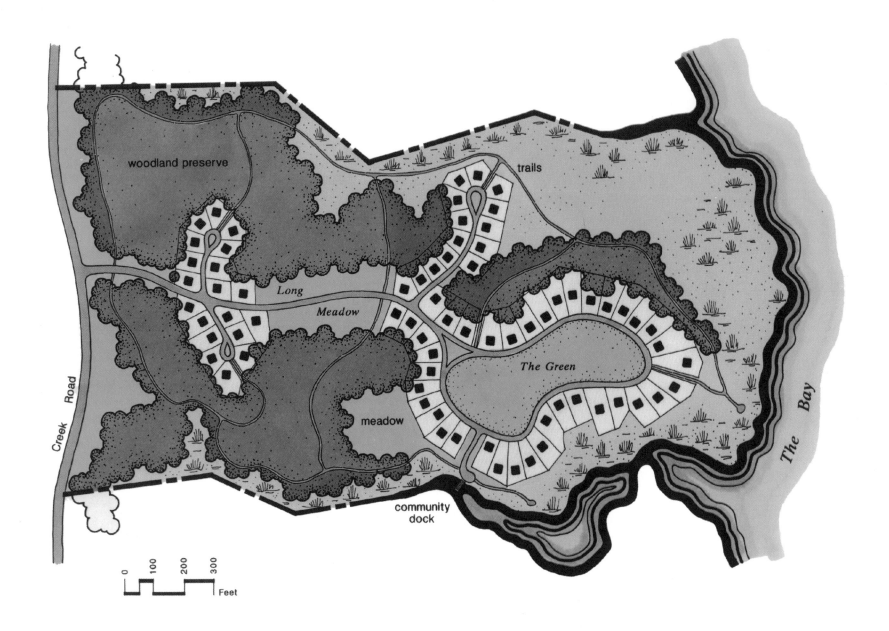

woodland preserve

trails

Long

Meadow

The Green

meadow

Creek Road

community dock

The Bay

0 100 200 300 Feet

Figure 7C-9. Site C: Drawing in the Lot Lines

82

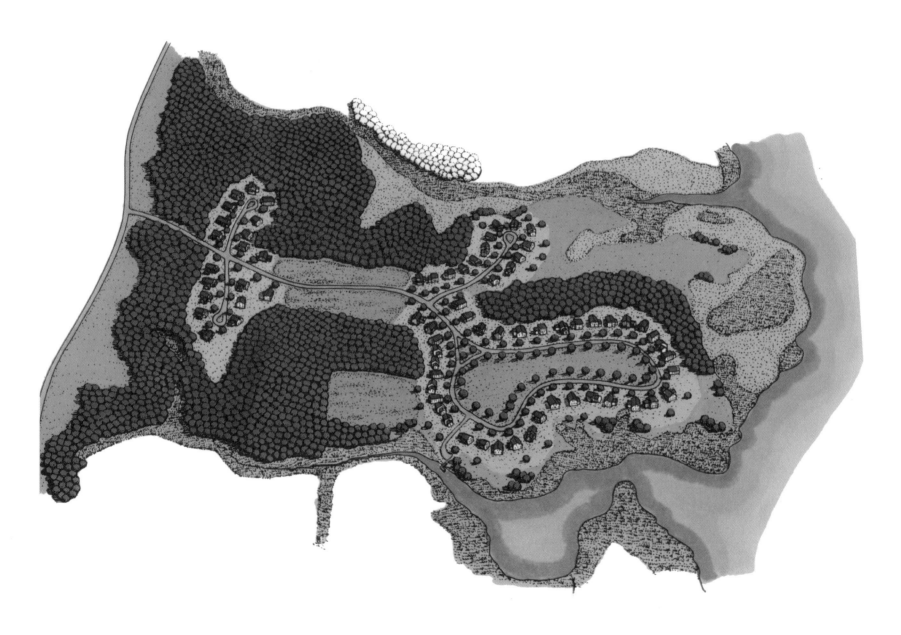

Figure 7C-10. Site C: With Conservation Design

ing strategy to a growing number of people who are seeking homes with less maintenance responsibility and greater opportunities to enjoy looking at and walking through natural areas, such as those located along the extensive soft-surfaced trail system provided by this successful developer. The woodland preservation areas and the continuous greenway buffer along the water comply fully with the recommendations of the state environmental agency, whose positive recommendation for plan approval can be expected to help smooth and expedite the review process. One of the concerns often raised by conservation biologists is that new development that fragments and diminishes formerly large woodland areas is having a negative impact on the "neo-tropical" songbirds that spend their summers here in North America, breeding and feeding, and which migrate to the southern hemisphere every fall. A development pattern such as the one illustrated on this site (and to a lesser extent on Sites A and D, as well) should mitigate those impacts and help to preserve the remaining woodlands in these predominantly agrarian areas.

On a more mundane level, street length is comparable in both plans—an estimated 5500 feet on the conventional layout versus 5400 feet on the conservation design layout. Street length could have been reduced on the conservation plan, but part of this design's attractiveness is due to the road segments that cross woodlands and meadows and have homes on only one side, rounding the central green. In the conventional layout the streetscape is always the same on both sides: lawns, housefronts, driveways, and garage doors.

Alternative Examples

In closing, it should be noted that this design approach, conserving 75% of Site C as open space, would also work well in other areas with lower zoning densities. For example, with base zoning of one acre per dwelling, the resulting lots would be one-quarter acre (instead of 5,000 square feet). Alternatively, with base zoning of two acres per dwelling, the lots would be one-half acre.

Site D: UPLAND PASTURE, WATER MEADOWS, AND SMALL CREEK

This 63-acre site, located in the rolling Pennsylvania countryside, lies at the edge of the Philadelphia metropolitan area where suburban development pressures and rising land values have combined to discourage commercial agriculture, which is steadily declining. Serious farmers are gradually moving westward into Lancaster County, where many townships have enacted effective agricultural zoning ordinances (which keep land costs to a reasonable level related to their resource value), and further west into rural Ohio and Indiana, where farmland is still inexpensive because of its greater distance from growing metropolitan centers.

This particular property contains no soils rated "prime" or "of statewide importance" and was last used for haying as part of a former dairy operation. About 90% of the site has been cleared for agriculture, including (uncharacteristically) most of the low-lying land along Lyons Run, where water meadows provided fresh pasture during the late summer when other parts of the property were dry. This small creek, which is fed by springs rising from the underlying limestone formations, is known for its brook trout. A favorite fishing spot for local fishermen, the creek flows through the site from township-owned land on the east to a state forest on the west. For a bird's-eye view of the site, as it presently appears, see Figure 7D-1.

The "background stage" begins with a site analysis and an understanding of the local context. In terms of its principal features, the site is notable for its central watercourse, floodplain, and associated wetlands. Significantly, the creek's water quality rating is in the highest category set by the state environmental agency. (Fishermen have reported increased populations of trout and perch since the dairying operation ceased eight years ago, with cows no longer stirring up the muddy bottom, trampling the highly erodible banks, and adding to background nitrogen loadings.) A quick botanical survey performed by a local high school biology teacher serving on the township's planning commission revealed the presence of a number of interesting plant and shrub species, including marsh buttercup, coreopsis, broomsedge (*Andropogon virginicus*), trout lily, buttonbush, swamp milkweed, Virgin's Bower, inkberry, silky dogwood, sweetspire, and winterberry. Locationally, the presence of public land on both the upstream and downstream ends of the property is an important feature. The potential of this corridor has been recognized by local planning officials as a high priority candidate for the township's first greenway trail project in their recent comprehensive plan.

According to the medium-intensity soil survey published by the USDA Natural Resources Conservation Service, only the higher land is at all suitable for on-site septic sewage disposal, and even then locations must be selected carefully. About one-third (19 acres) of the 63-acre site is constrained by periodic flooding, wet-

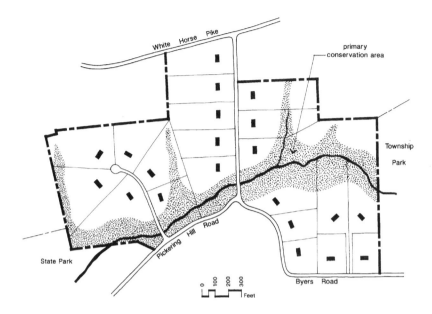

Figure 7D-2. Site D: Yield Plan

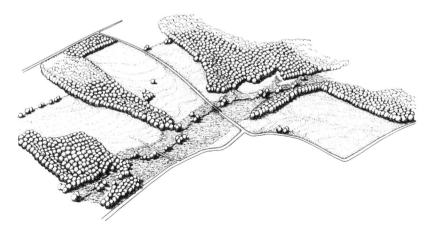

Figure 7D-1. Site D: Before Development

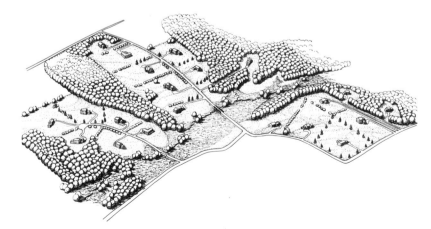

Figure 7D-3. Site D: With Conventional Development

lands, and hydric soils. These unbuildable soils constitute what is known as the "Primary Conservation Areas" on the site, shown in Figure 7D-4. To that are added the "Secondary Conservation Areas," which comprise roughly half the residual land (21 of the remaining 44 acres). Although by their nature these "Secondary Conservation Areas" encompass land that would otherwise be buildable, the landowner's development potential is not diminished because the open space design approach provides for full density to be accomplished on that part of the buildable land that is not designated for permanent conservation. On this relatively uncomplicated site, the obvious locations for designating "Secondary Conservation Areas" are the small wooded margins providing the only upland habitat on the parcel and the highly visible four-acre meadow located at a sharp right angle bend in Byers Mill Road. Within the woodland is a small area, less than half an acre, where the trees are skinnier and the ground layer of vegetation is not nearly as lush as it is in the surrounding woods. Several out-

croppings of a greenish hue confirm that this area is underlain by serpentine bedrock, a crystalline formation whose chemical composition contains certain elements that inhibit most species of plant life. The relatively few plant species that do inhabit these areas (such as the mountain pink and the serpentine-barrens aster) are rather rare, and for this reason serpentine "barrens" (as they are called) are considered to be somewhat special places by botanists. In the absence of any historic, archaeological, or cultural features, or any other notable wildlife habitats, the Secondary Conservation Areas are as shown in Figure 7D-3.

Outlining potential areas for conservation and development, as described above, constitutes the first step in the four-step design process. This step is shown in Figures 7D-4 through 7D-6.

The second step consists of locating house sites within the proposed development areas (Fig. 7D-7). As in golf course communities, a principal consideration involves maximizing the number of homes that will have views of the creek and the surrounding pro-

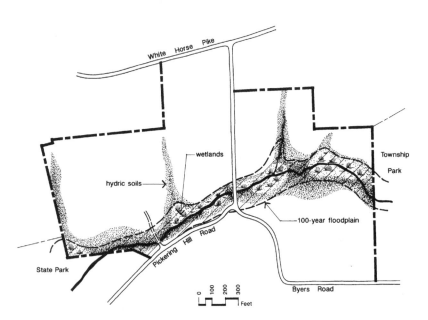

Figure 7D-4. Site D: Identifying Primary Conservation Areas

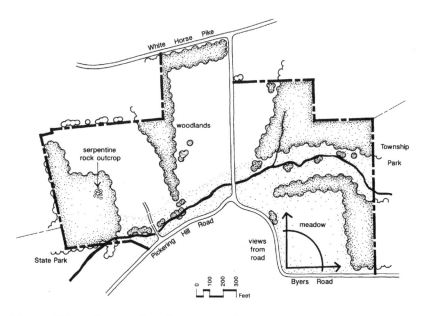

Figure 7D-5. Site D: Identifying Secondary Conservation Areas

tected open space. The total number of homes in a conservation design should be equal to the number that could realistically be built in a conventional "cookie-cutter" design. The conceptual "yield plan" in Figure 7D-2 shows that no more than 21 houselots could be created on this unserviced parcel, owing to environmental constraints and the township's density requirements for conventional subdivisions (two acres per dwelling, exclusive of wetlands, floodplains, and steep slopes on each lot). This pattern of "wall-to-wall houselots" is graphically illustrated in Figure 7D-3.

It should be noted that this result is consistent with that obtained by using the township's zoning formula for determining the number of allowable houselots in conservation subdivisions. According to that formula, the 63-acre site's net buildable area is calculated by first subtracting the 19 acres of wetlands, floodplains, hydric soils, and steep slopes and then deducting 10% of the remaining land to allow for new street rights-of-way. This exercise produces a net buildable area of 39.6 acres (63 minus 19 equals 44,

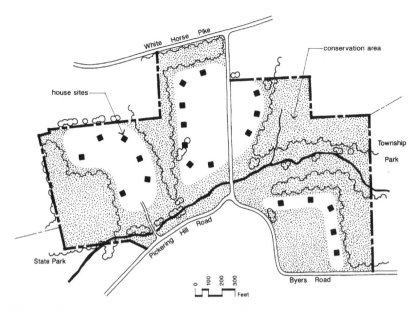

Figure 7D-7. Site D: Locating Potential House Sites

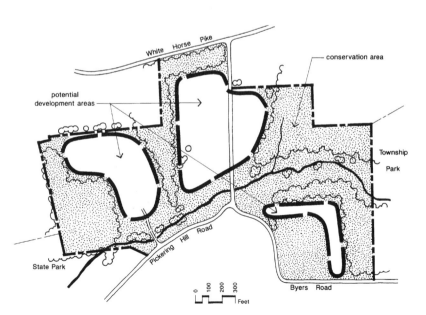

Figure 7D-6. Site D: Identifying Potential Development Areas

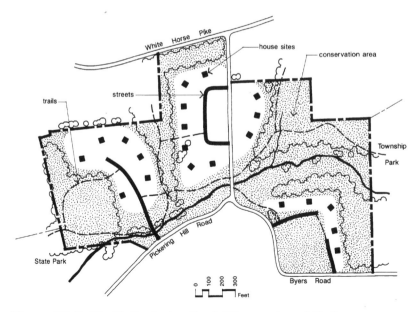

Figure 7D-8. Site D: Designing Road Alignments and Trails

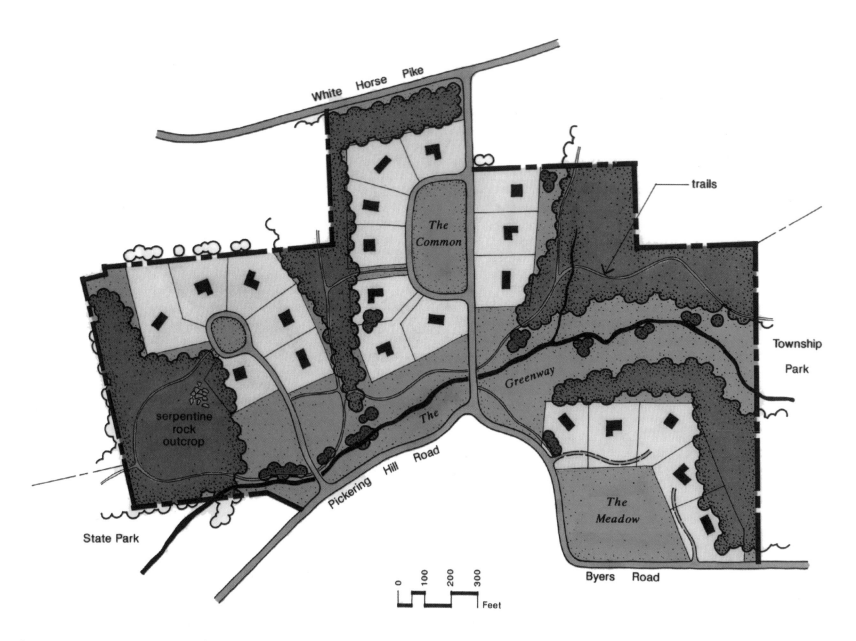

Figure 7D-9. Site D: Drawing in the Lot Lines

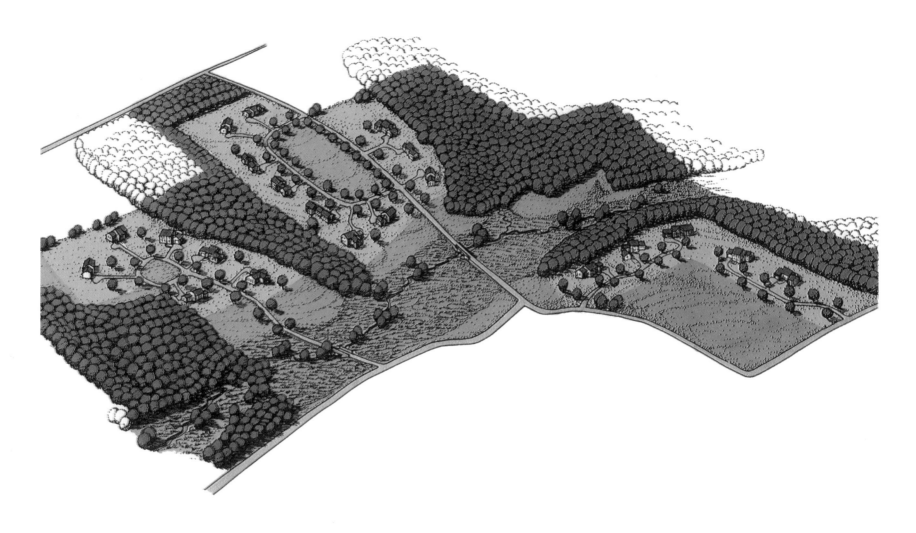

Figure 7D-10. Site D: With Conservation Design

minus 10% equals 39.6). Dividing 39.6 acres by the minimum amount of unconstrained land required per dwelling unit in this township in open space developments (82,000 square feet) produces a yield of 21 houselots.

The conventional layout on the "yield plan" observes the Primary Conservation Areas and locates the homes away from them, but it does nothing more in the way of resource protection or neighborhood access to the stream corridor. The entire site is divided into a large checkerboard pattern of houselots and streets, with lots typically ranging from two to three acres each, segmenting the stream into seven separate ownerships in a most unnatural and unneighborly way.

After identifying potential conservation and development areas and locating proposed house sites, the third step in this innovative design process is to access the homes with streets and common driveways (Fig. 7D-8), and the final step is to draw in the lot lines (Fig. 7D-9).

In contrast to the oversized "houselots" on the conventional layout—which are too large to mow but too small to plow—the conservation subdivision design provides more reasonably sized one-acre lots on the land that is most suitable for individual wells and septic systems. Each of these lots faces onto or abuts 40 acres of protected greenway open space, and a larger number (eight) enjoy views of the creek, compared with six or seven in the standard layout. Four homes along Byers Mill Road are located well back from the roadway at the far edge of a four-acre meadow whose permanent protection ensures that the scenic vistas from the public thoroughfare will always be enjoyed by passing motorists. The 1.5-acre "common" along Pickering Hill Road buffers a group of seven houses from traffic noise and creates a village-like setting for these homes that would otherwise be lined up along this fairly busy connector street. In addition to introducing fewer new driveway entrances along existing township roads, the conservation layout creates an extensive trail system linking every house with the creekside footpath, the state forest, and the future municipal park

to the west. In addition, the serpentine area and its associated plant community have remained undisturbed, instead of being cleared, loamed, and converted into a suburban backyard.

Although the conventional layout possesses the same overall density, its checkerboard development pattern with no undivided common land forecloses the possibility of a neighborhood footpath system and precludes the opportunity to manage the bulk of the property in an environmentally responsible manner. Instead of huge lawns around every house, with fertilizers and weed killers applied to the grass right down to the edge of the creek, the 40-acre conservation area will be managed according to a model *Maintenance and Operations Plan,* which the township has adopted to help developers prepare a mechanism and game plan to look after the open space in a way that will enlarge the wildlife habitat and help keep excessive nutrients from reaching the creek (see Chapter 9 for further details on such management plans). For example, part of that management plan would probably be to allow indigenous plants and shrubs to continue growing in the water meadows and upland margins along the creek, and it might also include the judicious introduction of compatible species from other areas to further certain wildlife objectives (such as planting buddleia bushes to supplement native milkweed, goldenrod, spearmint, red clover, and Queen Anne's lace, enhancing the habitat for monarch, swallowtail, and fritillary butterflies).

Both the conventional and the conservation layouts include several "flag-lots," a harmless variation on the ubiquitous "pie-shaped" lot found at the end of many cul-de-sacs. Although they are not inherently defective or detrimental, many jurisdictions prohibit lots resembling flags, pork chops, or pipe stems, as these shapes are variously referred to. Concerns about such lots containing excessively long extensions, providing too little land around their house sites, or reducing the backyard privacy of people living in homes in front of them are more appropriately addressed through design standards establishing parameters for the way such lots are laid out.

Site E: LAKEFRONT SITE IN THE NORTHERN WOODS

The fifth site in this series consists of a 46-acre parcel located alongside one of the many glacial lakes found in central Wisconsin. The parcel is heavily wooded except for an interior meadow and a small boggy area in which rises the headwaters spring for the small unnamed brook that flows diagonally across the site into Lake Leopold. Mixed hardwoods and conifers such as sugar maple, white pine, hemlock, and balsam fir dominate the second-growth woodland that is fairly typical of this part of the state. Several locations on the property, however, contain small groups of unusually tall and mature specimens.

The subject property is part of a much larger parcel owned by a prominent Milwaukee family that has maintained a large estate and hunting lodge on the lake for several generations, but which for financial reasons is compelled to liquidate part of its lakefront for development. Fortunately the family's orientation has traditionally been toward conservation, an approach that has been in-

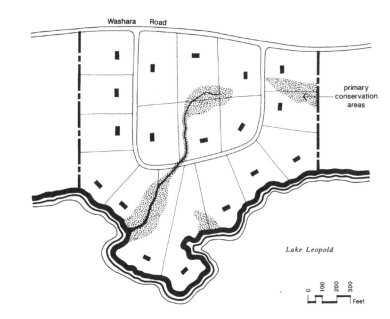

Figure 7E-2. Site E: Yield Plan

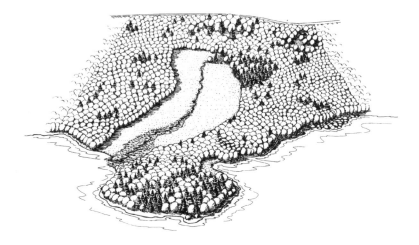

Figure 7E-1. Site E: Before Development

Figure 7E-3. Site E: With Conventional Development

fluenced by its long association with the Washington Highlands, a planned suburb of Milwaukee designed in 1916 on part of the old Pabst Farm by the distinguished team of Werner Hegemann and Elbert Peets, who incorporated parks and greenways into their original layout. Several generations of the family have all grown up in this neighborhood where the preservation of many natural features is a given fact. Therefore, when the family first considered the idea of selling part of their lake frontage, there was no question that a greenway approach would be taken.

The design team hired by the family was headed by a landscape architect working with a surveyor, engineer, and a conservation biologist. Their first task was to identify the legally unbuildable parts of the site, as defined by local ordinances and state law. The kinds of land categorized as "primary environmental corridors" in Wisconsin relate closely to the types of resource areas that are called "Primary Conservation Areas" in this handbook: bogs, flood-

plains, stream valleys, and steep slopes (shown in Fig. 7E-4). Of the 46 acres on the site, 5 were so classified, leaving 41 developable acres, of which a further 4.1 (10%) were deducted for new streets. Dividing the net land area of 36.9 acres by the two-acre minimum land requirement per dwelling produces a total of 18 potential houses. In order to demonstrate the feasibility of this to the local planning board, a "yield plan" was prepared, as shown in Figures 7E-2 and 7E-3. Because the property is located in an outlying section of an incorporated village that was exempted from the Wisconsin law mandating shoreline setbacks and severely limiting vegetative clearing within a buffer zone, the "yield plan" reflected a very conventional and insensitive approach.

No one was impressed by this layout, especially the design team members who were looking forward to doing something quite special with this property. Members of the local planning board were greatly relieved to learn that the family had no intention of sim-

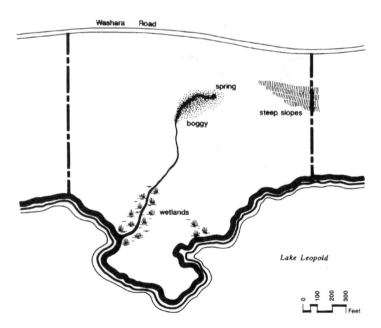

Figure 7E-4. Site E: Identifying Primary Conservation Areas

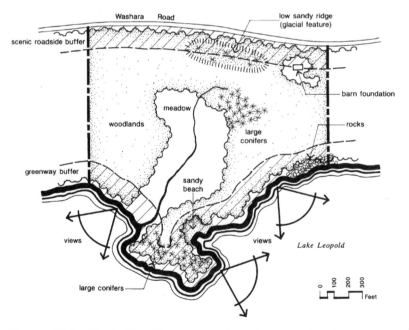

Figure 7E-5. Site E: Identifying Secondary Conservation Areas

ply refining this checkerboard layout as a preliminary plan submission—as local regulations in that village would allow, and as most developers would do.

After walking the site with board members and discussing the property's special features with members of the family—who seemed to know the location of every rock outcrop, large tree, and scenic viewpoint—the design team completed the first step by delineating "Secondary Conservation Areas." These areas included the upland meadow, a low sandy ridge created during the retreat of the last glacier, the most notable groupings of mature trees, the small sandy beach, an old barn foundation, an area parallel to Washara Road critical for screening and buffering purposes, a wooded lakeside greenway between the waterview lots and the shoreline, and several prominent viewpoints on the peninsula (Fig. 7E-5). In fact, the Secondary Conservation Areas identified during this stage involved even more resources than would have been protected had the village adopted the state's normal shore-

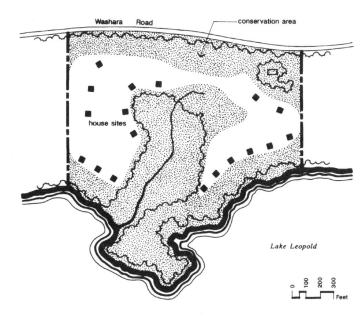

Figure 7E-7. Site E: Locating Potential House Sites

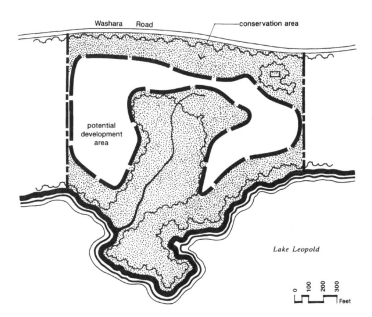

Figure 7E-6. Site E: Identifying Potential Development Areas

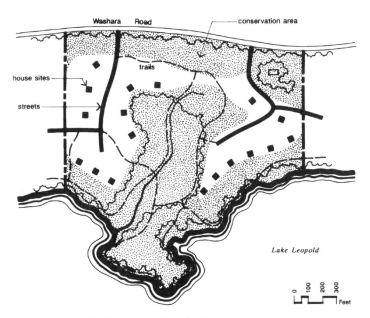

Figure 7E-8. Site E: Designing Road Alignments and Trails

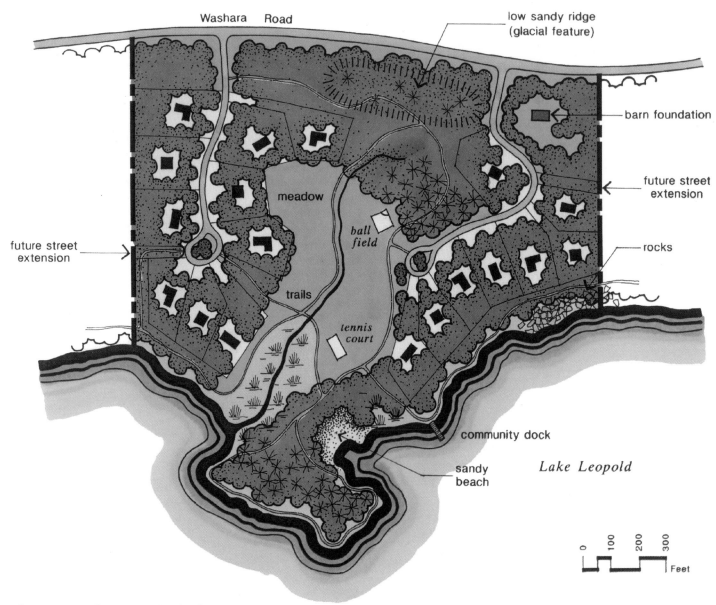

Washara Road

low sandy ridge
(glacial feature)

barn foundation

future street
extension

future street
extension

meadow

*ball
field*

rocks

trails

*tennis
court*

community dock

Lake Leopold

sandy
beach

0 100 200 300 Feet

Figure 7E-9. Site E: Drawing in the Lot Lines

Figure 7E-10. Site E: With Conservation Design

land standards (but without reducing the site's overall building potential). Among the plant species identified in the Secondary Conservation Areas were leatherwood, beaked filbert, dwarf bush-honeysuckle, Solomon's seal, trillium, bloodroot, hepatica, wood anemone, Dutchmen's breeches, cinnamon fern, wintergreen, partridgeberry, coreopsis, sundrops, coneflower, Indian grass, and big bluestem (*Andropogon gerardii*), none of which are listed in the state as rare or endangered species but all of which are certainly worth the effort of designing around wherever possible.

After greenlining half the site as potential open space and identifying "potential development areas" (Fig. 7E-6), the second major step—locating house sites—is undertaken. Here the skills of the landscape architect and the real estate professional come into full play, finding the most attractive settings on the property and maximizing the number of sites that would enjoy views of the water and/or the preserved open space. *Experienced developers recognize the importance of siting the homes before street alignments and lot lines have been set, because they realize that their principal sales products are the homes and not the street system or the lot boundaries.* Members of the family intuitively knew this and above all wanted the new houses on this property to fit comfortably onto the land in a low-key manner—in a way that would not dominate either the terrain or the lake itself. The approach they settled upon involved carefully opening up deliberate vistas to the lake from the nine lots nearest the water, through narrow "view tunnels" in which many lower limbs would be trimmed and a minimal number of trees would be removed.

The third and fourth steps were fairly straightforward at this advanced stage of the site analysis and design, and they were in fact simply the logical extension of the work that had already taken place. The street system was laid out to avoid disturbing the low sandy ridge (which could easily have been bulldozed and removed to another development site for fill) and to eliminate the need for

a costly and potentially contentious wetland crossing. Although the two streets do not connect with each other, trail linkages provide the opportunity for the neighborhood to function as a whole, through pedestrian movement (see Fig. 7E-8). The lot lines themselves are far less regular than those shown on the yield plan but relate well to the actual house sites, which is the most important thing (Fig. 7E-9). Several "flag lot" shapes were used to eliminate unnecessary street paving that might otherwise dominate the site. And members of the local planning board recognized the counter-productivity of requiring full street frontage on each lot simply for bureaucratic purposes. Ample room for emergency vehicle access and turning is provided by large asymmetrical cul-de-sac ends, which include generously proportioned wooded islands in their centers.

Altogether the development contains 13 view-lots, nine with water views (compared with seven on the conventional yield plan) plus four others that face onto the interior meadow. In addition, there is an extensive network of informal neighborhood footpaths leading to the sandy beach that all 18 families can enjoy, plus a tennis court and a small ballfield where residents can play softball in the spring or touch football in the autumn.

Site F: FARM WITH CIVIL WAR BATTLE-RELATED RESOURCES

The sixth site to be considered blends natural resource conservation with the preservation of significant historic features. Unlike the other properties examined in this handbook, Site F is a composite, incorporating attributes of several different farms in Spotsylvania County, Virginia, that witnessed troop movements and hosted army encampments during the Civil War. A great many farms and woodlands in the Old Dominion and other southern states possess "battle-related resources" that have not been incorporated into the network of historic properties administered by the National Park Service because they were the scene of minor skirmishes rather than major engagements, or because they represent positions where soldiers created such intimidating fortifications that those on the other side were deflected away and initiated battle action elsewhere. Alternatively, the historic significance of a property may lie in the fact that a certain division marched across it en route to or from some particularly bloody encounter, or because wounded soldiers received makeshift medical attention at a farmhouse hastily converted to serve as an emergency field hospital. The point here is that the historic resources need not be connected with any particular event, or listed on a state or national inventory of historic places, in order for them to merit sensitive and respectful treatment during the development design process.

Unlike predominantly wooded areas where the typical objective is to conserve open fields or pastures, and unlike agrarian regions where woodlands and tree groupings are often regarded as the most significant natural resources to be "designed around," on properties adjoining or near Civil War battlefields the historic and cultural features surviving from the 1860s are accorded the highest priority status when identifying the "Secondary Conservation Areas." These features include military fortifications (or "earthworks"), civilian structures (or their ruins), hedgerows, "traces" of old roads, the historic landscape, archaeological evidence of 1860s events, and a presumed cemetery.

This 130-acre site, known as the old Harrison homestead, is characterized by gently rolling terrain with gradual slopes, and it possesses only a small linear wetland running along both sides of Landrum Brook, a tributary of the Po River. The majority of the property lies in open field and pasture as it did in 1863 when soldiers in General Robert E. Lee's Army of Northern Virginia hurriedly dug a line of infantry and artillery fortifications running in

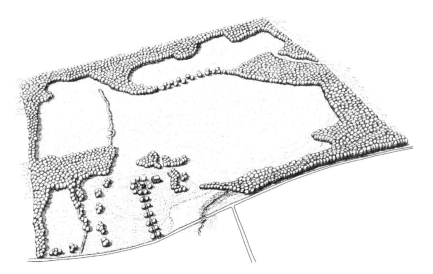

Figure 7F-1. Site F: Before Development

Figure 7F-2. Site F: Yield Plan

a general north–south direction across the western third of the farm. Although their design afforded reasonable cover at the time, 130 years of weathering has eroded these primitive earthworks substantially, so that much of what remains today appears to the untrained eye to be minor mounds and shallow depressions. There the troops remained in a blocking position for several days while other Confederate divisions maneuvered and fought around Chancellorsville, 12 miles to the northwest. When they departed the Confederates followed an old roadway that was abandoned thirty years later but whose visible remains survive as a dirt track or "trace," still deeply rutted by heavy wagon wheels that regularly sank into its muddy surface. The house and barn sit atop a slight knoll. Standing at the end of a long avenue of oak trees, this vernacular antebellum residence served as both a Confederate headquarters, during the construction and occupation of the nearby

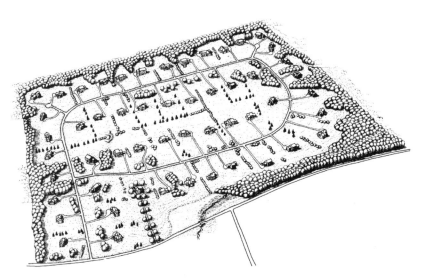

Figure 7F-3. Site F: With Conventional Development

fortifications line, and as a Confederate field hospital during an earlier battle. These facts are not officially commemorated by even a roadside historic marker, so numerous were such informal care facilities during the war.

In addition to the wetlands associated with Landrum Brook, the site's natural features include hedgerows, copses, several small woodlands, and a shady grove of tall oak trees where a number of Confederates who died in the hospital are believed to have been buried (and never disinterred). The wooded area along the brook provides habitat for a rich variety of trees, including red maple, shagbark hickory, persimmon, eastern redbud, tulip poplar, and flowering dogwood. Among the species found among the shrub layer are mapleleaf viburnum, elderberry, and sweetshrub Carolina allspice. Of the herbaceous plants the most notable are Virginia bluebells, columbine, wild snakeroot, spiderwort, and maidenhair fern. Along the field edges are found several varieties of wildflowers, including coreopsis, chicory, milkweed, Queen Anne's lace, brown-eyed susan, yarrow, and Indian blanket.

Despite their beauty and ecological value, none of these natural areas (except the actual wetland and floodplain) are protected under current county zoning or subdivision ordinances—a situation that is typical in rural areas across the country. A similar situation exists regarding many nonstructural historic resources, which Virginia law requires to be only studied and noted in county comprehensive plans (although counties have the legal authority to create historic districts to protect such features). On the Harrison Farm, only the presumed cemetery is necessarily protected under state law, if a survey documents its existence.

The first step in the design process consists of identifying both the Primary and Secondary Conservation Areas, which together comprise the features normally shown on a good site analysis map. This site is relatively uncomplicated in terms of Primary Conservation Areas, which consist of just the brook and its adjoining wetlands and floodplain, shown in Figure 7F-4. Of the various features that could be included in the Secondary Conservation Areas, the most significant in this context are the battle-related resources (earthworks, trace, hospital, and suspected burial area), closely followed by the hedgerows and woodlands, which offer the opportunity to enclose the new development from public view. (Please see Fig. 7F-5.)

From the standpoint of the county chamber of commerce and the National Park Service, protecting views from the well-travelled Fredericksburg Road (itself of post–Civil War vintage) is particularly important, given the large number of tourists who drive along this rural highway every year, travelling between the area's numerous Civil War battlefields. Although this thoroughfare has been officially named a Virginia Scenic Byway, the state legisla-

tion supporting that designation is rather toothless, and the scenic byway status is given real meaning only through the goodwill of adjoining landowners and/or special land-use development standards contained in local zoning and subdivision regulations.

Because most of the natural and historic resources on the property are unprotected under state and county laws, the land they occupy is included in the acreage figures used for computing permitted development density. However, in order to minimize the impact of new subdivisions on those resources, the new development is limited in its areal extent to the "potential development areas" outlined in Figure 7F-6. Under Spotsylvania's new comprehensive plan, new standards for development along such highways are being considered as part of the county's overall economic

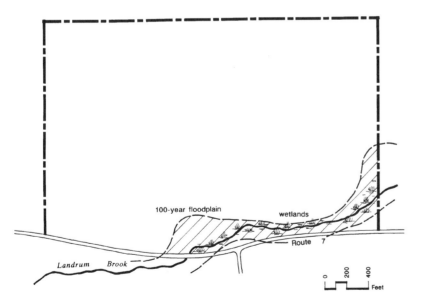

Figure 7F-4. Site F: Identifying Primary Conservation Areas

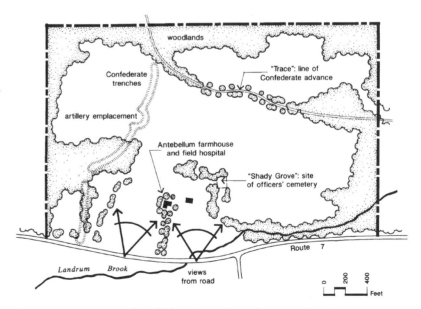

Figure 7F-5. Site F: Identifying Secondary Conservation Areas

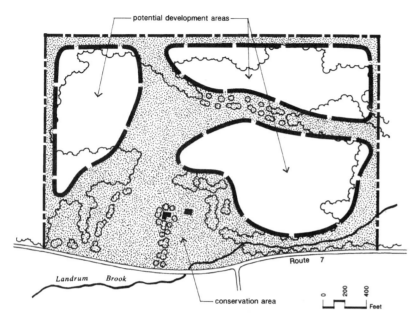

Figure 7F-6. Site F: Identifying Potential Development Areas

development strategy, recognizing the dollar value of tourism to the regional economy.

One process of computing the legal maximum number of homes allowed on this farm consists of drawing a simple "yield plan" showing lots with two or more acres of land, not including wetlands, floodplains, and steep slopes. The results of such an exercise show that 54 houselots could be created on the parcel. This agrees with the density formula contained in the county's new zoning ordinance for this transition zone (between more urban areas to the east and more rural lands to the west), allowing one houselot for every 88,000 square feet of net buildable land, less 10% for streets (130 acres minus 10 acres of wetland equals 120 acres, minus 12 acres for street circulation equals 108 acres, di-

vided by 2 acres per lot equals 54 lots). The "yield plan" for Site F shows 54 lots, all of which contain two acres exclusive of land that is wet, floodprone, or steep (see Figs. 7F-2 and 7F-3). The consequences of this large-lot checkerboard pattern is that virtually all of the special site features, both environmental and historic, would be destroyed—replaced with suburban lawns, driveways, and streets.

Locating the 54 new home sites comprises the second step in the design process, and they are arranged in such a way that nearly all of them face onto or back up to open space, in the manner of the choicest lots in golf course developments where views and convenient access are premium features. Both the earthworks and the trace are preserved intact, except for one minor segment in each case where the linear feature had to be breached to accommodate new street connections.

The third step consists of aligning those streets and informal walking trails, which follow both the trace and the trenches. In two instances the new streets also enclose central greens or commons, where neighborhood children may enjoy games of catch or throw frisbees in the afternoon light.

A special feature of the new regulations is a *density bonus* rewarding developers who create special viewscapes by "single-loading" their streets, a more expensive practice that maximizes the number of new homes enjoying views of the protected conservation lands. In this case the bonus consists of the historic farmhouse set on its own 16-acre mini-farm, an exceptionally valuable and marketable property which is additional to the 54 new houselots created behind it. (Needless to say, a permanent conservation easement, such as those required to be placed on the undivided open space, will be placed on the mini-farm as well, as a condition of approval.)

The main access street to the Fredericksburg Road has been concealed between two groups of trees and follows a somewhat

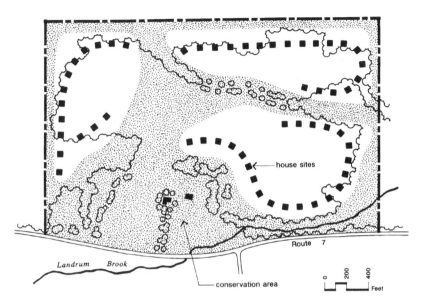

Figure 7F-7. Site F: Locating Potential House Sites

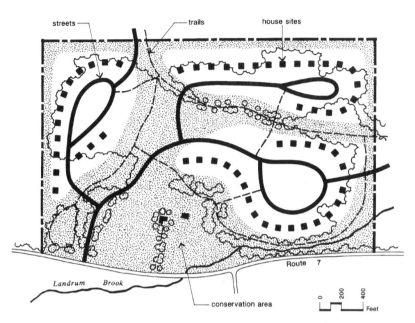

Figure 7F-8. Site F: Designing Road Alignments and Trails

curving path offering changing vistas of the open space. Historical markers with interpretive texts are placed where the new streets cross the 1860s trace and the fortification line and at a wayside offering a panoramic view of the farmhouse, thus emphasizing the uniqueness of this development: *this ground, and no other, was the scene of these historic events.*

After locating house positions and street alignments, the last step consists merely of setting in the lot lines. Lots in this example are 30,000 square feet (approximately 125 ft × 240 ft), large enough to accommodate individual wells and septic systems. Alternatively, either the individual wells or the individual septic fields could be located within the adjoining undivided open space, in specific places designated for such use on the final plan.

As a result of scaling houselots down to 30,000 square feet from

88,000 square feet, almost two-thirds of the site can be preserved as permanent open space. Views from the highway are protected, battle-related resources remain essentially undisturbed, the developer obtains a unique marketing advantage, and residents enjoy living in a truly parklike setting. Equally as important, the current owner of this hypothetical composite site, a locally prominent gentleman named Robbie McAllister, will receive full value for the property when he sells it to a developer from Richmond, ensuring that his retirement years will be financially secure. He will also be able to look back on the transaction with a large measure of pride because the design solution outlined here has preserved the rural character of his property as well as all of its most significant natural and historic features.

future street extension — "Trace": line of
Confederate trenches Confederate advance

The Green

future street extension

The Common

Antebellum farmhouse and field hospital

Route 7

"Shady Grove": site of officers' cemetery

Landrum Brook

0 200 400 Feet

Figure 7F-9. Site F: Drawing in the Lot Lines

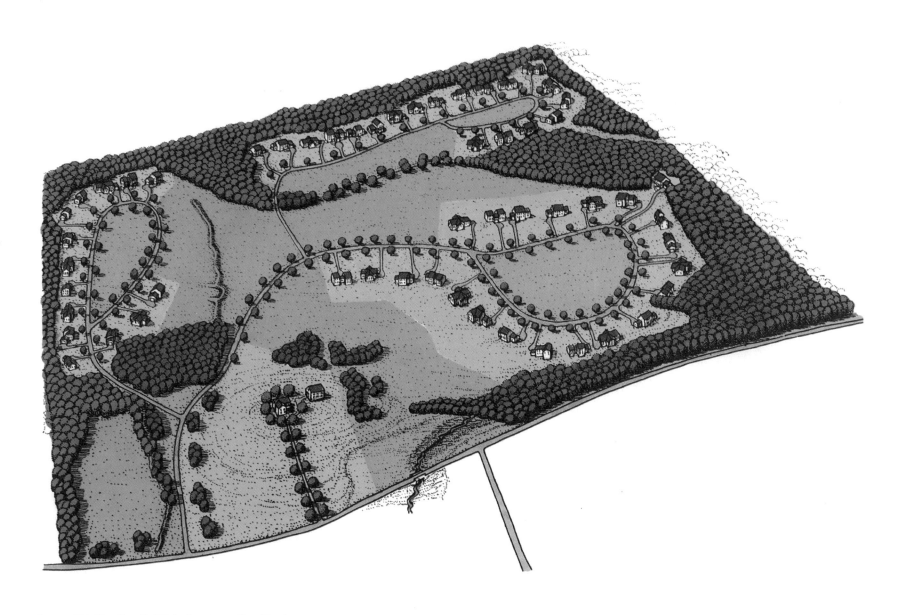

Figure 7F-10. Site F: With Conservation Design

Site G: OLD FIELDS, SWAMP FOREST, AND ARCHAEOLOGICAL SITES ON THE SOUND

This 50-acre site is situated along the lower reaches of the North Landing River as it enters Currituck Sound, part of the huge Albemarle–Pamlico estuarine system that dominates the low country of northeastern North Carolina (see Fig. 7G-1). This extensive estuary provides vital resources for the farming, recreation, and fishing industries that form the region's economic base. As family farms continue to decline in number, much of the land they formerly occupied is gradually being converted to new subdivisions serving commuters to the Hampton Roads area of Chesapeake, Norfolk, and Virginia Beach, Virginia, and both vacationers and retirees who are drawn by the area's peaceful atmosphere, plentiful fishing, and quietly attractive coastal scenery.

This part of North Carolina is also particularly rich in archaeological and historic resources, reflecting the close relationship of older cultures and peoples with the sound. The property examined in this case study demonstrates how new development can be readily accommodated in a practical way that protects historic and prehistoric resources and also respects the natural and scenic qualities that continually draw visitors and new residents to this remarkable corner of the state.

Currituck County is experiencing tremendous development pressure due to its location between Hampton Roads, Virginia, and North Carolina's Outer Banks. With 1200 feet of frontage on the sound and its close proximity to the Virginia state line, this site is almost certain to be subdivided within the near future. On coastal properties such as this one, the typical development pattern is for the valuable waterfront lots to be "stripped off" and sold first. Afterward, the remaining backland is gradually developed according to standard suburban subdivision practices but, without views of the sound and with limited water access, these interior lots command far lower prices than do those on the water. Furthermore,

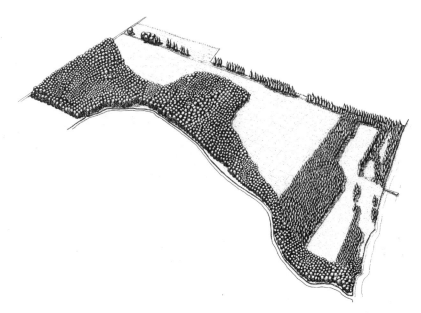

Figure 7G-1. Site G: Before Development

the resulting pattern of standard houselots and streets is completely out of character with the traditional rural landscapes it replaces.

In contrast, by thoughtfully siting the same number of homes on selected parts of a property, and by preserving the remaining land as an amenity for all the residents to enjoy, conservation subdivision design can enable landowners and developers to meet or exceed the net financial return likely to be produced by conventional development plans. To ensure that the conservation subdivision plan will realize the full development potential offered by this property, a maximum-yield layout based on lot standards in the existing zoning ordinance and following conventional "cookie-cutter" design methods is drawn up. This "standard" pattern is illustrated in the "yield plan" (Fig. 7G-2) and in the aerial sketch of that layout (Fig. 7G-3).

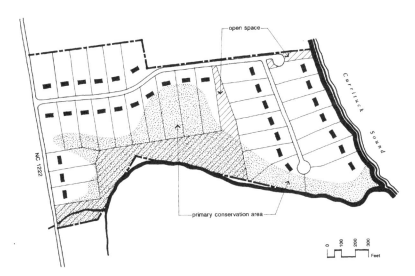

Figure 7G-2. Site G: Yield Plan

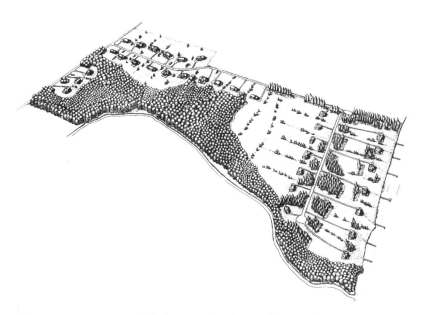

Figure 7G-3. Site G: With Conventional Development

The maximum density allowed in this part of the county is one house per 40,000 square feet of land, with a minimum lot width of 125 feet. All lots must contain an adequate area of dry upland soils to accommodate septic drain fields. However, as public water is available, private wells are not needed. Finally, street standards limit cul-de-sacs to 1000 feet in length, for emergency access reasons. These regulations also require that at least five percent of the total parcel area must be left as usable open space, no less than half of which must consist of buildable land. Within this required open space there must also be at least 20,000 square feet of land providing public water access. Under these conditions, 33 lots could be created on this property, seven of which could have water frontage. This lot count is then used as the target to be achieved using the conservation subdivision design process.

The conservation subdivision design process begins with a fairly thorough site analysis and investigation of the local context. This property, like many in the area, is comprised largely of wet-

lands and farm fields. The traditional land-use pattern, which shows up very clearly on aerial photographs, is determined by the large, irregular areas of swamp and hardwood forest with high water tables at or near the surface. Farm fields are located on upland areas of sandy loam and are often drained by ditches that help remove excessive moisture from the seasonally wet soils. Farm boundaries follow the natural landscape units, with roads and homes generally located on the highest points.

At one time this property was part of a larger farm, but it now contains a single contemporary house near the water and a few small watermelon fields. Almost half the site is covered by swamp forest adjacent to a small creek that defines the southern edge of the property, with the remainder in fields or pine woods. An entrance drive lined with oaks and pines, displaying the characteristics of a rural lane or farm road, parallels the north property line, turning near the water to reach the house. The adjacent property to the north has already been divided into the conventional pattern of farm fields along the state road and residential lots along the waterfront.

The site can be best described in terms of three distinct open areas—or "outdoor rooms"—bounded by the wet woods and the pine stands. The upper field, adjacent to the public road, enjoys views across neighboring farmland and encompasses a small stand of oaks lining the existing drive. The central field, bordered on three sides by woods and on the fourth by the drive, is a comfortably enclosed space focused inwardly on itself. And the waterfront area possesses a park-like quality with its tall pines, meadow grasses, and wildflowers framing outward views across the sound.

The grouping of mature oak trees on the small rise near the road suggests that a farmhouse might once have been located on this property. Most significant historically, however, is the presence near the shore of a Native American archaeological site. Remains have been found dating back to the Woodland period (1000 B.C. to 1000 A.D.), including shell middens and pottery. Remarkably intact pieces have been unearthed, suggesting that the site is largely undisturbed and could be of National Register significance. Sites of this kind are in extreme danger of being destroyed by earth-moving and excavation machinery during the "normal" course of development, or of being lost to coastal erosion. Like habitat areas, archaeological sites are threatened by fragmentation resulting from development. Subdivision of large farms into many private hands reduces the chance that evidence will ever be pieced together to form a coherent picture of past activities.

Following conventional development techniques, this important resource would clearly be endangered. By contrast, the conservation subdivision design process makes it possible to preserve not only the entire archaeological site but also the property's natural and scenic features—such as the entrance drive, the formal line of oaks and pines, and the small fields that create the feeling

of "outdoor rooms"—all subtle elements of the property's traditional landscape that collectively form its rural character, and none of which are afforded any protection by existing county regulations. Conservation subdivision design also helps protect water quality and wetland and upland ecosystems, since large areas of the site could easily be left undisturbed, with development shifted to the least sensitive and best suited areas. Under a conventional layout such as typified by the "yield plan," it is likely that individual owners would gradually clear and fill much of the swamp forest vegetation occupying the back portions of their deep houselots, compromising the wildlife habitat and possibly lowering the water quality (through lawn runoff rich with fertilizers and weed-killing agents). In contrast to the methods used in laying out conventional plans, *the process of designing conservation subdivisions begins by prioritizing the site features most worthy of protection and then fitting development areas around them.*

The first step in the design process is therefore to delineate the Primary and Secondary Conservation Areas noted in the site analysis. The Primary Conservation Area encompasses the wetlands along the creek where the water table is at or near the surface throughout the year (Fig. 7G-4). The native swamp forest in this part of the property consists of a canopy layer of bald cypress, water tupelo, red maple, American elm, loblolly pine, pond pine, sweetgum, tulip poplar, and several species of oak. The understory contains ironwood, American holly, sweetbay, and red bay.

Shrubs and vines are quite dense, with fetterbush, highbush blueberry, Virginia sweetspire, and titi entwined with catbrier, Virginia creeper, muscadine, and trumpetvine. Several fern species are present including cinnamon fern and Virginia chainfern, while maidencane, pickerelweed, and green arrow-arum inhabit the wettest places. Other species observed nearby were sugar hackberry, mulberry, inkberry, black cherry, yaupon, sassafras, and loblolly bay.

These native plants provide an extensive palette that could be selectively used in landscaping developed areas so they may blend more successfully into the natural landscape and extend the habitat for local wildlife. A mix of native species that approximates the layered structure of the natural forest offers a much richer and more productive landscape system than the typical pruned and mulched collection of exotic tropical species seen in so many coastal developments in the South. This kind of mix would also be more resistant to drought and low temperatures, less vulnerable to insects and disease, and would require far less maintenance than would nonnative plants and trees. In addition, it would blend in with the surrounding natural areas much more successfully than would standard suburban landscape treatments, capturing "the spirit of the place." These characteristics offer clear advantages for developments with landscaped areas that must be maintained by homeowners' associations.

The Secondary Conservation Areas are identified by delineating the other features of the site that are noteworthy for their historic or scenic values, or that contribute significantly to its rural character, such as the property's "outdoor rooms" (open fields bounded by "walls" of trees). Among the Secondary Conservation Areas are the public viewshed from the state road (including the foreground meadow and most of the oaks and pines that line the entrance drive), parts of the inner field and the pines that frame its eastern edge, the views outward toward the sound, the pine grove and meadow near the water, and, most importantly, the Woodland-era archaeological site. This site has been determined to contain unusual flat-bottomed shell-tempered cermanic beakers and bowls in a variety of sizes and styles, according to the North Carolina Department of Cultural Resources, and is wholly unprotected.

Once these conservation areas have been mapped (see Fig. 7G-5), those parts of the site that are best suited for development can be identified as "potential development areas" (see Fig. 7G-6), with

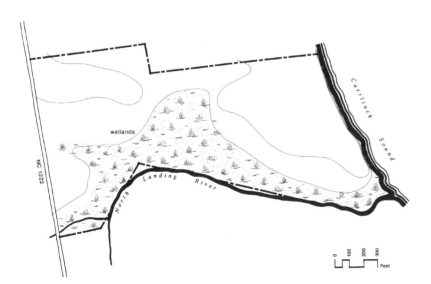

Figure 7G-4. Site G: Identifying Primary Conservation Areas

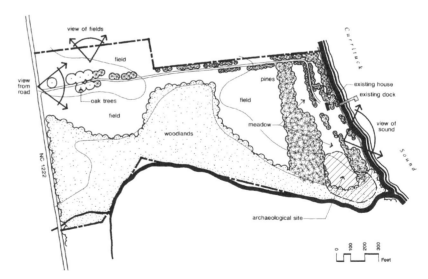

Figure 7G-5. Site G: Identifying Secondary Conservation Areas

house sites and streets located thereafter. Another criterion for Secondary Conservation Areas on this particular property should include soil conditions that are highly appropriate for individual or shared septic leaching fields, within several large common conservation meadows or neighborhood "greens." These portions of the parcel should not be used for house sites or streets and constitute another significant resource that should be deliberately "designed around."

The second step in the design process involves locating house sites around the edges of the various conservation areas. Although potential development areas readily emerge once the property's conservation elements have been prioritized, when locating the home sites care must be taken to maximize homeowners' views of the special site features. The waterfront area, typically divided into a few exclusive lots for the sole use of their owners, becomes instead a resource for the entire neighborhood to enjoy. When wa-

ter*view* lots are substituted for water*front* lots, the land along the shoreline can be conserved as a private park for use by *all* residents of the subdivision. Taking advantage of the county's planned residential development (PRD) ordinance that allows lot sizes to be reduced to one-quarter acre (10,000 square feet), ten lots with direct views and easy access to the water can be created, three more than would be possible under the conventional yield plan. The value of the remaining lots is also increased by the presence of a neighborhood park along the water's edge (which could also accommodate individual or shared septic systems, except at the southern end where the archaeological remains are located). The archaeological site, once mapped, could be covered with a layer of turf and used as a softball field, which would not disturb any remaining prehistoric artifacts.

The other 25 homesites are situated around the edges of the two upper fields, so that their central areas may be managed as mead-

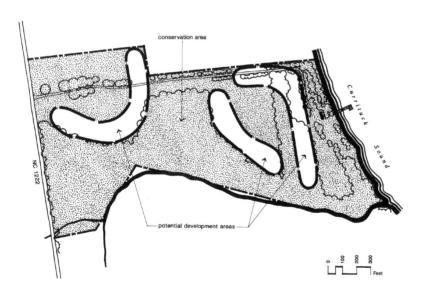

Figure 7G-6. Site G: Identifying Potential Development Areas

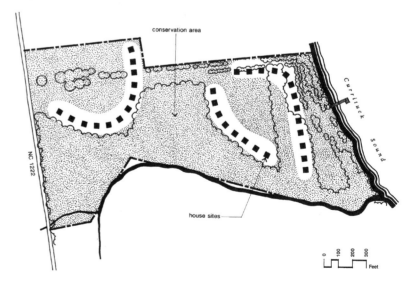

Figure 7G-7. Site G: Locating Potential House Sites

ows or "village greens" for visual enjoyment, casual recreational use, and subsurface sewage disposal (Fig. 7G-6). Each of these housing groups possesses a slightly different character, providing residents with a stronger community atmosphere, a greater sense of place, and a real appreciation for the fields, woods, and shoreland that comprise their very special neighborhood. Sadly, basic elements such as these are missing in most conventional subdivisions where every street tends to look just like every other, and where most of the natural landscape features have been swept away by layouts insensitive to them. The interior lots in the conservation design are slightly larger than those on the waterfront and are extended psychologically and visually by the adjacent open land in front and in back. As a result, residents should perceive a greater sense of space than they would in standard subdivisions, where front windows stare blankly at garage doors across the street and where rear decks often look out over one another.

Step Three involves laying out a street and pathway network to access the proposed homes and recreation areas (see Fig. 7G-8). The principal street follows the existing "country lane" (or drive) under the large oak trees. Care should be taken to minimize root damage during construction by directing heavy vehicle traffic and utility trenching outside the root zone. A stub connection to the adjoining property keeps the street from exceeding the maximum length allowed for cul-de-sacs. Pavement widths on the two short streets, which serve only five homes each, could be allowed to be as little as 12 feet because of their low traffic levels, with gravel shoulders provided to create 20 feet of vehicle-bearing surface. (Those shoulders could be surfaced with traditional materials such as clamshells or could be covered with several inches of loam and seeded with a tough but attractive groundcover, such as white clover, to reduce dust and help retain the site's rural character.) Curbs and gutters should not be necessary at these overall building densities on such sandy soils, and casual footpaths of clamshell or beach gravel could be substituted for suburban side-

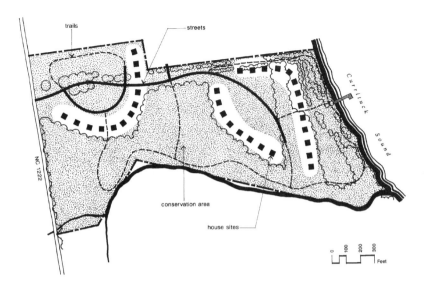

Figure 7G-8. Site G: Designing Road Alignments and Trails

walks of asphalt or concrete. Woodland trails could simply be cleared, slightly mounded, and mulched so they will remain dry, allowing residents to stroll about the open space while enjoying the property's natural features and outward views.

Finally, in Step Four, all that remains is to draw in the lot lines, making sure that each lot possesses at least 10,000 square feet, as required by the PRD ordinance (see Fig. 7G-9). Individual lots may vary in size according to the features of the site and market demands, thereby appealing to a broad spectrum of home buyers. Two "flag-lots" have been created at the eastern end of the upper green so that these homes can face this open space. (Had these lots been located at the opposite end of this green near the road, their owners would have had less backyard privacy and their houses would have obstructed public views of this conservation area.) In other instances this creative lot shape has been used to reduce cul-de-sac length, thereby reducing future public street

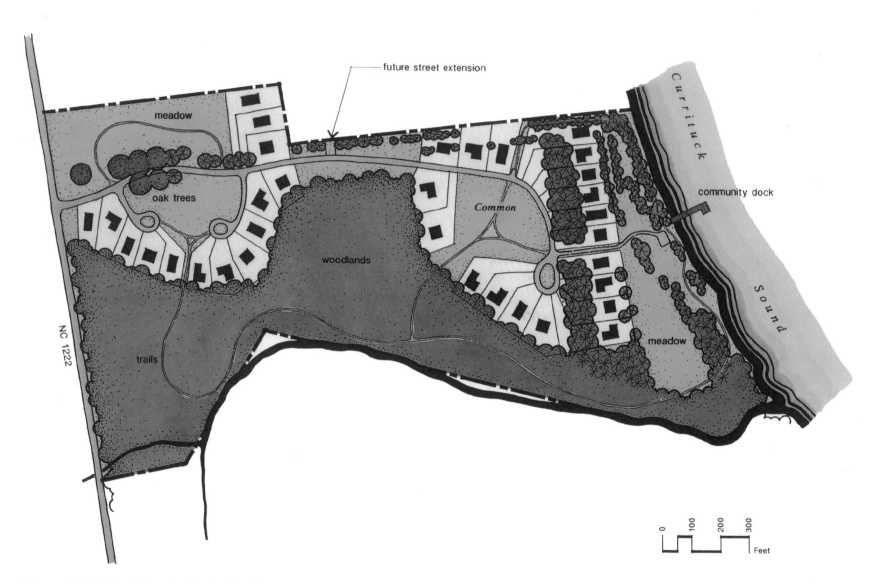

Figure 7G-9. Site G: Drawing in the Lot Lines

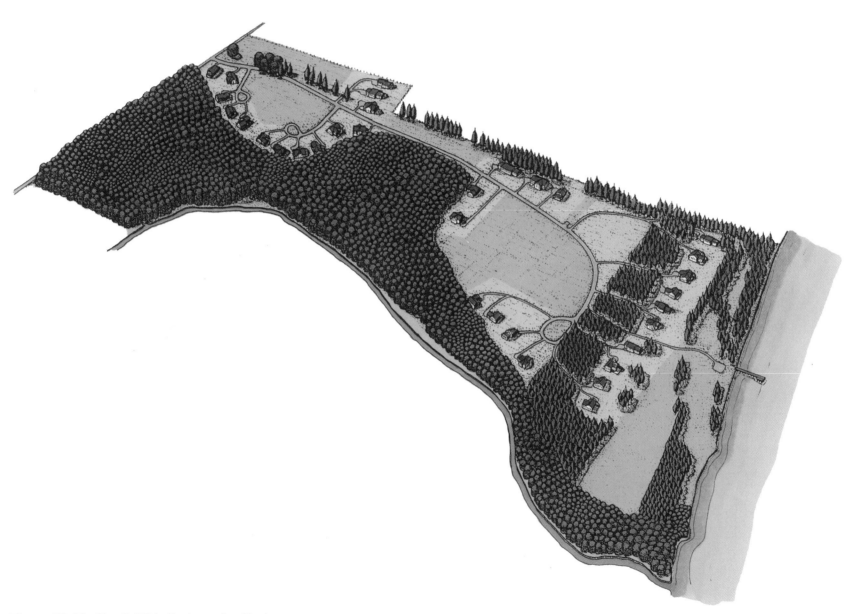

Figure 7G-10. Site G: With Conservation Design

maintenance costs and the total amount of site disturbance. In areas where lots extend into the woodlands, it would be desirable to require that residents respect the existing forest edge, while allowing some additional plantings or selective cutting to occur. The goal is to blend the new development into the existing landscape rather than to impose a new geometry onto the traditional pattern.

In unsewered developments with lots of the size shown here (10,000 square feet), it is also important that lot lines should be drawn so that each houselot will have fairly direct access to contiguous open space, where individual (or shared) off-lot septic drainage fields can be situated, within the open space, in locations earmarked for such use on the final plan.

This four-step process maintains much of the original character of the property while accommodating a substantial change in land use, as illustrated in the third aerial perspective sketch (Fig. 7G-10). Development blends more gracefully into the surrounding landscape and has less negative impact on the site's cultural and natural resources, as compared with the conventional "checkerboard" approach. All this is accomplished by making certain design improvements that increase real estate values, produce faster sales, and create a greater sense of community for the new residents who can also enjoy more of the rural landscape views that originally attracted them to the area.

8

Regulatory Improvements

This chapter describes a number of refinements to existing zoning and subdivision ordinances that would facilitate, encourage, and in some cases require the kind of "conservation subdivisions" illustrated in Chapter 7. They begin with responses to concerns frequently expressed by developers themselves, namely the need to provide clear standards governing layout and design of houselots, streets, and open space, and the desirability of straightforward review procedures for "flexible development" in which creatively designed subdivisions are given at least equal status with conventional layouts for which plan approvals are "by right" (and not subject to more burdensome and discretionary reviews as conditional uses or special exceptions).

Two other areas explored in this chapter include authorizing the township or county to set minimum standards requiring open space design in certain kinds of locations (especially along potential greenway corridors), and offering density bonuses to encourage certain kinds of socially desirable actions. As dealt with in this chapter, those actions include providing public access to at least part of the subdivision conservation land (such as along well-defined greenway trail corridors), securing endowment funds to help cover ongoing open space maintenance cost, and encouraging well-designed housing in conservation subdivisions where homes will be affordable to people who currently have no home equity and modest incomes (such as young couples working in entry-level positions—in other words, your children and mine).

CLEAR AND DETAILED STANDARDS FOR CONSERVATION DESIGNS

At the present time many rural townships and counties allow little flexibility in the layout of subdivisions. Any provisions that might exist in their codes to permit more creative layouts through clustering are frequently limited by restrictive regulations that make this alternative unattractive to most applicants. In such cases the most important remedial action is to modify existing ordinances so that conservation-based developments are classified as permitted uses. If a township or county wishes to encourage natural areas preservation through land-conserving conservation subdivision design, it only makes sense to treat this approach even-handedly and no more restrictively than proposals for conventional "checkerboard" designs that produce only more houselots and streets. (In fact, an excellent argument could be made to favor conservation designs over the checkerboard alternative, by classifying the latter as special exceptions, allowing them only at lower gross densities, or prohibiting them altogether—at least in certain overlay districts where open space protection is critically important.)

Some of the recommended remedial actions relate to points discussed in Chapter 5, "Steps Involved in Designing Conservation Subdivisions," such as providing for:

- an "Existing Features and Site Analysis" Map,
- a "yield plan" to demonstrate density potential (especially useful for unsewered sites), and
- a conceptual sketch plan or at least a conceptual preliminary

plan (without expensive engineering at this formative stage) showing Primary and Secondary Conservation Areas in addition to proposed development locations.

Model ordinance language addressing these items is included in Appendix H for use by interested readers. Without getting into the details here, it would be helpful to recap some of the main points, based upon recommendations that stem from developers' legitimate concerns. Above all, developers really want to know where they stand, with regulations that are sufficiently specific and detailed that they can be reasonably certain of approval provided they meet all the standards. In other words, they prefer rules that are clear and unambiguous, that straightforwardly describe what they are expected to submit, and that allow for their proposals to be evaluated solely on the basis of fairly objective written criteria.

Seven general recommendations follow from the above findings:

1.   Regulations for creatively designed developments should state that all applications meeting the requirements established for such proposals shall be approved, subject of course to conformance with other pertinent local, state, or federal regulations.

2.   The public (specifically abuttors and others with property within a certain distance of the proposal) should be invited to attend the first public meeting on the proposal, to learn about the general outline of the development, and to offer comment on the overall layout of streets, houselots, and conservation areas before heavy engineering costs are incurred (after which there is understandable reluctance to make major changes).

3.   Ground rules for public meetings and the more formal hearings should be expanded to include clarification that all comments must be directed to the official review criteria contained in the zoning and subdivision ordinances (to discourage statements of general sentiment or complaints about the legally permitted density—issues that are not germane to the review process and that should be addressed to local officials separately in a request for regulatory changes).

4. Design standards should be clearly defined for both the developed area and for the conservation lands. With respect to houselots and setbacks, consideration should be given to specifying both minimum and maximum distances to ensure a reasonably compact form, consistent with the building pattern in the region's historic small towns and villages. Certain allowances should also be made to permit "flag lots" and shared driveways, according to reasonable design criteria. Conservation area standards should include requirements relating to the *quantity* of protected land, its *quality* (in addition to environmentally constrained ground it should also contain otherwise buildable land providing a diversity of habitat), and its *configuration* or shape with respect to the existing roads and to proposed houses and streets. These provisions should also require that all or most of the conservation land must be owned and managed by a single entity according to a set of approved land management standards (such as those described in Chapter 9).

5. Approvals granted at the sketch plan stage should be firm enough to assure applicants that the broad outline of their proposal will not be requestioned and possibly disapproved at subsequent meetings.

6. General language giving officials broad latitude to render arbitrary decisions should be eliminated, to avoid potential future problems.

7. At the minimum, conservation subdivisions should be approvable "by right" or "as of right" and should not be required to meet the standards of special exceptions or special permits. In fact, if conventional subdivisions are not classified as conditional uses, conservation subdivisions should not be either. The "playing field" should at least be level, if open space development design is going to be given an even chance of being proposed. Applicants typically select the path of least resistance when deciding what kind of development to propose. The fewer the obstacles and the clearer the signposts (or standards), the more applications that are likely to be submitted for any given development type. If a township or county wishes to actively encourage conservation subdivisions and to actively discourage conventional layouts (at least in certain parts of its jurisdiction, such as in potential greenway corridor planning areas), the playing field

could be tilted to require that only conventional development proposals be subject to conditional use, special permit, or special exception review processes.

AUTHORIZATION TO REQUIRE CONSERVATION DESIGN

The idea that a township or county could assume a proactive role in encouraging land-conserving subdivision design, while discouraging standard "houselot-and-street" development, can be taken another step forward. A growing number of townships and counties from Maine to Washington State have adopted zoning provisions that set basic standards effectively *requiring* conservation subdivision design, at least in certain environmentally sensitive areas, in order to protect resources as diverse as prime farmland, mature woodlands, and steep slopes. In these new zoning districts, applicants are either required to submit conservation-based layouts, or are given the option of submitting a conventional "checkerboard" design at a reduced gross density (providing, for example, only one-third fewer lots). In other words, full density is achievable only with open space layouts, in which a minimum of 50 to 75 percent of the buildable land is permanently protected within *undivided* conservation areas (with density credits to allow homes to be built in a more compact fashion in other parts of the site).

The legal basis for such a requirement is that local governments have a legitimate public interest in ensuring that upland areas supporting terrestrial habitat or helping to protect water quality, or which are capable of producing high crop yields, represent irreplaceable natural features that they can ill-afford to squander on land-consumptive low density suburban sprawl development. Because many natural resource areas (such as underground aquifers, wetland complexes, and wildlife habitats) are interconnected in ways that are sometimes obvious and other times subtle or difficult to determine with precision, the only way that local governments can possibly ensure that these networks are not fragmented or adversely affected is to adopt certain design standards that would apply to developments proposed within new "overlay districts." The boundaries of such districts would be determined, in part, by the "area-wide maps of conservation and development" described in Chapter 6.

Although such an approach might at first be regarded as being somewhat extreme, it would not violate any constitutionally protected property rights. Because it is based upon the notion of allowing full density, limiting only the pattern of new development, it is difficult to imagine how anyone could mount a credible legal challenge. The case law regarding "takings" has consistently supported far more restrictive measures and has reaffirmed local and state land-use regulations that allow only a small fraction of the development that would ordinarily have been permitted. In the courts' view, even a small amount of development has usually been deemed to be enough, the usual standard for a "taking" being the absence of *any* reasonable and beneficial use.

The design technique advocated in this handbook does not even come close to approaching the line at which a "taking" argument could be sustained, and in fact this approach has been publicly endorsed by proponents of the conservative "Wise Use" movement in both California and Virginia as striking a reasonable compromise between conservation and development. There appears to be very little that property rights activists and land preservationists agree upon these days. Conservation subdivision design (even when it becomes a requirement to protect interconnected greenways) seems to be about the only thing they both look upon favorably, because it does not negatively affect the financial "bottom line."

In most suburban subdivision situations, land designated for protection according to the design principles described in this handbook should remain within undivided conservation areas and should not be allowed to be split into the back portions of large individual houselots, a situation in which the potential headaches involved in monitoring and enforcing easements tend to multiply and intensify. ("Backyard easements" also make it nearly impossible to ensure that the various kinds of natural resource areas on the property will be managed according to any commonly agreed principles, as each lot owner would be responsible for taking care of his or her own piece.) Again, requiring that conservation land remain undivided does not constitute a "taking" because none of it would be designated for public use, unless that were the joint wish of the developer and the local officials.

NEGOTIATING FOR LIMITED PUBLIC ACCESS

In light of the Supreme Court decision in *Tigard v. Dolan,* conservative advice to communities wishing to promote public access across private conservation land within new subdivisions would be to offer developers density incentives in exchange for easements permanently conferring such privileges for the purposes of walking, hiking, and cross-country skiing, at least within "green ribbon" corridors along certain trails, especially those that could potentially connect with other existing or future trails on adjoining lands. Although statutes in a number of states grant local governments the authority to require that five to ten percent of the land within proposed subdivisions be dedicated to public use, the constitutionality of such legislation is at least open to question as a result of several more recent decisions on property rights issues by federal courts, including the Supreme Court.

To ensure that the potential for a community-wide trail system through the interconnected open space network envisioned in this handbook is not diminished by gaps along certain critical sections passing through future subdivisions where the developer initially objects to limited public usage as described above, the zoning ordinance should contain provisions allowing local officials to offer the enticement of a certain percentage of additional lots. Another approach, not involving density incentives, would be to request "term easements" that would grant access privileges on a temporary but renewable basis, such as annually. These arrangements, sometimes called "access agreements," allow the developer (and ultimately the homeowners' association) to retain continuing control over the situation, so that if problems arise they can threaten to withhold the renewal unless the problems are corrected. Clearly, it would be in the best interests of all parties to work together to avoid and/or correct such problems, because everyone stands to benefit when trails in different subdivisions are connected with one another, providing longer and more interesting walking opportunities both for people in the proposed subdivision and for those residing in adjoining developments.

ENDOWMENT FUNDS FOR ONGOING MAINTENANCE

Although homeowners' associations can easily raise annual operating funds to cover the costs of maintaining their conservation land, the same is not true of nonprofit conservation organizations (such as land trusts). Even though the cost to individual members of homeowners' associations can be quite modest (typically $75 to $250 annually when elaborate facilities are not part of the open space), the total costs not reimbursed to a land trust, especially when viewed cumulatively, can be extremely burdensome. Whenever all or part of the open space within a conservation subdivision is offered to such a group, an endowment should be provided. Funds for this endowment could come from the developer through the sale of additional lots over and above the normal permitted density, provided the zoning ordinance contains specific language providing for such bonuses. The size of this endowment should be such that the interest it generates annually would be sufficient to cover the ongoing expenses of managing the prop-

erty, in terms of property tax payments, liability insurance premiums, mowing grassy areas and meadows, maintaining trails, bridges, and any other facilities, controlling erosion, and keeping the woodlands clear of invasive plants, trees, and especially woody vines. Even when the conservation area given to a land trust consists entirely of farmland, whose lease income can offset taxes and liability insurance premiums, the possibility of those fields reverting to second-growth woodland in 25 years (or whenever agriculture may become inviable in the area) should be factored in, along with estimated annual costs related to forest management and trails maintenance. This topic is also discussed in Chapter 9, under the section heading "Management Plans and Permanent Funding Sources."

DESIGN STANDARDS FOR AFFORDABLE HOUSING

Because real estate sold at prices affordable to local residents earning less than the median household income tends to be less profitable than larger residences marketed to more affluent people, it is usually not provided in the quantity that is needed. Another important factor in pricing out homes that can be afforded by your children and mine is the local zoning ordinance that typically requires considerably more land per dwelling unit today than it did 10 or 15 years ago. Therefore the key to reducing housing costs lies not so much in constructing smaller homes with the least expensive materials that still meet building codes, but in *reducing the land cost per dwelling.* In most areas, house price inflation has far exceeded the rising cost of materials and labor, and is directly linked to soaring land prices, which in turn reflect contemporary zoning densities. Therefore, whenever a landowner or developer seeks to have land rezoned for higher density (a decision that will surely increase its value and his or her potential profit), the township or county should be able to cite an official policy that requires a *quid pro quo* in the form of an enforceable condition stating that a certain percentage of the additional dwellings made possible by the rezoning must be made available to local first-time homebuyers with household incomes below a certain figure.

In other cases, where such rezoning is not requested, the local government could offer a substantial density bonus to encourage the provision of new homes that would be priced at levels that local teachers, nurses, public safety personnel, and others could afford, even if they have no real estate equity to apply toward the purchase. In order that new development built under such provisions not look like low-income housing projects, the density bonus should be large enough to cover the additional cost of designing the buildings and the site layout in such a way that they would be appealing to the eye and enjoyable to live in. Design standards governing certain features such as building volume, massing, roof shape and pitch, window size, proportions and "rhythm" (on the facades), exterior materials, and maximum number of dwellings per building could all be drafted and adopted.

As a general suggestion, to avoid the problem of designs that are inappropriate to your community (but which might not be out of place in other areas or in more suburban locations), standards could be related to the vernacular architecture, as expressed in the traditional nineteenth century buildings found in your region's small towns and villages. "Twins" and three-family homes can easily be designed to resemble large single-family residences, and there is no shortage of building plans—in current issues of house design catalogs—for modest, compact starter homes based upon historical precedents.

It would also be helpful to all parties involved if the standards were to be illustrated. An excellent case in point is the new 100-page ordinance amendment adopted by Manheim Township, Lancaster County, Pennsylvania, pertaining solely to planned residential developments—which is so lengthy because it contains 86 photos, elevations, perspective sketches, and site plans showing applicants, regulators, and the public the kind of development that is expected at these higher densities. Such large undertakings could easily include a wide range of house sizes and prices, as are offered at the award-winning Woodlake development outside Richmond, Virginia, where buyers may choose from apartments and condos, to homes varying from $80,000 to $650,000, depending on their distance to the water. (For the best description of the standards adopted in Manheim, see Nelessen, *Visions for a New American Dream,* 1994.)

Another condition of approval should definitely pertain to the minimum percentage of usable upland that is reserved as undivided conservation areas within the new affordable developments. If there is any group in society that is more likely to have the need for convenient and accessible open space, it is those who can least afford it, at least in the way this amenity is usually provided (in golf course developments, for example). Families with young children and single-parent households would both benefit greatly from the provision of open space near their homes, including active and passive recreational facilities.

Management Techniques for Conservation Lands

This chapter deals with a number of issues related to the management of the conservation lands that are preserved through creative residential development layouts. Among the topics discussed are how to afford permanent protection to conservation areas, how to create effective homeowners' associations, how to create a permanent funding source to maintain the open space, and how to deal with property tax and accident liability issues.

PERMANENT PROTECTION THROUGH CONSERVATION EASEMENTS

The most effective and most common method used to protect land set aside for conservation purposes, in this and other contexts, is the "conservation easement." This is a legally enforceable agreement permitting the easement holder (or other co-signers) to take action to prevent alterations to the designated land, and to require that incursions be removed and that the land be restored to its preexisting state, if altered in a manner not allowed by the easement. Such easements are restrictive in nature and are generally written to prohibit all but a certain number of types of activities to occur upon the land (such as specific types of farming, nature conservation, and passive recreation). In developments containing different kinds of open space, including active recreation facilities, those uses can also be permitted, but the easement document should be accompanied by a map identifying those parts of the property that are subject to different levels of restriction.

Easements run with the title and are recorded in the county Register of Deeds. They may be altered only with the express written permission of the easement holder and any other co-signers. Easements are typically granted to land conservation organizations such as land trusts or conservancies. They may also be granted to units of government at the municipal, county, or state levels. When held by a governmental body it is advisable that these easements also be co-signed by an independent conservation organization to act as a check or balance, in the event that future office holders seek to alter long-standing conservation policies for short-term reasons, or simple expediency.

Granting a conservation easement can sometimes provide financial advantages in terms of federal taxation, but only when the conservation restriction serves a legitimate public purpose and when the building density has been lowered to such a degree that the land's economic value has been reduced. As this does not occur with "density-neutral" conservation subdivision design, this is not an issue here.

Organizations holding easements are required to visit the land at least once yearly, to inspect it and to prepare a brief report (with photographic documentation of any infractions). To cover such monitoring costs, a growing number of conservation organizations request an "endowment" from the developer, in an amount sufficient to produce annual interest income equal to its out-of-pocket expenses. Techniques for generating such endowments are discussed later in this chapter.

As mentioned in Chapter 8, it is highly recommended that the protected conservation land within subdivisions be delineated *outside* individual houselots and that its boundaries be clearly marked. These steps should help reduce potential problems related to monitoring and enforcing conservation easements on such areas, and would enable those lands to be managed according to a set of uniform standards (rather than being neglected or mismanaged).

CREATING EFFECTIVE HOMEOWNERS' ASSOCIATIONS

The natural lands (and possible recreational facilities) that are established in conservation subdivisions are typically owned and managed by homeowners' associations, or HOAs. (They are sometimes owned by local land trusts, and even more rarely they are donated to the local government for use as a public park.) The vast majority of such associations have long track records of smooth and successful operation, although some of them have experienced a variety of problems.

There are three key ways to avoid difficulties when establishing homeowners' associations. First, *membership must be automatic* for all purchasers of houselots or homes. This is accomplished by making membership a condition of sale, and the membership document is only one of many that purchasers must sign at the closing or settlement. Second, the association bylaws (which should be reviewed by the township or county attorney before final plan approval is granted) must *authorize the HOA to place liens* on the real property of members who fail to pay their dues. The lien clouds the title, preventing the owner from selling until he or she pays all back dues, with interest. (Very few homeowners would withhold dues payment and risk becoming known as a deadbeat or freeloader in their own neighborhood—but this is always a wise preventive measure.) Third, it is advisable to *minimize regular maintenance costs* so that dues may remain low. Except in large-scale developments, fancy physical improvements that cost a lot to operate (such as swimming pools, hot tubs, and buildings of any sort) should be very carefully considered to ensure that their ongoing maintenance will not be a burden for the number of residents involved. In smaller developments, open space maintenance might consist of mowing several greens every week, mowing a meadow once or twice a year, and pruning branches and clearing occasional trees that have fallen across a woodland trail. At this level, annual HOA dues can be as low as $75 or $100 per family.

MANAGEMENT PLANS AND PERMANENT FUNDING SOURCES

Zoning regulations should be amended not only to require HOAs to have automatic membership and lien authority but also to require that developers submit management plans for the conservation lands and other open spaces in their subdivisions. Such plans would establish management objectives, outline procedures, and define responsibilities for maintaining the conservation areas. Typically, grassy commons require fertilization, irrigation, and mowing; meadows are mown after wildflower seeds have been set; and woodlands frequently require annual pruning not only to keep trails clear but also to check the growth of invasive tree species (such as Norway maple) and exotic vines (Oriental bittersweet, Japanese honeysuckle, multiflora rose, etc.), especially along their outer edges.

After several years of reviewing proposals for conservation subdivisions (which their local zoning requires for all residential developments encompassing more than five acres), officials in Lower Merion Township, Montgomery County, Pennsylvania, engaged the Natural Lands Trust to prepare a model *Maintenance and Operations Plan* on which developers may base their proposals for ongoing land stewardship activities. Such an approach is helpful to all parties involved, clarifying what the municipality wants, while at the same time helping applicants to satisfy township requirements. The three basic principles of designing conservation areas are:

1. *Conservation areas should include the most sensitive resource areas of a property.* In addition, they should include locally significant features of the property, such as hedgerows, hillocks, and scenic viewpoints.

2. *Fragmentation of conservation land should be minimized so that these resource areas are not divided into numerous small parcels located in various parts of the development.* To the greatest extent practicable, this land should be designated as a single block with logical straightforward boundaries. Long, thin strips of conservation land should be avoided, unless necessary to connect other significant areas, or when they are designed to protect linear resources such as streams or trails.

3. *Conservation areas should be designed as part of larger continuous and integrated open space systems.* Whenever possible, they should connect with existing or potential conservation areas on adjoining parcels.

Another principle is that conservation land should not be permitted to be divided into individual backyard areas, unless it is located in a "limited development" with a gross density of ten acres per dwelling, or lower.

The cost of ongoing maintenance is normally supported entirely through annual dues paid by members of HOAs. When land trusts agree to accept open space, in any location, they usually stipulate that a reserve fund be established by the donor, interest from which would cover its anticipated operational costs. Assuming interest income accruing at a rate of five percent per annum, the size of that fund must be twenty times as large as the projected average yearly maintenance costs. Because most donors are not in a financial position to make that kind of contribution in addition to the land itself, land trusts routinely work with donors to generate this needed endowment through the simple expedient of creating certain additional "endowment lots." Recognizing the benefits of creating such endowments for new HOAs, local zoning regulations should be amended specifically to permit a small density bonus for the purpose of ensuring that future HOAs will have the financial means to implement Maintenance and Operations Plans of the kind currently required by progressive townships such as Lower Merion. (See Model Ordinance language in Appendix H, Section I.B.)

DEALING WITH LIABILITY AND TAX ISSUES

Rural landowners who do not charge a fee for the recreational use of their land are shielded from liability suits by statutes and case law which set tougher standards requiring that "gross negligence" be proven by accident victims. Simply stepping into a rabbit hole along a trail or tripping on a stone or tree root protruding from the forest floor are not sufficient grounds to win suits against rural landowners who allow casual public access. The same applies to land trusts and to homeowners' associations, which are not obligated to maintain woodland trails as if they were level city sidewalks, or to fence paths along creeks.

Courts have generally looked favorably on noncommercial providers of open space, unless they are guilty of "willful or malicious failure to guard or warn against a dangerous condition." Failure to undertake regular inspection of facilities that might contain unnatural dangers—such as rusty nails protruding from docks or rafts—could, however, result in at least partial damages against a HOA. For these and other reasons, HOAs should be required by the local government to carry sufficient insurance coverage to meet possible court judgments against them.

Regarding payment of property taxes on any conservation land that is permanently protected in an open space subdivision, responsibility falls to the owner of record, usually a HOA. Tax assessments on such land should be minimal because it has no current or potential future use other than as open space, as per restrictions in the conservation easement. For this reason, assessments on conservation land could be expected to be similar to those levied on wetlands, or on unbuildable land within high-velocity flood zones.

When one pauses to think about it, there is no reason that conservation subdivisions should pay property taxes that are lower or higher than would conventional developments, if the same total acreage and the same number of dwelling units are involved. Tax bills to 60 homeowners for their homes and "cluster" lots, taken together with the tax bill for their common open space (paid by the HOA) should produce the same total amount that would be generated by 60 homes on standard dimension lots with no open space. Put simply, tax responsibility for the open space is typically transferred to the owners of each lot or unit who would pay it either as part of the taxes on their dwelling, or as an additional and separate tax bill, prorated among the total number of co-owners. (The practice of sending one separate tax bill, on the total conservation lands, to the HOA is not practiced by some local governments due to a worst-case scenario fear that someday the HOA might decide not to pay, as a means of forcing the township or county to assume ownership and maintenance responsibilities on it, for nonpayment of taxes. Although this is an unlikely scenario, that potential situation could probably be avoided by including the open space assessment as part of each homeowner's tax bill.)

Toward a New Land Ethic in Your Community

The idea of a "land ethic" represents an evolution from the first two kinds of ethics long recognized by our predominantly Judeo-Christian culture: those that govern relations among individuals, and those that govern relations between individuals and society. Sixty years ago Professor Aldo Leopold, who founded the discipline of game management at the University of Wisconsin, suggested a third kind of ethic, to deal with "man's relation to the land."

In ancient Greece and Rome, even the first kind of ethic had not yet become fully formed: wealthy men were expected to be faithful and treat their wives with dignity, but were free to buy and sell other human beings in the slave market. As Leopold wrote, "During the three thousand years which have since elapsed, ethical criteria have been extended to many fields of conduct, with corresponding shrinkages in those judged by expediency only."

The second major kind of ethic governs one's relations to society and is characterized by the Golden Rule and the creation of democratic institutions for self-governance.

However, as Leopold observed in 1933,

> There is yet no ethic dealing with man's relation to the land and the animals and plants which grow upon it. Land, like

Odysseus' slave-girls, is still property. The land-relation is still strictly economic, entailing privileges but not obligations.

Ethics essentially limit one's freedom of action. Since Leopold's day government has begun to fill the vacuum caused by the absence of a general land ethic, not only in the United States but in every major industrialized country. Individual actions that would produce long-term damage to the environment at great cost to the larger community (such as pollution of rivers, lakes, and aquifers through use or disposal of hazardous or toxic chemicals), but which would also produce short-term profit for the individual landowner or businessman, are now limited or prohibited by laws and regulations.

The idea of a land ethic is probably very much alive in the minds and hearts of many rural residents, including many landowners. What farmer, for example, would truly prefer the noise of traffic or the hum of air conditioners over the sound of birdsong or the rustle of wind through the leaves? Who would prefer to see rooftops defining the horizon line instead of treetops, or parking lots instead of fields and meadows?

In Leopold's time there were few financial alternatives for those who depended upon the value of their land to ease their retirement years, or to pay for health care costs. Today a variety of options exist, allowing landowners to realize the economic value of their farms and woodlands, without destroying the wildlife and ecological values of their property. This handbook illustrates one of these options, one that could be used along with others to strike a better balance between development and natural areas conservation.

Among those other options are the purchase of development rights, the transfer of development rights, "landowner compacts" involving density shifts among contiguous parcels, bargain sales to land conservancies, and "limited development" into mini-farms or country estates. Of the entire range of alternatives, it is likely that *the approach described in this handbook offers the greatest potential because it does not require public expenditure, does not depend upon landowner charity, does not need a special "high end" market, does not involve complicated regulations for transferring rights to other sites, and does not depend upon the cooperation of two or more adjoining landowners to make it work.*

This is not to imply that the other options should not be actively encouraged in your community, but rather to place those techniques in a realistic perspective as supporting elements to an area-wide program of conservation and development that is most logically based upon the flexibility and advantages offered by "conservation subdivision design." The great advantage of some of those other options is that many of them preserve parcels in their entirety (or a larger proportion of their land area), although they are implemented less frequently. The great advantage of conservation subdivision design is that it will probably be used much more frequently than the other techniques because the implementation of development regulations and standards is more of a day-to-day occurrence than PDR, TDR, etc.

Leopold would not be entirely happy with the approach advocated in this handbook, for he was uncompromising in his strong conservation philosophy. In fact, in *A Sand County Almanac,* he specifically warned against trying to appeal to landowners' economic self-interest as a basis for their adopting a land ethic, because many elements in the natural world that lack commercial value are nevertheless vital to its healthy functioning. However, if one accepts that most people have legitimate economic concerns and expectations regarding their land, based upon their legal rights under local zoning and subdivision codes, a more balanced approach would involve appealing to *both* economic and ethical considerations at the same time. This could increase the possibility that at least one of the messages will be heard, and that the other message will help to persuade the undecided listener that the "conservation subdivision" approach will enable him or her to "do well while also doing good."

Leopold was absolutely right when he pointed out that "We can be ethical only in relation to something we can see, feel, understand, love, or otherwise have faith in." Tangible examples of what can be easily lost or almost as easily saved help us to appreciate how much of our community's rural character is needlessly at risk of gradually disappearing under a blanket of conventional development. People who love their communities should take a fresh look at the remaining unbuilt and unprotected land through the eyes of a typical developer. Unless local ordinances governing subdivision design are modified to reflect conservation principles, every parcel that is not inherently unbuildable will ultimately be cleared, graded, and converted to standard subdivisions or other forms of suburban development—unless it is donated to a conservation organization or purchased at fair market value with private or public money.

In such communities—which unfortunately are the norm rather than the exception—it is not unrealistic for residents to suggest parallels with familiar places that were recently rural but are now thoroughly developed: areas such as Long Island—once famed for its fresh vegetables, tomato catsup, and baking potatoes, but now better known for its clogged highways and polluted tidal creeks.

For, without an enlightened land ethic, communities that are hamstrung by conventional zoning and subdivision ordinances are destined to repeat the same mistakes and to experience similar fates.

Sixty years on, the country's leading environmental thinkers acknowledge the significance of Leopold's observations and warnings. They frequently quote his dicta that all ethics rest upon the premise that "the individual is a member of a community of interdependent parts," and that "the land ethic simply enlarges the boundaries of the community to include soils, waters, plants and animals, or collectively: the land."

As Leopold taught us, ethical attitudes toward the land are necessarily based on respect and admiration for its various life forms. In their recent collection of essays on man's relation to other elements in the natural world, *The Biophilia Hypothesis,* Stephen Kellert and E.O. Wilson assert that humans are inherently dependent on nature not only for food and sustenance but also for "aesthetic, intellectual, and spiritual meaning and satisfaction" (Kellert and Wilson, 1993). In other words, "much of the human search for a coherent and fulfilling existence is ultimately dependent upon our relationship with nature."

The other side of the coin is that people can become quite capable of consciously damaging the environment when they have become alienated or estranged from nature. Those who feel no connection with the natural world are certainly incapable of possessing the kind of land ethic Leopold described. It may help to minimize the number of such individuals, who grow up lacking any conscious connection with the natural world, if greater opportunities were provided for people of all ages (especially those in their formative years) to have frequent, informal, and positive contacts with the natural world, so that their inborn tendencies to relate to nature and all forms of life may be gently stimulated and encouraged.

These opportunities generally do not arise in suburbia today, where one must typically drive miles to the nearest "nature center" simply to go for a walk in the woods. Such opportunities should be consciously designed to exist in every new neighborhood, supplemented by wider opportunities to explore entire stream valleys and related upland meadows or forests.

Situations such as these would be commonplace 20 years from now in our developing communities if residents and local officials were to take steps to create community open space networks through the principles of conservation subdivision design, approaches that would dovetail well with the development of new or expanded settlements designed around New Urbanist principles, and with more traditional but limited approaches to land protection, such as encouraging easements and donations, or raising public or private funds to purchase land or its development rights.

To the extent that readers of this volume become aware of practical ways to conserve some of the familiar and well-loved elements of their local landscapes that they see and nearly take for granted every day—features they would miss dearly if they disappeared next year (including fields, woodlands, meadows, hedgerows, riverbanks, bayshores, and lakefronts)—this handbook will have served its purpose.

Appendix A

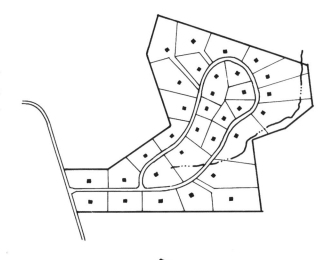

Schematic graphics and summary statistics are provided here for the seven conservation subdivisions detailed in Chapter 7. The purpose of this appendix is to offer a brief overview of the results obtained on these seven very different sites and to enable readers to compare them more easily.

Site A: GENTLY SLOPING SITE IN THE PIEDMONT REGION

Land Type	Percentage	Acreage
Primary Conservation Area	21%	17.0 acres
Secondary Conservation Area	44%	36.5 acres
Total conservation land	65%	53.5 acres
Developed area	35%	28.5 acres

Density Calculations:

82.0 acres total

−17.0 acres Primary Conservation Area

65.0 acres remaining (buildable)

−6.5 acres for streets (10%)

58.5 acres net

58.5 acres divided by 80,000 square feet per dwelling equals 32 lots

- Total developed area comprises 28.5 acres (consisting of 32 lots @ 30,000 square feet, plus 6.5 acres for streets), or 35% of the site.

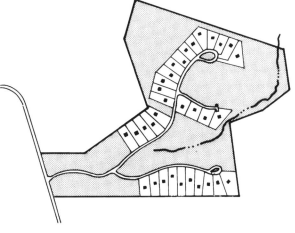

Site B: MOSTLY WOODED SITE AT THE BASE OF THE FOOTHILLS

Land Type	Percentage	Acreage
Primary Conservation Area	21%	15.0 acres
Secondary Conservation Area	31%	22.0 acres
Total conservation land	53%	37.0 acres
Developed area	47%	33.0 acres

Density Calculations:

　　70.0 acres total

　−15.0 acres Primary Conservation Area

　　55.0 acres remaining (buildable)

　　−5.5 acres for streets (10%)

　　49.5 acres net

　　49.5 acres divided by 60,000 square feet per dwelling equals 36 lots

- The developed area comprises 33 acres (consisting of 36 lots @ 35,000 square feet plus 3 acres for streets), or 47% of the site.

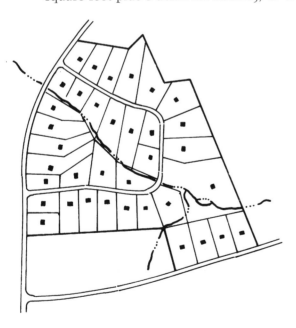

Site C: ADJACENT TO A SHALLOW BAY AND TWO TIDAL CREEKS

Land Type	Percentage	Acreage
Primary Conservation Area	31%	18.0 acres
Secondary Conservation Area	48%	27.7 acres
Total conservation land	79%	45.7 acres
Developed area	21%	12.3 acres

Density Calculations:

    58.0 acres total

    −18.0 acres Primary Conservation Area

    40.0 acres remaining (buildable)

    −4.0 acres for streets (10%)

    36.0 acres net

    36 acres divided by 20,000 square feet per dwelling equals 72 lots

- The developed area comprises 12.3 acres (consisting of 72 lots @ 5,000 square feet, plus four acres for streets), or 21% of the site.

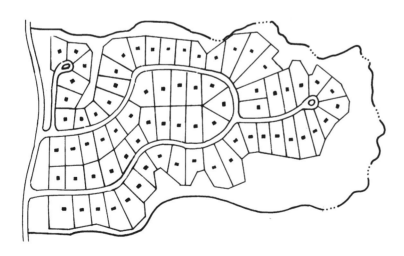

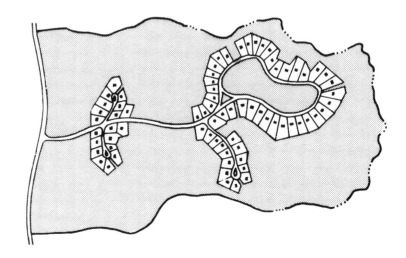

Site D: UPLAND PASTURE, WATER MEADOWS, AND SMALL CREEK

Land Type	Percentage	Acreage
Primary Conservation Area	30%	19.0 acres
Secondary Conservation Area	33%	21.0 acres
Total conservation land	63%	40.0 acres
Developed area	37%	23.0 acres

Density Calculations:

    63.0 acres total

    −19.0 acres Primary Conservation Area

    44.0 acres remaining (buildable)

    −4.4 acres for streets (10%)

    39.6 acres net

    39.6 acres divided by 82,000 square feet per dwelling equals 21 lots

- The developed area comprises 23 acres (consisting of 21 one-acre lots plus two acres for streets), or 37% of the site.

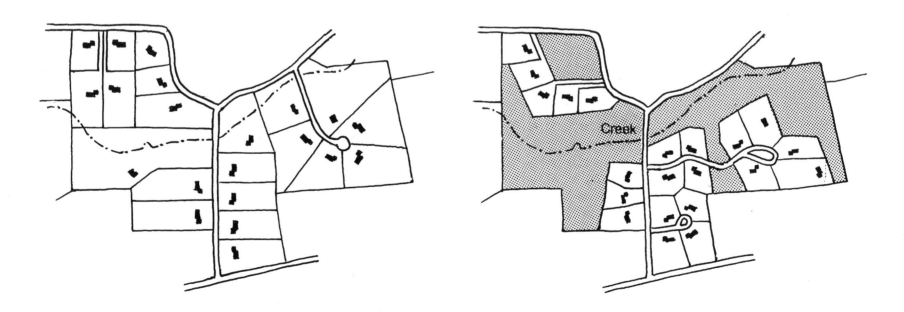

Site E: LAKEFRONT SITE IN THE NORTHERN WOODS

Land Type	Percentage	Acreage
Primary Conservation Area	11%	5.0 acres
Secondary Conservation Area	53%	24.5 acres
Total conservation land	64%	29.5 acres
Developed area	36%	16.5 acres

Density Calculations:

46.0 acres total

−5.0 acres Primary Conservation Area

41.0 acres remaining (buildable)

−4.1 acres for streets (10%)

36.9 acres net

36.9 acres divided by 2 acres per dwelling equals 18 lots

- Total developed area comprises 16.5 acres (consisting of 18 lots @ 30,000 square feet, plus 4.1 acres for new streets), or 36% of the site.

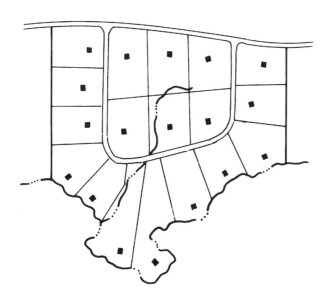

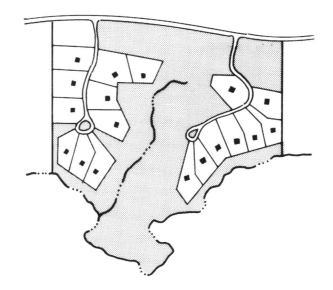

Site F: FARM WITH CIVIL WAR BATTLE–RELATED RESOURCES

Land Type	Percentage	Acreage
Primary Conservation Area	8%	10 acres
Secondary Conservation Area	55%	71 acres
Total conservation land	62%	81 acres
Developed area	38%	49 acres

Density Calculations:

> 130.0 acres total
> –10.0 acres Primary Conservation Area
>
> 120.0 acres remaining (buildable)
> –12.0 acres for streets (10%)
>
> 108.0 acres net
>
> 108.0 acres divided by two acres per dwelling equals 54 lots

- The developed area comprises 49 acres (54 lots of 30,000 square feet each, plus 12 acres for streets), or 38% of the site.

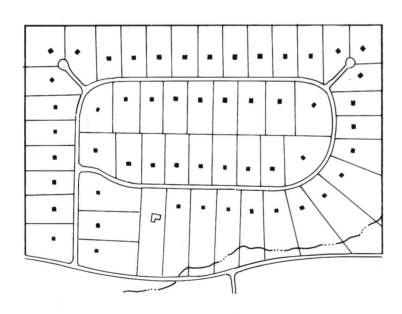

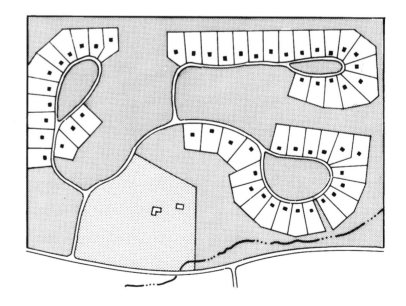

Site G: OLD FIELDS, SWAMP FOREST, AND ARCHAEOLOGICAL SITES ON THE SOUND

Land Type	Percentage	Acreage
Primary Conservation Area	28%	14.4 acres
Secondary Conservation Area	37%	18.6 acres
Total Conservation Land	65%	33.0 acres
Developed Area	35%	17.7 acres

Density Calculations:

    50.7 acres total

    –14.4 acres Primary Conservation Area

    36.3 acres remaining (buildable)

    –3.3 acres for streets (10%)

    33.0 acres net

    33.0 acres divided by one acre per dwelling equals 33 lots

- The developed area comprises 17.7 acres, or 35% of the site.

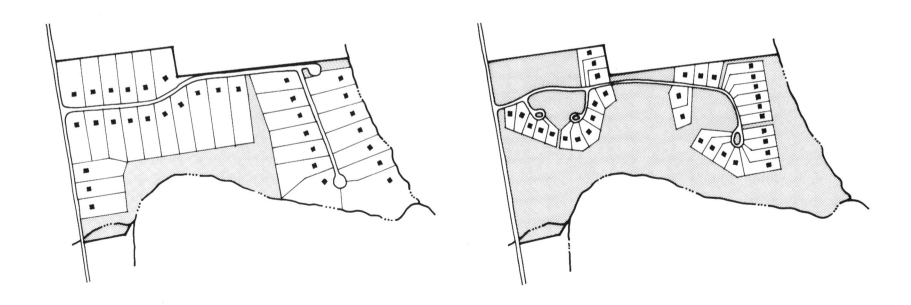

Appendix B

Alternative layouts generated by citizen participants during a workshop on conservation design indicate that use of the "four-step" methodology described in this handbook is likely to produce consistent results regarding open space conservation, albeit with different street alignments and different lot shapes and arrangements. Held in Stroudsburg, Pennsylvania, in January 1994, the workshop—directed toward local developers and municipal officials—was underwritten by the Terrestrial Ecosystem Protection Initiative of the U.S. Environmental Protection Agency and by the National Park Service, Division of Park and Resource Planning (Region III).

The great majority of participants were municipal officials from Monroe County (primarily township supervisors and planning commissioners) with no prior experience in site design. Others included members of county conservation districts, developers of well-planned but essentially conventional subdivisions and their engineering consultants, realtors, and a county commissioner and a lay member of the county planning board. Although some of these other participants had considerable site planning experience, none had ever designed a true conservation subdivision before.

After a slide presentation on conservation subdivision design techniques by the author (with numerous built examples illustrating what such neighborhoods look like on the ground), workshop participants divided into three groups and were given drawings of the yield plan and of the Primary and Secondary Conservation Areas for Site B in this handbook.

Without any knowledge of the final layout for this site (shown in Fig. 7B-9) and without any cross-discussion among the groups, three different solutions were independently generated. Reproduced in schematic form here in this appendix, they show broad agreement with regard to the overall pattern of conservation and development, but exhibit different internal approaches to the design of street systems and individual lot configurations. All of the design solutions were judged successful by the workshop organizers, a pronouncement that added to the satisfaction felt by the participants themselves.

The results of this exercise indicate that *it is probably difficult to generate a truly inappropriate or disappointing design solution when the four-step method is followed.* Whatever else the exercise might or might not have proven, it demonstrated to the participants that when laypersons are provided with the basic background site in-

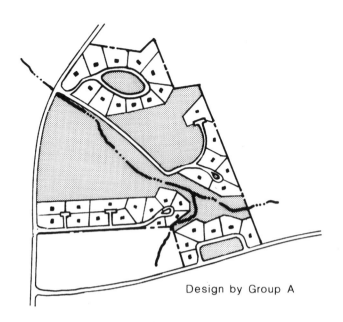

Design by Group A

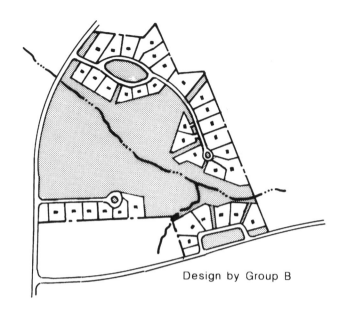

Design by Group B

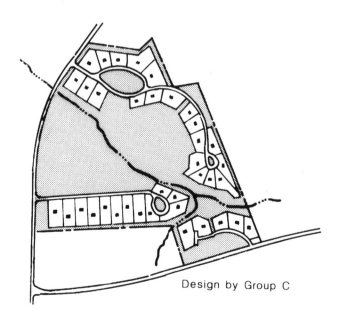

Design by Group C

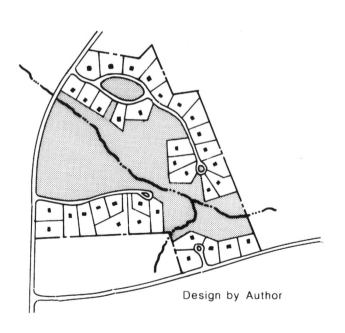

Design by Author

formation described in Chapter 5, they are capable of designing good conservation subdivisions with a minimum of training. It is expected that this experience is likely to lead them to demand more of developers and their consultants in the future. It was also clear that the participants genuinely enjoyed their "hands-on" design experience, and that the extra time involved in setting up and conducting this exercise was well worth the effort.

Another interesting feature of the workshop was a "lottery" in which various categories of winners received "free" consultations from the Natural Lands Trust, under contract with the EPA and the National Park Service. Among the winners were townships desiring guidance in updating their zoning and subdivision standards, developers seeking design assistance on current and future projects, and joint township–developer combinations in which both parties had volunteered to collaborate to produce mutually workable solutions in their communities.

Part of the success of the workshop is due to the fact that the two federal agencies that organized it had secured co-sponsorships from the regional homebuilders association and from the regional chamber of commerce. A local builder and a local realtor, both well-known in the area, participated formally as speakers, adding their views that everyone can benefit and profit from open space development designs that protect the environment.

Another factor in the workshop's success was that instead of consuming an entire day, it was divided into two sessions, each held on a Saturday morning two weeks apart. Scheduling in January ensured that it would not conflict with many other events or diversions. (Other good times of the year are early November, February, and—in more northern states—March, which is "mud season.") And scheduling the workshops two weeks apart avoided consuming time on consecutive weekends, time that many participants might have been unwilling to commit to such an exercise.

One upshot of the workshop is that a number of "local partners" emerged from various professions interested in promoting the

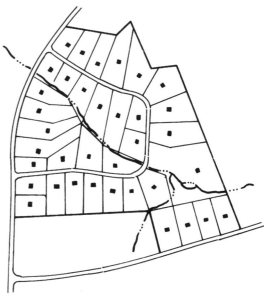

"Yield Plan"

idea of open space design. Among the participants who expressed interest in helping to "spread the word" were professional developers, planners, engineers, architects, landscape architects, and foresters. These individuals could become key figures at the local and regional levels in keeping these concepts alive, given the 100-mile distance between the federal agency offices and the Poconos.

Postscript

A year after the Poconos workshop described above, I conducted one in the Pittsburgh area in which I learned more about how to make these design exercises even more fun for participants. Co-sponsored by the Pennsylvania Environmental Council and the Allegheny Land Trust, this workshop took place at a local hotel one week before Hallowe'en. Noticing that each of the tables had a goblet filled with candy corn kernels, and that the kernels were about the size of houses on the site plan base maps, I suggested that each group take 35 kernels from these containers and locate them on their worksheets, as if they were actual houses. People generally liked this offbeat idea quite a lot, as it enabled them literally to play around with the house locations and experiment with different layouts, before using their pencils. The flexibility these kernels provided was part of their appeal. Their unusual shape and bright colors made them interesting objects to move around, and the thought of using them to represent houses was unusual enough to strike their fancy. In addition, the ability to eat them up at the end of the exercise may have held some symbolic meaning. Whatever the reason, several people remarked that this was the most enjoyable planning workshop they had ever attended. School teachers have known for generations that students generally learn better and faster if they are actively involved and if they are not bored by the activity. One lesson that emerges from this experience is that the use of offbeat props can be a great help when conducting design workshops for conservation subdivisions.

Appendix C

DETAILED HOUSELOT DESIGNS AT HIGHER NET DENSITIES

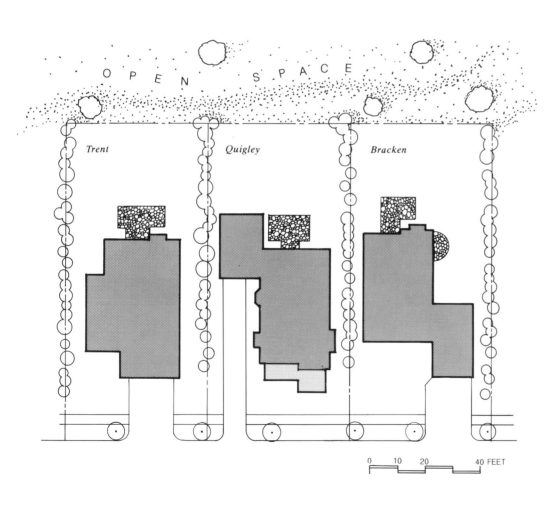

This sketch shows how single-family detached homes could be located on the most compact lots recommended in this handbook in a manner that would provide private outdoor areas in backyards buffered along their side lot lines by trees, shrubs, and garden fences. Front elevations and floor plans for the three houses in the layout at left are shown in Appendix D, along with a number of other examples. On some of the homes designed for particularly narrow lots, windows are minimized or absent on one of the side walls to maximize privacy between homes. The open space abutting their rear lot lines psychologically extends these properties through long views across the conservation land.

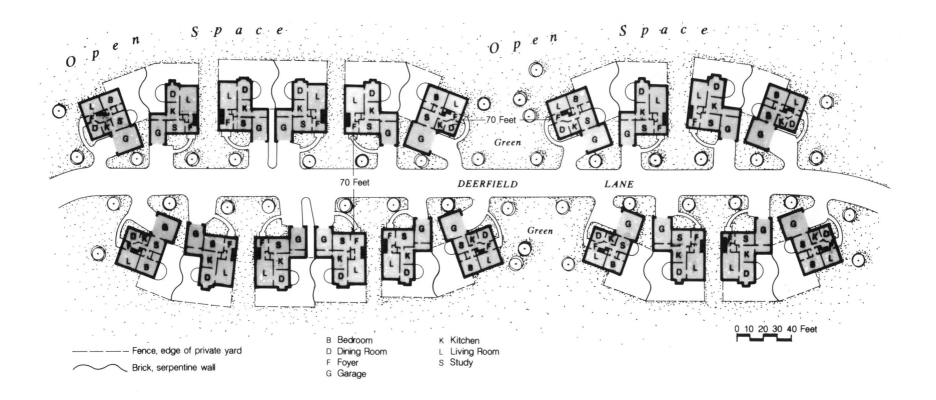

As shown in the layout above, single-family detached homes containing 2,100 square feet and having one- and two-car garages can be located on 50-foot frontages in an attractive and workable fashion, when they back up to open space. Privacy issues are dealt with by limiting the number of side-wall windows and by separating backyards with wooden fencing and curving brick walls. A special design feature of this layout is the siting of end units at a 70-degree angle from the road, so that end units in neighboring groups face each other across 70 feet of green space. This door-to-door distance is similar to that of homes facing each other on opposite sides of the street and is based on measurements taken in small villages and hamlets in the surrounding rural district.) This building pattern can be seen in the successful "Deerfield Knoll" development in Willistown Township, Chester County, Pennsylvania (shown in the photograph on the facing page).

Single-family homes grouped around a pond at Deerfield Knoll illustrate the physical relationships of the houses shown on the site plan on the preceding page. Garages are located quite close together (6 to 10 feet apart), and windowless endwalls on the other sides of the houses are between 12 and 18 feet apart. An end unit, just to the right of the center, is set at an angle to the road and faces another end-unit about 70 feet away (both can be seen reflected in the pond).

Another view of the homes at Deerfield Knoll, taken from the front yard of one of the houses across the street. The average width of these houselots is 55 feet, which is sufficient to accommodate each 25-foot wide house with attached one-car garage. End units come with two-car garages. All homes contain 2,100 square feet of floorspace, in addition to their full basement.

Appendix D

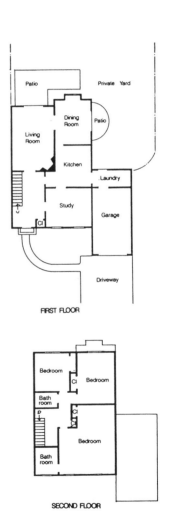

FIRST FLOOR

SECOND FLOOR

The Bracken: This 2,100 square foot home measures 40 feet wide, including its single-car garage. Because the house itself is just 25 feet in width, one side yard can be 20 feet wide in the area behind the garage, creating additional usable yard space in addition to the patio and rear lawn, off the dining room. This house includes a living room, dining room, study/family room, eat-in kitchen, three bedrooms, and 2 ½ baths. (Courtesy of Leonard Blair, Blair & Son, Bryn Mawr, Pennsylvania. This is one of the classic designs that Blair has built at Deerfield Knoll in Willistown Township, Chester County, Pennsylvania.)

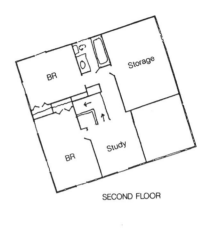

SECOND FLOOR

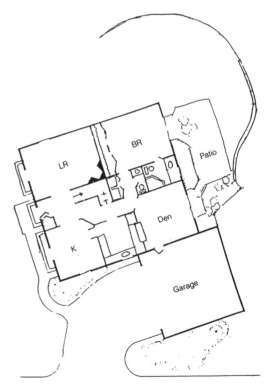

FIRST FLOOR

The Abbott: This design is one of several offered at Deerfield Knoll, Willistown Township, in Chester County, Pennsylvania. Containing 2,100 square feet of living space (with a full basement as well), this home features a master bedroom and a den with a cathedral ceiling on the ground floor, both of which open onto an enclosed patio, in addition to a living room with fireplace, kitchen, dining room, and full bath. The second floor contains two bedrooms, a study loft, and a large storage area. By locating this end unit at a 30-degree angle from the street and facing the main entrance onto open space, the developer has been able to minimize the garage door as a visual element. (Readers are referred to the photo on page 141.) And by enclosing the patio with a serpentine brick wall, the developer has been able to provide backyard privacy for these homes, despite the fact they are located on lots that are just 55 feet wide.

Second Floor

The Chaucer: This 2,500 square foot home is one of several models built at Malvern Hills in the Borough of Malvern, Pennsylvania, by SBCM and Kahn Properties. The ground floor plan includes a foyer, dining room, study, great room with a fireplace and cathedral ceiling, and a large kitchen with a breakfast area, plus a powder room and a two-car garage. On the second floor are three bedrooms (one with a large walk-in closet), two full bathrooms, and a linen closet. A fourth bedroom is optional, in place of the cathedral ceiling in the great room. From a streetscape perspective, an advantage of this design is that the garage doors face to the left (not toward the front) and therefore do not dominate the home's appearance, as seen head-on from the street.

First Floor

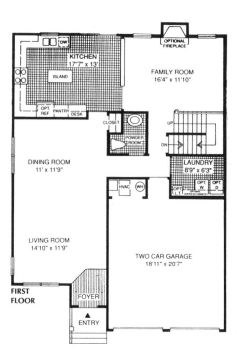

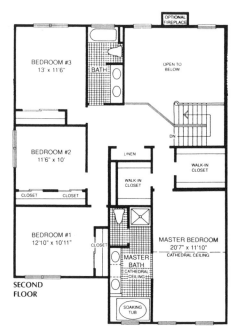

The Buckingham: This 2,400 square foot residence is one of five models (each with a choice of fa-cades) built at Fox Heath in Perkiomen Township, Montgomery County, Pennsylvania, by Hovnanian Homes. This model features a spacious living room/dining room, a family room with fireplace and cathedral ceiling, eat-in kitchen, and a laundry room and a powder room on the ground floor, with four bedrooms, two full baths, and two large walk-in closets on the second floor. The front elevation comes with a choice of front porches, and although the garage doors face the street, their visual prominence is reduced by the second-story windows and the two roof dormers. By incorporating the garage into the ground floor plan, the architect was able to design this home at an efficient 32-foot width, allowing it to be sited on 40-foot wide lots.

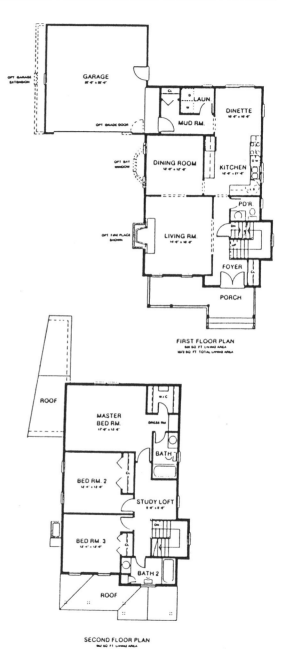

The Quigley: This design is based on a measured drawing of a "Queen Anne" style home in Canandaigua, New York, and has been used in the "Canandaigua Classics" subdivision in that town. The garage has been set back from the front facade in order to reduce its visual presence as seen from the street, and it connects to the eat-in kitchen through a mudroom and laundry. The 1,924 square foot home also features a large front porch, a living room with fireplace, a dining room, a study loft, three bedrooms, and 2 ½ baths.

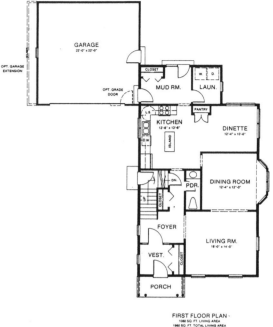

FIRST FLOOR PLAN
1080 SQ. FT. LIVING AREA
1960 SQ. FT. TOTAL LIVING AREA

The Phelps: This design is another in the "Canandaigua Classics" series (see preceding page). It is an adaptation of the ever-popular Greek Revival style home built extensively during the 1840s. In this two-story, three-bedroom home, the front door opens into a vestibule, which serves to prevent drafts sweeping into the principal chambers. Other features of this 1,960 square foot house include a two-story foyer, a mudroom/laundry leading from the attached garage, an eat-in kitchen, and 2 ½ baths.

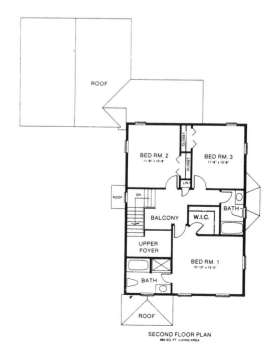

SECOND FLOOR PLAN
880 SQ. FT. LIVING AREA

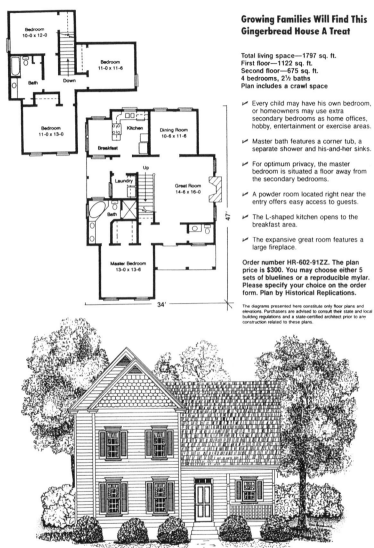

Growing Families Will Find This Gingerbread House A Treat

Total living space—1797 sq. ft.
First floor—1122 sq. ft.
Second floor—675 sq. ft.
4 bedrooms, 2½ baths
Plan includes a crawl space

- Every child may have his own bedroom, or homeowners may use extra secondary bedrooms as home offices, hobby, entertainment or exercise areas.

- Master bath features a corner tub, a separate shower and his-and-her sinks.

- For optimum privacy, the master bedroom is situated a floor away from the secondary bedrooms.

- A powder room located right near the entry offers easy access to guests.

- The L-shaped kitchen opens to the breakfast area.

- The expansive great room features a large fireplace.

Order number HR-602-91ZZ. The plan price is $300. You may choose either 5 sets of bluelines or a reproducible mylar. Please specify your choice on the order form. Plan by Historical Replications.

The diagrams presented here constitute only floor plans and elevations. Purchasers are advised to consult their state and local building regulations and a state-certified architect prior to any construction related to these plans.

To Order, Phone Toll Free 1-800-393-7379   PB&R Zero Lot Line/9

Inviting Porch Welcomes Guests

The inspiration for this charming turn-of-the-century house is found in Natchez, Mississippi. The inviting porch extends a gracious invitation to friends and neighbors.

Once inside, a very impressive foyer leads to the living room or the great room. A formal dining room, located conveniently between the kitchen and the living room, lends itself to easy entertaining.

The master bedroom has a bath with a separate shower stall, as well as an oversized tub. A large walk-in closet completes the amenities of this spacious room. The other bedrooms share a compartmentalized bath.

This plan is especially well-suited for a narrow lot.

First floor: 1,066 sq. ft.
Second floor: 913 sq. ft.

Total living area: 1,979 sq. ft.

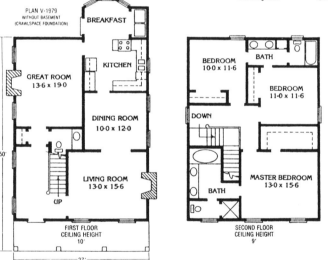

PLAN V-1979
WITHOUT BASEMENT
(CRAWLSPACE FOUNDATION)

Blueprint Price Code B

Plan V-1979

TO ORDER THIS BLUEPRINT,
CALL TOLL-FREE 1-800-547-5570
(prices and details on pp. 12-15.)

Shutters And Shakes Bring Country Charm To This Affordable Plan

Total living space—1098 sq. ft.
First floor—702 sq. ft.
Second floor—396 sq. ft.
3 bedrooms, 2 baths

✔ The vaulted ceiling in the great room lends volume to the gathering space that is warmed by a fireplace.

✔ The open kitchen/dining room area is well located to easily serve the accessible deck for outdoor dining on warm summer nights.

✔ The master bedroom location affords privacy, while providing close proximity to the full hallway bath.

✔ Secondary bedrooms are located on the upper level and share a full bath.

Order number HR-689-88MM-AF91. Use plan price schedule A. Plan by Historical Replications Inc.

The diagrams presented here constitute only floor plans and elevations. Purchasers are advised to consult their state and local building regulations and a state-certified architect prior to any construction related to these plans.

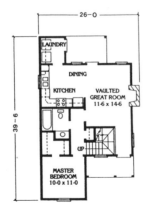

Chimney Plays Prominent Role In Exterior Intrigue

Total living space—1690 sq. ft.
First floor—845 sq. ft.
Second floor—845 sq. ft.
3 bedrooms, 2½ baths

✔ The side entry is an unusual design twist.

✔ The living room boasts a fireplace and a sitting area at the front window.

✔ The dining room features French doors that access the back yard. The corner countertop can also serve as a snack bar.

✔ All bedrooms are located on the second floor. The master suite features a compartmented bath, dual vanity and garden tub in a corner setting.

✔ Secondary bedrooms share a full bath. A linen/plant ledge conveniently sits nearby, in the hall corner.

Order number LWG-1086-89MM-AF91. Use price plan schedule A. Plan by Larry W. Garnett & Associates Inc.

The diagrams presented constitute only floor plans and elevations. Purchasers are advised to consult their state and local building regulations and a state-certified architect prior to any construction related to these plans.

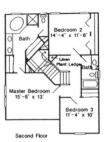

Second Floor

First Floor

8' Clg. Throughout

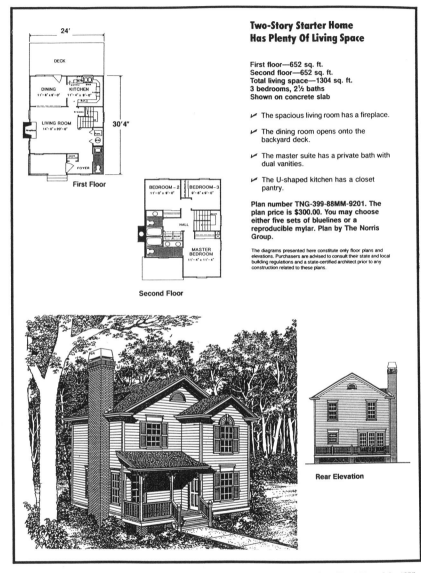

Two-Story Starter Home Has Plenty Of Living Space

First floor—652 sq. ft.
Second floor—652 sq. ft.
Total living space—1304 sq. ft.
3 bedrooms, 2½ baths
Shown on concrete slab

✔ The spacious living room has a fireplace.

✔ The dining room opens onto the backyard deck.

✔ The master suite has a private bath with dual vanities.

✔ The U-shaped kitchen has a closet pantry.

Plan number TNG-399-88MM-9201. The plan price is $300.00. You may choose either five sets of bluelines or a reproducible mylar. Plan by The Norris Group.

The diagrams presented here constitute only floor plans and elevations. Purchasers are advised to consult their state and local building regulations and a state-certified architect prior to any construction related to these plans.

First Floor

Second Floor

Rear Elevation

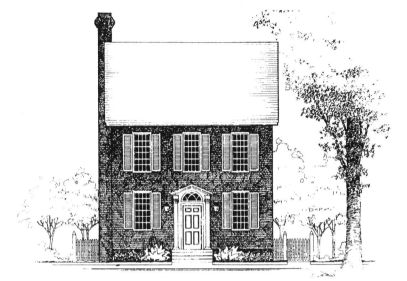

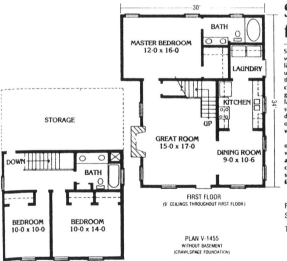

Stately Charm for Small Lot

Small but stately, this charming dwelling with its classic and perfectly proportioned lines is ideal for a diminutive lot in an urban setting. Economical to construct, this enchanting design will generate compliments from all who see it. The generously sized living room appears even larger than it is, due to the open-stringed stairway which rises from it. The formal dining room, framed by a large cased opening, is filled with light from its long windows.

The master bedroom suite supplies the owners with a particularly inviting bath. A well-placed skylight will flood the dressing area with light. If desired, the owners could postpone the completion of the second floor until the expansion of their family requires additional space.

First floor:	936 sq. ft.
Second floor:	519 sq. ft.
Total living area:	1,455 sq. ft.

FIRST FLOOR
(9' CEILINGS THROUGHOUT FIRST FLOOR)

SECOND FLOOR
(8' CEILINGS ON SECOND FLOOR)

PLAN V-1455
WITHOUT BASEMENT
(CRAWLSPACE FOUNDATION)

Blueprint Price Code A

Plan V-1455

TO ORDER THIS BLUEPRINT,
CALL TOLL-FREE 1-800-547-5570
(prices and details on pp. 12-15.) **109**

All-Brick Home Has Stately Appearance

First floor—2066 sq. ft.
Second floor—601 sq. ft.
Total—2667 sq. ft.
3 bedrooms, 2½ baths
Plan includes basement

✔ With its open floor plan, this is a perfect home in which to entertain.

✔ The island kitchen shares space with the bayed breakfast area.

✔ The dining room features French doors and skylights.

✔ The living room and the family room each have a fireplace.

✔ The first-floor master suite has French doors to the backyard and a luxury bath with oval tub, separate shower, his-and-her vanities and compartmented toilet.

✔ Upstairs, bedrooms two and three share a large, compartmented bath.

Order number LWG-1001-91ZZ. Price is $400.05 for five sets of bluelines or one reproducible mylar. Please specify your choice on the order form. Plan by Larry Garnett & Associates Inc.

The diagrams presented here constitute only floor plans and elevations. Purchasers are advised to consult their state and local building regulations and a state-certified architect prior to any construction related to these plans.

Clerestory Windows Shower Loft With Light

Total living space—1551 sq. ft.
First floor—1067 sq. ft.
Second floor—484 sq. ft.
2 bedrooms, 2½ baths

✔ A cathedral ceiling embellishes the living/dining room areas. Window interest and a cozy fireplace make it an elegant gathering spot.

✔ The kitchen affords a sunny spot that can be used as a breakfast nook.

✔ The first-floor study can be used as a guest room.

Order number CMA-486-88MM-AF91. Use plan price schedule A. Plan by Claude Miquelle & Associates.

The diagrams presented here constitute only floor plans and elevations. Purchasers are advised to consult their state and local building regulations and a state-certified architect prior to any construction related to these plans.

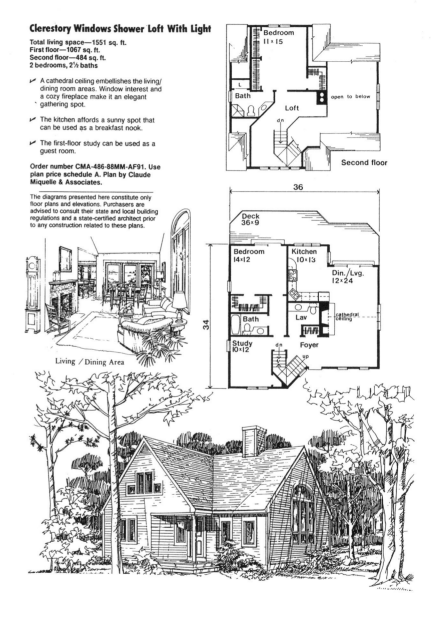

Living / Dining Area

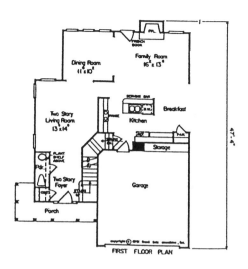

FIRST FLOOR PLAN

The Trent: This house is essentially 34 feet wide (not including the six-foot extension of the front porch) and contains 1,800 square feet of living space plus a two-car garage. Features include a foyer and living room with cathedral ceilings, a family room with fireplace, a dining room, an eat-in kitchen, three bedrooms, and 2 ½ baths.

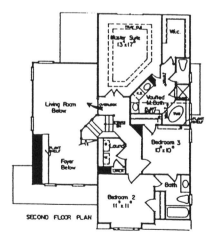

SECOND FLOOR PLAN

Appendix E

ECONOMIC BENEFITS OF OPEN SPACE UPON REAL ESTATE

REAL PROPERTY VALUES

Greenway corridors provide a variety of amenities, such as attractive views, open space preservation, and convenient recreation opportunities. People value these amenities. This can be reflected in increased real property values and increased marketability for property located near open space. Developers also recognize these values and incorporate open space into planning, design, and marketing new and redeveloped properties.

Increased Property Values—Quantified

The effect on property values of a location near a park or open space has been the subject of several studies. Statistical analyses have been a common method of attempting to measure this effect. These analyses attempt to isolate the effect of open space from

other variables which can affect property values, such as age, square footage, and condition of homes. Isolating the effect of open space can be difficult and results have been varied. Nevertheless, many studies have revealed increases in property values in instances where the property is located near or adjacent to open spaces. Most studies have addressed traditional parks or greenbelts (large open space areas), though a few studies are available for greenways.

- A study of property values near greenbelts in Boulder, Colorado, noted that housing prices declined an average of $4.20 for each foot of distance from a greenbelt up to 3,200 feet. In one neighborhood, this figure was $10.20 for each foot of distance. The same study determined that, other variables being equal, the average value of property adjacent to the greenbelt would be 32 percent higher than those 3,200 feet away (Correll, Lillydahl, and Singell, 1978).

- The amenity influence of greenbelt land on property values also applies to privately held greenbelt land, according to a study of the Salem metropolitan area in Oregon. In this case, the greenbelt was comprised of rural farmland. Greenbelt zoning had been applied to this prime farmland beginning in 1974 in an effort to contain urban sprawl and preserve farmland. The study found that urban land adjacent to the greenbelt was worth approximately $1,200 more per acre

Excerpted from *Economic Impacts of Protecting Rivers, Trails, and Greenway Corridors,* National Park Service (Rivers, Trails and Conservation Assistance Section), 1993. Note that references cited in this excerpt do not appear in this handbook. The interested reader should refer to the original publication for reference listings.

than urban land 1,000 feet away from the greenbelt boundary, all other things being equal. However, rural land values within the restrictive zoning actually decreased in value by $1,700 per acre (Nelson, 1986).

•   A recent study of market appreciation for clustered housing with permanently protected open space in Amherst and Concord, Massachusetts, found that clustered housing with open space appreciated at a higher rate than conventionally designed subdivisions. Appreciation was measured as the percent increase in open-market sales price. The study compared one clustered development and one conventional subdivision in each community. The clustered homes studied in Amherst appreciated at an average annual rate of 22%, as compared to an increase of 19.5% for the more conventional subdivision. This translated into a difference in average selling price of $17,100 in 1989 between the two developments. In both Amherst and Concord, the homes in the clustered developments yielded owners a higher rate of return, even though the conventional subdivisions had considerably larger lot sizes (Lacy, 1991).

•   An analysis of property surrounding four parks in Worcester, Massachusetts, showed a house located 20 feet from a park sold for $2,675 (1982 dollars) more than a similar house located 2,000 feet away (More, Stevens, and Allen, 1982).

•   In the neighborhood of Cox Arboretum, in Dayton, Ohio, the proximity of the park and arboretum accounted for an estimated 5 percent of the average residential selling price. In the Whetstone Park area of Columbus, Ohio, the nearby park and river were estimated to account for 7.35 percent of selling prices (Kimmel, 1985).

•   In the vicinity of Philadelphia's 1,300 acre Pennypack Park, property values correlate significantly with proximity to the park. In 1974, the park accounted for 33 percent of the value of a plot of land (when the land was located 40 feet away from the park), nine percent when located 1,000 feet away, and 4.2 percent at a distance of 2,500 feet (Hammer, Coughlin and Horn, 1974).

The effects of proximity to open space may not be as simply quantified as in the above studies. Many studies (Brown and Connelly; Colwell, 1986) have found the potential for an increase in property value depends upon the characteristics of the open space and the orientation of surrounding properties. Property value increases are likely to be highest near those greenways which:

– highlight open space rather than highly developed facilities

– have limited vehicular access, but some recreational access

– have effective maintenance and security

•   Similar residential properties near a park in Columbus, Ohio, were compared to determine if proximity to the park affected property values. Conclusions showed properties where the homes that faced the park sold for between seven to 23 percent more than homes one block from the park. Those homes that backed up onto the park sold at values similar to properties one block away (Weicher and Zerbst, 1973).

One implication of these studies might be that increases in nearby property values depend upon the ability of developers, planners, and greenway proponents to successfully integrate neighborhood development and open space. Designing greenways to minimize potential homeowner–park user conflicts and maximize the access and views of the greenway can help to avoid a decrease in property values of immediately adjacent properties.

Increased Property Values—Surveyed

Survey methodology has also been used to document perceived increases in property values. Surveys can be less time-consuming, less expensive, and generally require less specialized expertise than detailed statistical analyses. The following findings are based upon surveys of property owners and real estate professionals.

•   In a recent study, *The Impacts of Rail-Trails,* landowners along three rail-trails reported that their proximity to the trails had not adversely affected the desirability or values of their properties. Along the suburban Lafayette/Moraga Trail in California, the majority of the owners felt that the trail would make their properties sell more easily and at increased values. The other two trails studied included the Heritage Trail in eastern Iowa and the St. Marks Trail in Florida (National Park Service and Pennsylvania State University, 1992).

• A study completed by the Office of Planning in Seattle, Washington, for the 12 mile Burke-Gilman trail was based upon surveys of homeowners and real estate agents. The survey of real estate agents revealed that property near, but not immediately adjacent to the trail, sells for an average of 6 percent more. The survey of homeowners indicated that approximately 60% of those interviewed believed that being adjacent to the trail would make their home sell for more or have no effect on the selling price (Seattle Office of Planning, 1987).

•   In a survey of adjacent landowners along the Luce Line rail-trail in Minnesota, the majority of owners (87 percent) believed the trail increased or had no effect on the value of their property. Fifty-six percent of farmland residents thought the trail had no effect on their land values. However, 61 percent of the suburban residential owners noted an increase in their property value as a result of the trail. New owners felt the trail had a more positive effect on adjacent property values than did continuing owners. Appraisers and real estate agents claimed that trails were a positive selling point for suburban residential property, hobby farms, farmland proposed for development, and some types of small town commercial property (Mazour, 1988).

INCREASED PROPERTY TAX REVENUES

An increase in property values generally results in increased property tax revenues for local governments. Many arguments made for park and open space investment claim these acquisitions pay for themselves in a short period of time, due in part to increased property tax revenues from higher values of nearby property. A point to remember, however, is that in many jurisdictions, assessments of property values often lag behind market value. Furthermore, in those states which have passed legislation limiting real estate tax increases, such as California's Proposition 13, property tax revenues also lag behind increases in market value.

•   California's Secretary for The Resources Agency anticipated that $100 million would be returned to local economies each year from an initial park bond investment of $330 million. The returns were to be in the form of increased value of nearby properties and stimulated business (Gilliam, 1980).

•   A study of the impacts of greenbelts on neighborhood property values in Boulder, Colorado, revealed the aggregate property value for one neighborhood was approximately $5.4 million greater than if there had been no greenbelt. This results in approximately $500,000 additional potential property tax revenue annually. The purchase price of the greenbelt was approximately $1.5 million. Thus, the potential increase in property tax alone could recover the initial cost in only three years. In the study, the authors did note that this potential increase is overstated in part because actual assessments may not fully capture greenbelt benefits (Correll, Lillydahl, and Singell, 1978).

CONSTRUCTION/DEVELOPMENT PERSPECTIVES

Proximity to greenways, rivers, and trails can increase sales price, increase the marketability of adjacent properties, and promote faster sales. Clustering the residential development to allow for establishment of a greenway might also decrease overall development costs and result in greater profits for the developer.

•   A land developer from Front Royal, Virginia, donated a 50-foot wide seven-mile easement for the Big Blue Trail in northern Virginia after volunteers from the Potomac Appalachian Club approached him to provide a critical trail link along the perimeter of his second-home subdivision. The developer recognized the amenity value of the trail and advertised that the trail would cross approximately 50 parcels. All tracts were sold within four months (American Hiking Society, 1990).

•   Thirty-five acres were set aside as a protected corridor through a 71-lot subdivision for approximately one-half mile of the Ice Age Trail in Wisconsin. The Ice Age Trail Foundation had purchased the parcel when the land became available for sale and was being considered for development. Later the Foundation sold the parcel to a subdivision developer, after placing an easement on the trail corridor. The developer now touts the easy access to the Ice Age Trail in promotional subdivision brochures (Pathways Across America, Winter 1991).

- Hunters Brook (Yorktown Heights, New York), a cluster development of 142 townhouse-style condominium units ranging in price from $170,000 to $260,000, was designed to capitalize on the amount of open space in the development. The homes were clustered on 30 acres, preserving 97 acres of natural sloping woods, including a dense pine forest. Care had been taken to retain local wildlife, thus adding to the rural setting. One of the developers commented, "It may not be the woods that bring (buyers) to us initially, but it seems to make all the difference when they see what it's like" (Brooks, 1987).

- In a 1970 study of a 760 square mile area in Maryland, noted planner Ian McHarg projected that uncontrolled development would yield $33.5 million in land sales and development profits by 1980. Profits resulting from development plans designed to accommodate the same population level, while preserving desirable open spaces, would exceed $40.5 million. The resulting additional $7 million translated into an increase in value of $2,300 per acre for the planned 3,000 acres of open space (Caputo, 1979).

SAMPLE OF REAL ESTATE ADS MENTIONING
PROXIMITY OF HOMES TO GREENWAYS

On any given Sunday in Raleigh and Durham, North Carolina, one can find numerous newspaper advertisements for homes and houselots citing proximity to the greenway network. Shown here is a sampling from the October 7, 1990 issue of the *Raleigh News and Observer*. (Note that phone numbers from the original advertisements have been partially omitted and italics have been added for emphasis.)

WELL LOVED RANCH WITH FULL BASEMENT—*backs up to city greenway,* follow the path to Shelley Lake. 2 finished rms. in basement. Sandra 870-xxxx (xxxx) $87,900

FARMINGTON WOODS Walk to school, perfect for growing family, *greenway,* 4 bedrooms, 3 baths, (65451) 859-xxxx/xxxx $144,900

UNIQUE CORNER cul-de-sac in Lochmere, *backs up to greenway,* build your own dreamhome! (64075) 859-xxxx $57,000

TRANSITIONAL RANCH *Backs up to greenway,* tongue-in-groove, cathedral ceiling, very open, (62617) 859-xxxx $89,900

NEW LISTING 3 bedrm 2½ bath home under construction in Planter's Walk. Fabulous 1st floor master with champagne bath. Lots of storage and 1 car garage. Deck. Great lot—*adjacent to greenway.* Only $106,475. Call Gina at 266-xxxx. Pulle homes.

VILLAGE ON GREEN Assume $6,000 townhome FHA 10.5%. End unit *backs to greenway.* Motivated! (59527) 876-xxxx

PREMO VIEW, privacy and *access to greenway* for exercise, affordable 2.5 bath townhome at $63,500. Nelson Bunn H563

SPACIOUS CARY TWNHSE, Pirate's Cove, 3 bedrms, 2.5 baths, living room, formal dining rm., large private *deck overlooks greenway.* exc. schools. $64,900. Owner pays closing costs. 467-xxxx

This appendix contains two newspaper articles that discuss the use of open space in subdivision development. The first is an article about golf course developments from *The Philadelphia Inquirer* (Real Estate Section, Sunday, September 26, 1993). The second is an article from *The Washington Post* (Saturday, January 7, 1995) on new interest in open space among homebuyers.

A Front Yard on the Front Nine

By Tom Belden
INQUIRER STAFF WRITER

When retirees Dick and Loretta Fagan began looking for a new townhouse in Montgomery County, having a view of golf-course greenery out the front and back doors was not their first requirement.

Dick Fagan admits to liking golf — he's addicted to it, in fact. And now that he has the time, he plays every day. But it was Loretta Fagan, a non-golfer, who actually found the couple's three-bedroom home in Pine-Crest, a housing development on a golf course in Montgomeryville.

All of the homes planned for Pine-Crest, a community developed by the Klein Co. that will eventually have 49 single-family homes and 270 townhouses, will overlook PineCrest's public golf course, providing one of the most sought-after amenities in housing today: a view of trees, flowers, gardens and open space that is unlikely to be marred anytime soon by construction.

"We looked for the ideal situation of a townhouse, and we think we found it," said Dick Fagan, whose home has a view of PineCrest's third fairway out the back and the first fairway from the front. "I play golf every day here, but really, we liked everything about it."

The Fagans are among those being drawn to the increasing number of verdant housing developments taking root in the midst of a local golf course or next to one.

While such communities have been popular for years in places where golf is a year-round game, including Florida, the Carolinas and the Southwest, developers say their numbers are increasing here because of the open space they provide as well as the growing interest among baby boomers in playing golf.

The developments provide a diversity of housing, ranging from townhouses priced at less than $80,000 to single-family homes for more than $500,000.

In this area, golf-course living is a surprisingly affordable luxury. But in a higher-priced real estate markets

See **GOLF**

Here, the Open Spaces Are Par for the Course

From **GOLF**

such as Washington and Miami-Fort Lauderdale, FL., many new homes fronting golf courses carry price tags of $1 million or more.

Officials at PineCrest, as well as other builders and real estate agents, say that people like the Fagans, empty nesters with grown children, make up the largest group of buyers of both townhouses and detached homes in area golf-course communities.

Single people and younger couples making their first investments in homes also are a major part of the townhouse market in the communities, builders say.

And at PineCrest and other developments, the buyers of single-family homes also include small bands of professionals moving in from the South or Southwest and other places where golf-course living has deep roots.

"Our homes have golf-course views from the rooms of the house where you live, from the kitchen and family and master bedrooms," said Don Brecker, PineCrest's vice president of sales and marketing. "That appeals to a lot of people. We have buyers here from the South, like people moving from Houston, who are used to golf-course living and won't consider anything else but a house on a golf course."

Undoubtedly helping to push sales in the golf-course developments is the number of people taking up the game these days. The National Golf Foundation, a trade organization of the golf business, has estimated that as many as 30 million adults could be playing the game by the mid-1990s, compared with fewer than 24 million in the early 80s.

"What's helped push the development in this part of the country is an incredible explosion in the popularity of golf," said Larry Henry, a senior associate in the Philadelphia office of PKF Consulting, a national real estate consulting firm.

A golf-course community also can give itself added cachet, and increase the asking prices of its homes, by having a prominent architect or famous professional player design its course.

Blue Bell Country Club, a Toll Bros. development in Blue Bell where a total of 850 homes are planned, is taking that approach, with a course whose original design was conceived by Arnold Palmer. Homes in the development command from $175,000 to more than $300,000 and are clustered in villages named after famous golf courses.

Although some golfers are drawn naturally to consider living along a golf course, playing the game isn't the main attraction for many of those buying property overlooking courses, developers and salespeople say.

As many as four out of five sales in some developments are to people who have little or no interest in dressing in funny-colored clothes and spending four or five hours batting a little white ball along the ground. Those people are buying the parklike views of open space, *views that can command both a premium in a home's initial sale price and its resale value.* (emphasis added)

"Anything along a golf course will bring a premium because of the open space," said Ann White of Weichert Realtors in West Chester, project manager for Twin Ponds, a Parec Construction Co. development in Douglas Township, Montgomery County, that overlooks a public course.

New Jersey builder John D'Anastasio learned a lot about the interests of buyers of property with a golf-course view when his D'Anastasio Corp. was selling his Fairway Townhomes development just off Haddonfield Road in Pennsauken Township five years ago. He thought some members of the adjacent Pennsauken Country Club would be eager to move in, he said.

The Fairway development and a smaller cluster of eight twin houses, The Twins of Iron Rock Court, that D'Anastasio now has under construction are along the fourth and fifth holes of the club, which is a public course operated by Pennsauken Township.

"We did a mailing to the members...because we thought that would be a primary market, but it's not been," the developer said. *"Maybe 20 percent of the buyers play golf."*

What has helped most, D'Anastasio said, has been the huge, landscaped 'yards' the townhouses have, the form of a golf course. And in the case of Pennsauken Country Club, it is very likely to be kept as a golf course because it is both a money-maker for the township and helps the municipality meet planning requirements to keep lands as open space, he said.

There is no guarantee, of course, that the golf course that draws a home buyer in the first place will stay that way. Numerous older courses in the Philadelphia area in recent years have been turned into residential or commercial developments.

Likewise, from a golfer's perspective, there is no guarantee that a golf course will have much aesthetic appeal if homes are built along all of its fairways and loom over some of its greens and tees. Some townhouse developments are packed so densely along golf courses that they can be distracting, to both a golfer hitting a shot and to a homeowner who lives in the line of fire.

Dick Fagan, the PineCrest resident, said that an expected part of living on a course is having an occasional stray golf ball land in the backyard and having a player wander up to the deck looking for it.

"There are times when you get some rowdy guys who'll come right up and play it off your air conditioner," he said, laughing. "Others won't come in the yard at all even if they know the ball is there."

Fagan added that among the reason he and his wife like their townhouse is that it's probably out of range of all but the longest and most errant of drives off of PineCrest's third tee. But, he added, the proximity of some homes to tee boxes means, "You'd have to be crazy to want to live there."

Community Living: Look for Bike Paths, Not Golf Courses

By Kenneth R. Harney

Hot attractions for 1995: Bike paths, hiking trails, outdoor living rooms and interactive community amenities.

Not so hot: Tennis courts, golf courses, fancy clubhouses and splashy subdivision entrances.

Extra security services, especially private guards patrolling the neighborhood in vehicles while you're asleep at night—are de rigueur. In fact, you probably wouldn't even buy without them.

And some new concepts, such as "community concierges" who will provide you all sorts of time-saving, free services—buying theater tickets, making reservations, helping with catering arrangements or shopping—are on the verge of taking off.

These are just a few of the findings emerging from a major, unreleased poll of what American home shoppers want—and will pay a premium for—in a newly developed community.

Conducted for a group of the largest-volume home builders in the country, the study is based on the responses from more than 800 consumers who bought or shopped for a home in planned communities last August and September in California, Texas, North Carolina, Florida and Georgia.

The research was performed by American Lives Inc., a San Francisco-based firm that interviews 80,000 to 100,000 consumers a year, primarily for the real estate industry.

Brooke Warrick, president of American Lives and designer of the study, said "what really jumps out at you" is that consumers now want features designed into new communities that not only allow—but promote—"interaction with other families, children and community organizations," far more than they did just five or 10 years ago. (emphasis added)

Consumers also are putting an increasingly high premium on interaction with the outdoor environment through the inclusion of wooded tracts, nature paths and even "wilderness areas" where possible, Warrick said. Back in the mid-1980s by contrast, he said, the top consumer draws in newly developed communities were tennis courts, swimming pools, golf courses and golf clubhouses. (emphasis added)

"Everybody wanted to look out at rolling greens from their own windows," Warrick said. But that has changed dramatically.

"The reality," he said, "is that after living on the edge of a golf course for a while, those homeowners discovered that golfers can be a pain. I mean, they hit balls into your windows, they intrude on your privacy and that's no fun."

Tennis courts used to be ranked as "essential" amenities by a high percentage of shoppers, but no longer.

"Tennis courts are nice," Warrick said, but they ranked only 28th out of 39 features that 1994 buyers defined as crucial in persuading them to buy in a particular new community. Having a golf course within the community came in 29th, and a golf clubhouse and pro shop ranked 34th.

So what features will command premium prices in 1995? Here are the top several:

- *No. 1. Community designs that deliver low traffic and quiet. Fully 93 percent of all home buyers and shoppers in the study rated this either "essential" or "very important." In Warrick's description, "if a builder or developer doesn't provide this, he's out of the game."*

- *No. 2. About 77 percent of consumers put "lots of natural, open space" in the must-deliver category, along with street designs that take the shape of cul-de-sacs, circles and courts.*

- *No. 3. Plenty of "walking and biking paths." Ideally Warrick said, the paths meander through wooded areas and parklands, and abut some homeowners' lots to enhance "a sense of interactivity among private houses and leisure-time,*

fun activities" by residents of all ages. (emphasis added)

Among other high-value, we'll-pay-premium-price features that emerged in the new study:

- An exercise or fitness center, run or overseen by the community itself, should be in the subdivision. Nearly 51 percent of consumers said this was essential or very important to their daily lifestyles.

"They don't want to have to go outside for this anymore," Warrick said. "It's got to be a place where you meet and interact with people from your own community."

- Wilderness areas. The idea here, according to Warrick, is to set aside substantial wooded acreage with the fauna and flora that existed before the development of the subdivision itself.

Along with other open, natural spaces, gardens and vest pocket parks, wilderness areas become part of what Warrick calls the new "outdoor living room" concept that buyers expect—and will pay extra to get—in a planned development.

After all, he said, "who cares if your lot is small or even your house is small when you've got an interactive, outdoor living room that goes on for acres?" (emphasis added)

Appendix H

OUTLINE OF CONTENTS

I. STANDARDS FOR "CONSERVATION SUBDIVISION DESIGN"

A. Determining Density or "Yield"

Applicants shall have the option of estimating the legally permitted density on the basis of mathematical percentages and formulas contained in this ordinance, or on the basis of a "yield plan." Such "yield plans" consist of conventional lot and street layouts and must conform to the township's regulations governing lot dimensions, land suitable for development (for example, not including wetlands), street design, and parking. Although such plans shall be conceptual in nature, and are not intended to involve significant engineering costs, they must be realistic and must not show potential house sites or streets in areas that would not ordinarily be legally permitted in a conventional layout.

In order to prepare a realistic "yield plan," applicants generally need to first map the Primary Conservation Areas on their site. Typical "yield plans" would include, at minimum, basic topography, location of wetlands, 100-year floodplains, slopes exceeding 25%, and soils subject to slumping, as indicated on the medium-intensity maps contained in the county soil survey published by the USDA Natural Resources Conservation Service.

On sites not served by public sewerage or a centralized private sewage treatment facility, soil suitability for individual septic systems shall be demonstrated. The Planning Commission shall select a small percentage of lots (10 to 15%) to be tested, in areas considered to be marginal. If tests on the sample lots pass the percolation test, the applicant's other lots shall also be deemed suitable for septic systems, for the purpose of calculating total lot yield. However, if any of the sample lots fail, several others (of the township's choosing) shall be tested, until all the lots in a given sample pass.

B. Density Incentives

1. To Endow Maintenance Fund. The township may allow a density bonus to generate additional income to the applicant for the express and sole purpose of endowing a permanent fund to offset continuing open space maintenance costs. Spending from this fund should be restricted to expenditure of interest, in order that the principal may be preserved. Assuming an annual average interest rate of 5%, the amount designated for the Endowment Fund should be twenty (20) times the amount estimated to be required on a yearly basis to maintain the open space. On the assumption that additional dwellings, over and above the maximum that would ordinarily be permitted on the site, are net of development costs and represent true profit, 75% of the net selling price of the lots shall be donated to the Open Space Endowment Fund for the preserved lands within the subdivision. Such estimates shall be prepared by an agency or organization with experience in open space management acceptable to the Planning Commission. This fund shall be transferred by the developer to the designated entity with ownership and maintenance responsibilities (such as a homeowners' association, a land trust, or the township).

2. To Encourage Public Access. Dedication of land for public use, including trails, active recreation, municipal spray irrigation fields, etc., in addition to the 10% public land dedication required under other provisions of this ordinance, may be encouraged by the supervisors who are authorized to offer a density bonus for this express purpose. The density bonus for open space that would be in addition to the 10% public land dedication that may also be required shall be computed on the basis of a maximum of one dwelling unit per five acres of publicly accessible open space. The decision whether to accept an applicant's offer to dedicate open space for public access shall be at the discretion of the board of supervisors, who shall be guided by the recommendations contained in the township's *Open Space Recreation, and Environmental Resources Plan,* particularly those sections dealing with trail networks and/or recreational facilities.

3. To Encourage Affordable Housing. A density increase is permitted where the conservation subdivision proposal provides on-site or off-site housing opportunities for low- or moderate-income families. The amount of the density increase shall be based on the following standard: *For each affordable housing unit provided under this section, one additional building lot or dwelling unit shall be permitted, up to a maximum 15% increase in dwelling units. Affordable housing is herein defined as units to be sold or rented to families earning 70 to 120 percent of the county median income, adjusted for family size, as determined by the U.S. Department of Housing and Urban Development.*

C. Minimum Percentage of Open Space

The minimum percentage of land that shall be designated as permanent open space, not to be further subdivided, and protected through a conservation easement held by the township or by a recognized land trust or conservancy, shall be as specified below:

1.   A minimum of fifty percent (50%) of the total tract area, after deducting the following kinds of unbuildable land (which are also required to be deducted when calculating net permitted density for conventional subdivisions as well):

- wetlands (both tidal and fresh) and land that is generally inundated (land under ponds, lakes, creeks, etc.),
- all of the floodway and floodway fringe within the 100-year floodplain, as shown on official FEMA maps,
- land with slopes exceeding 25%, or soils subject to slumping,
- land required for street rights-of-way (10% of the net tract area),
- land under permanent easement prohibiting future devlopment (including easements for drainage, access, and utilities).

The above areas shall generally be designated as *undivided open space,* to facilitate easement monitoring and enforcement, and to promote appropriate management by a single entity according to approved land management standards. [However, in subdivisions where the gross density is one dwelling per ten acres (or lower), the required open space may be included within individual lots.]

2.   All undivided open space and any lot capable of further subdivision shall be restricted from further subdivision through a permanent conservation easement, in a form acceptable to the township and duly recorded in the County Register of Deeds Office.

3.   At least twenty-five percent (25%) of the minimum required open space shall be suitable for active recreation purposes, but no more than fifty percent (50%) shall be utilized for that purpose, in order to preserve a reasonable proportion of natural areas on the site. The purposes for which open space areas are proposed shall be documented by the applicant.

4.   The required open space may be used, without restriction, for underground drainage fields for individual or community septic systems, and for "spray fields" for spray irrigation purposes in a "land treatment" sewage disposal system. However, "mound" systems protruding above grade and aerated sewage treatment ponds shall be limited to no more than ten percent of the required minimum open space.

5.   Stormwater management ponds or basins may be included as part of the minimum required open space, as may land within the rights-of-way for underground pipelines. However, land within the rights-of-way of high-tension power lines shall not be included as comprising part of the minimum required open space.

D. Location of Open Space

The location of open space conserved through compact residential development shall be consistent with the policies contained in the Open Space, Recreation, and Environmental Resources Element of the township's comprehensive plan, and with the recommendations contained in this section and the following section ("Evaluation Criteria").

Open space shall be comprised of two types of land: "Primary Conservation Areas" and "Secondary Conservation Areas." All lands within both Primary and Secondary Conservation Areas are required to be protected by a permanent conservation easement, prohibiting further development, and setting other standards safe-guarding the site's special resources from negative changes.

1. Primary Conservation Areas. This category consists of wet-lands, lands that are generally inundated (under ponds, lakes, creeks, etc.), land within the 100-year floodplain, slopes exceeding 25%, and soils subject to slumping. These sensitive lands are de-ducted from the total parcel acreage to produce the "Adjusted Tract Acreage," on which density shall be based (for both conventional and conservation subdivisions).

2. Secondary Conservation Areas. In addition to the Primary Conservation Areas, at least fifty percent (50%) of the remaining land shall be designated and permanently protected. *Full density credit shall be allowed for land in this category that would otherwise be buildable under local, state and federal regulations, so that their de-velopment potential is not reduced by this designation.* Such density credit may be applied to other unconstrained parts of the site.

Although the locations of Primary Conservation Areas are pre-determined by the locations of floodplains, wetlands, steep slopes, and soils subject to slumping, greater latitude exists in the desig-nation of Secondary Conservation Areas (except that they shall in-clude a 100-foot deep greenway buffer along all waterbodies and watercourses, and a 50-foot greenway buffer alongside wetlands soils classified as "very poorly drained" in the medium-intensity county soil survey of the USDA Natural Resources Conservation Service).

The location of Secondary Conservation Areas shall be guided by the maps and policies contained in the Open Space, Recreation, and Environmental Resources Element of the township's compre-hensive plan, and shall typically include all or part of the follow-ing kinds of resources: mature woodlands, aquifer recharge areas, areas with highly permeable ("excessively drained") soil, signifi-cant wildlife habitat areas, sites listed on the Pennsylvania Natural Diversity Inventory, prime farmland, historic, archaeological or cultural features listed (or eligible to be listed) on national, state or county registers or inventories, and scenic views into the prop-erty from existing public roads. Secondary Conservation Areas therefore typically consist of upland forest, meadows, pastures, and farm fields, part of the ecologically connected matrix of nat-ural areas significant for wildlife habitat, water quality protection, and other reasons. Although the resource lands listed as potential Secondary Conservation Areas may comprise more than half of the remaining land on a development parcel (after Primary Con-servation Areas have been deducted), no applicant shall be re-quired to designate more than 50% of that remaining land as a Sec-ondary Conservation Area.

3. General Locational Standards. Subdivisions and planned resi-dential developments (PRDs) shall be designed around both the Primary and Secondary Conservation Areas, which together con-stitute the total required open space. The design process should therefore commence with the delineation of all potential open space, after which potential house sites are located. Following that, access road alignments are identified, with lot lines being drawn in as the final step. This "four-step" design process is fur-ther described in Section II.B.6 below.

Both Primary and Secondary Conservation Areas shall be placed in undivided preserves, which may adjoin housing areas that have been designed more compactly to create larger areas that may be enjoyed equally by all residents of the development.

Undivided open space shall be directly accessible to the largest practicable number of lots within a conservation subdivision. To achieve this, the majority of houselots should abut undivided open space in order to provide direct views and access. Safe and conve-nient pedestrian access to the open space from all lots not adjoin-ing the open space shall be provided (except in the case of farm-land, or other resource areas vulnerable to trampling damage or human disturbance). Where the undivided open space is desig-nated as separate, noncontiguous parcels, no parcel shall consist of less than three (3) acres in area nor have a length-to-width ratio in excess of 4:1, except such areas that are specifically designed as village greens, ballfields, upland buffers to wetlands, waterbodies or watercourses, or trail links.

4. Interconnected Open Space Network. As these policies are implemented, the protected open spaces in each new subdivision will eventually adjoin each other, ultimately forming an interconnected network of Primary and Secondary Conservation Areas across the township. To avoid the issue of the "taking of land without compensation," the only elements of this network that would necessarily be open to the public are those lands that have been required to be dedicated for public use, never more than 10% of a development parcel's gross acreage, and typically configured in a linear fashion as an element of the township's long-range open space network.[1]

E. Evaluation Criteria

In evaluating the layout of lots and open space, the following criteria will be considered by the Planning Commission as indicating design appropriate to the site's natural, historic, and cultural features, and meeting the purposes of this ordinance. Diversity and originality in lot layout shall be encouraged to achieve the best possible relationship between development and conservation areas. Accordingly, the Planning Commission shall evaluate proposals to determine whether the proposed conceptual preliminary plan:

1. *Protects and serves all floodplains, wetlands, and steep slopes* from clearing, grading, filling, or construction (except as may be approved by the township for essential infrastructure or active or passive recreation amenities).

2. *Preserves and maintains mature woodlands, existing fields, pastures, meadows, and orchards, and creates sufficient buffer areas* to minimize conflicts between residential and agricultural uses. For example, locating houselots and driveways within wooded areas is generally recommended, with two exceptions. The first involves significant wildlife habitat or mature woodlands that raise an equal or greater preservation concern, as described in items #5 and #8 below. The second involves predominantly agricultural areas, where remnant tree groups provide the only natural areas for wildlife habitat.

3. *If development must be located on open fields or pastures because of greater constraints in all other parts of the site,* dwellings should be sited on the least prime agricultural soils, or in locations at the far edge of a field, as seen from existing public roads. Other considerations include whether the development will be visually buffered from existing public roads, such as by a planting screen consisting of a variety of indigenous native trees, shrubs, and wildflowers (specifications for which should be based upon a close examination of the distribution and frequency of those species found in a typical nearby roadside verge or hedgerow).

4. *Maintains or creates an upland buffer* of natural native species vegetation of at least 100 feet in depth *adjacent to wetlands and surface waters,* including creeks, streams, springs, lakes and ponds.

5. *Designs around existing hedgerows and treelines between fields or meadows, and minimizes impacts on large woodlands* (greater than five acres), especially those containing many mature trees or a significant wildlife habitat, or those not degraded by invasive vines. Also, woodlands of any size on highly erodible soils with slopes greater than 10% should be avoided. However, woodlands in poor condition with limited management potential can provide suitable locations for residential development. When any woodland is developed, great care shall be taken to design all disturbed areas (for buildings, roads, yards, septic disposal fields, etc.) in locations where there are no large trees or obvious wildlife areas, to the fullest extent that is practicable.

6. *Leaves scenic views and vistas unblocked or uninterrupted,* particularly as seen from public thoroughfares. For example, in open agrarian landscapes, a deep "no-build, no-plant" buffer is recommended along the public thoroughfare where those views or vistas are prominent or locally significant. The concept of "foreground meadows,"

---

[1]The legality of requiring public land dedication is open to question in light of the recent *Dolan v. Tigard* decision.

with homes facing the public thoroughfare across a broad grassy expanse (as illustrated in Fig. 5-5 of *Conservation Design for Subdivisions: A Practical Guide to Creating Open Space Networks*) is strongly preferred to mere buffer strips, with or without berms or vegetative screening. In wooded areas where the sense of enclosure is a feature that should be maintained, a deep "no-build, no-cut" buffer should be respected, to preserve existing vegetation.

7. *Avoids* siting new construction on prominent *hilltops or ridges,* by taking advantage of lower topographic features.

8. *Protects wildlife habitat areas* of species listed as endangered, threatened, or of special concern by the U.S. Environmental Protection Agency and/or by the Pennsylvania Natural Diversity Inventory.

9. *Designs around and preserves sites of historic, archaeological, or cultural value,* and their environs, insofar as needed to safeguard the character of the feature, including stone walls, spring houses, barn foundations, cellar holes, earthworks, and burial grounds.

10. *Protects rural roadside character* and improves public safety and vehicular carrying capacity by avoiding development fronting directly onto existing public roads. Establishes buffer zones along the scenic corridor of rural roads with historic buildings, stone walls, hedgerows, and so on.

11. *Landscapes common areas* (such as community greens), cul-de-sac islands, and both sides of new streets with native specie shade trees and flowering shrubs with high wildlife conservation value. Deciduous shade trees shall be planted at forty-foot intervals on both sides of each street, so that the neighborhood will have a stately and traditional appearance when they grow and mature. These trees shall generally be located between the sidewalk or footpath and the edge of the street, within a planting strip not less than five feet in width.

12. *Provides active recreational areas* in suitable locations that offer convenient access by residents and adequate screening from nearby houselots.

13. *Includes a pedestrian circulation system* designed to assure that pedestrians can walk safely and easily on the site, between properties and activities or special features within the neighborhood open space system. All roadside footpaths should connect with off-road trails, which in turn should link with potential open space on adjoining undeveloped parcels (or with existing open space on adjoining developed parcels, where applicable).

14. *Provides open space that is reasonably contiguous,* and whose configuration is in accordance with the guidelines contained in the *Design and Management Handbook for Preservation Areas,* produced by the Natural Lands Trust. For example, fragmentation of open space should be minimized so that these resource areas are not divided into numerous small parcels located in various parts of the development. To the greatest extent practicable, this land shall be designed as a single block with logical, straightforward boundaries. Long thin strips of conservation land shall be avoided, unless the conservation feature is linear or unless such configuration is necessary to connect with other streams or trails. The open space shall generally abut existing or potential open space land on adjacent parcels (such as in other subdivisions, public parks, or properties owned by or eased to private land conservation organizations). Such subdivision open space shall be designed as part of larger contiguous and integrated greenway systems, as per the policies in the Open Space, Recreation, and Environmental Resources Element of the township's *comprehensive plan.*

II. SITE PLANNING PROCEDURES FOR CONSERVATION SUBDIVISIONS

A. General

1. Process Overview. The sequence of actions prescribed in this article is as listed below. These steps shall be followed sequentially and may be combined only at the discretion of the Planning Commission:

a. Pre-application discussion

b. Existing Features (Site Analysis) Plan (90-day clock starts with the submission of this plan at the on-site walkabout or at a regularly scheduled meeting of the Planning Commission)

c. On-site walkabout by planning commissioners and applicant

d. Pre-submission conference

e. Conceptual Preliminary Plan (*conceptual illustration* of greenway land, potential house sites, street alignments, and tentative lot lines, prepared according to the four-step design process described herein)

f. Preliminary Plan submission, determination of completeness, review of overall planning concepts, and decision

g. Preliminary engineering certification

h. Final Plan submission, determination of completeness, review, and decision

i. Supervisors' signatures

j. Recording at County Recorder of Deeds

B. Elements of the Preliminary Plan Process

1. Pre-Application Discussion. A pre-application discussion is strongly encouraged between the applicant, the site designer(s), and the Planning Commission. The purpose of this informal meeting is to introduce the applicant and the site designer(s) to the township's zoning and subdivision regulations and procedures, and to discuss the applicant's objectives in relation to the township's official policies and ordinance requirements. The township may designate a consultant experienced in development design and in the protection of natural features and greenway lands to meet with the applicant and to attend or conduct meetings required under this ordinance. (The cost of these consultant services shall be paid for through subdivision review fees received by the township.)

2. Existing Features (Site Analysis) Plan. Plans analyzing each site's special features are required for all proposed subdivisions, as they form the basis of the design process for greenway lands,

house locations, street alignments, and lot lines. The applicant or his/her representative shall bring a copy of the Existing Features (Site Analysis) Plan to the on-site walkabout. Detailed requirements for Existing Features (Site Analysis) Plans are contained in another section of this ordinance, but at the minimum must include (1) a contour map based at least upon topographical maps published by the U.S. Geological Survey; (2) the location of severely constraining elements such as steep slopes (over 25%), wetlands, watercourses, intermittent streams and 100-year floodplains, and all rights-of-way and easements; (3) soil boundaries as shown on USDA Natural Resources Conservation Service medium-intensity maps; and (4) the location of significant features such as woodlands, treelines, open fields or meadows, scenic views into or out from the property, watershed divides and drainage ways, fences or stone walls, rock outcrops, and existing structures, roads, tracks and trails, and any sites listed on the Pennsylvania Natural Diversity Inventory.

These Existing Features (Site Analysis) Plans shall identify both Primary Conservation Areas (floodplains, wetlands, and steep slopes, as defined in the process for computing "Adjusted Tract Acreage") and Secondary Conservation Areas, as described in Sections I.C.1 and I.D.1 of this ordinance. Together, these Primary and Secondary Conservation Areas comprise the development's proposed open space, the location of which shall be consistent with the locational design criteria listed in the Open Space, Recreation, and Environmental Resources Element of the township's *comprehensive plan*. The Existing Features (Site Analysis) Plan shall form the basis for the conceptual Preliminary Plan, which shall show the tentative location of houses, streets, lot lines, and greenway lands in new subdivisions, according to the four-step design process described in Section II.B.6 below.

3. On-Site Walkabout. After the Existing Features (Site Analysis) Plan has been prepared, the Planning Commission shall schedule a mutually convenient date to walk the property with the applicant and his/her site designer. The purpose of this visit is to familiarize township officials with the property's special features, and to provide them an informal opportunity to offer guidance (or at least a response) to the applicant regarding the tentative location of the Secondary Conservation Areas and potential house locations and street alignments. If this visit is not scheduled before submission of the sketch plan or the Conceptual Preliminary Plan, it should occur soon thereafter.

4. Pre-Submission Conference. Prior to the submission of the sketch plan or a Conceptual Preliminary Plan, the applicant shall meet with the Planning Commission to discuss how the four-step approach to designing subdivisions, described in Section II.B.6 below, could be applied to the subject property. At the discretion of the Planning Commission this conference may be combined with the on-site walkabout.

5. Conceptual Preliminary Plan. After the pre-submission conference, a sketch plan or a *Conceptual* Preliminary Plan shall be submitted for all proposed subdivisions. As used in this ordinance, the term "Conceptual Preliminary Plan" refers to a preliminarily engineered sketch plan drawn to illustrate initial thoughts about a conceptual layout for greenway lands, house sites, and street alignments. This is the stage where drawings are *tentatively* illustrated, before heavy engineering costs are incurred in the design of any proposed subdivision layout. These drawings shall be prepared by a team that includes a landscape architect and a civil engineer.

A Conceptual Preliminary Plan shall be submitted by the applicant to the township zoning officer who will then submit it to the Planning Commission for review for the purpose of securing early agreement on the overall pattern of streets, houselots, Primary and Secondary Conservation Areas, and potential trail linkages (where applicable), prior to any significant expenditure on engineering costs in the design of streets, stormwater management, or the accurate delineation of internal lot boundaries.

Within thirty days of receiving the Conceptual Preliminary Plan the Planning Commission shall approve it, disapprove it, or approve it with conditions, stating its reasons in writing. The remaining 60 days of the statutory 90-day review period for Preliminary Plans (as provided for in the state enabling legislation) shall therefore remain for the applicant to submit a Detailed Preliminary Plan (which shall contain all the customary engineering data) and for the Planning Commission to review said plan and to render its decision in writing. Either or both of these time periods may be formally extended if mutually agreeable to the applicant and the Planning Commission.

6. Four-Step Process. Each sketch plan or Conceptual Preliminary Plan shall follow a four-step design process, as described below. When the conceptual Preliminary Plan is submitted, applicants shall be prepared to demonstrate to the Planning Commission that these four design steps were followed by their site designers in determining the layout of their proposed streets, houselots, and greenway lands. This process shall be accomplished during the first 30 days of the statutory 90-day review period for Preliminary Plans.

a.   *Designating the Open Space.* During the first step, all potential conservation areas (both primary and secondary) are identified, using the Existing Features (Site Analysis) Plan. Primary Conservation Areas shall consist of wetlands, floodplains, slopes over 25%, and soils susceptible to slumping. Secondary Conservation Areas shall comprise 50% of the remaining land, and shall include the most sensitive and noteworthy natural, scenic, and cultural resources on that remaining half of the property.

Guidance on which parts of the remaining land to classify as Secondary Conservation Areas shall be based upon:

- the procedures described in *Conservation Design for Subdivisions: A Practical Guide to Creating Open Space Networks,* produced by Natural Lands Trust and published by Island Press,

- on-site visits or "walkabouts,"
- the open space locational criteria contained in Section I.E above,
- the evaluation criteria listed in Section I.E above,
- information from published data and reports, and
- conversations with existing or recent owners of the property, and members of the township Board of Supervisors and Planning Commission.

b.   *Location of House Sites.* During the second step, potential house sites are tentatively located. Because the proposed location of houses within each lot represents a significant decision with potential impacts on the ability of the development to meet the 14 evaluation criteria contained in Section I.E. above, subdivision applicants shall identify tentative house sites on the Conceptual Preliminary Plan and proposed house sites on the detailed Final Plan. House sites should generally be located not closer than 100 feet from Primary Conservation Areas, but may be situated within 50 feet of Secondary Conservation Areas, in order to enjoy views of the latter without negatively impacting the former. The building "footprint" of proposed residences may be changed by more than fifty feet in any direction with majority approval from the members of the Planning Commission. Changes involving less than fifty feet do not require approval.

c.   *Street and Lot Layout.* The third step consists of aligning proposed streets to provide vehicular access to each house in the most reasonable and economical way. When lots and access streets are laid out, they shall be located in a way that avoids or at least minimizes adverse impacts on both the Primary and Secondary Conservation Areas. To the greatest extent practicable, wetland crossings and streets traversing existing slopes over 15% shall be strongly discouraged. Street connections shall generally be encouraged to minimize the number of new cul-de-sacs to be maintained by the township and to facilitate easy access to and from homes in different parts of the property (and on adjoining parcels). Where cul-de-sacs are necessary, those serving six or fewer homes may be designed with "hammerheads" facilitating three-point turns. Cul-de-sacs serving more than six homes shall generally be designed with a central island containing indigenous trees and shrubs (either conserved on site or planted).

The township generally encourages the creation of single-loaded residential access streets, in order that the maximum number of homes in new developments may enjoy views of open space.

Note that in situations where more formal, "neo-traditional," or village-type layouts are proposed, Steps Two and Three may be reversed, so that the location of house sites follows the location of streets and squares.

d.   *Lot Lines.* The fourth step is simply to draw in the lot lines (where applicable). These are generally drawn midway between house locations and may include L-shaped "flag-lots" meeting the township's minimum standards for the same.

7. Preliminary Engineering Certification. Prior to approval of the Conceptual Preliminary Plan, the applicant shall submit to the Planning Commission a "Preliminary Engineering Certification" that the approximate layout of proposed streets, houselots, and open space lands complies with the township's zoning and subdivision ordinances, particularly those sections governing the design of subdivision streets and stormwater management facilities. This certification requirement is meant to provide the township with assurance that the proposed plan is able to be accomplished within the current regulations of the township. The certification shall also note any waivers needed to implement the plan as drawn.

III. OWNERSHIP AND MAINTENANCE OF OPEN SPACE

A. General

Different ownership and management options apply to the permanently protected open space created through the development process. The open space shall remain undivided and may be owned and managed by a homeowners' association, the township, or a recognized land trust or conservancy. (However, in low-density rural subdivisions with ten or more acres per dwelling, all or part of the required open space may be located within the house-lots.) A public land dedication, not exceeding 10% of the total parcel size, may be required by the township, through this open space, to facilitate trail connections. A narrative describing ownership, use and maintenance responsibilities shall be submitted for all common and public improvements, utilities, and open spaces.

B. Ownership Standards

Common open space within a development shall be owned, administered, and maintained by any of the following methods, either individually or in combination, and subject to approval by the township.

1. Offer of Dedication. The township shall have the first and last offer of dedication of undivided open space in the event said land is to be conveyed. Dedication shall take the form of a fee simple ownership. The township may, but shall not be required to accept undivided open space provided: (1) such land is accessible to the residents of the township; (2) there is no cost of acquisition other than any costs incidental to the transfer of ownership such as title insurance; and (3) the township agrees to and has access to maintain such lands. Where the township accepts dedication of common open space that contains improvements, the township may require the posting of financial security to ensure structural integrity of said improvements as well as the functioning of said improvements for a term not to exceed eighteen (18) months from the date of acceptance of dedication. The amount of financial security shall not exceed fifteen percent (15%) of the actual cost of installation of said improvements.

2. Homeowners' Association: The undivided open space and associated facilities may be held in common ownership by a home-owners' association. The association shall be formed and operated under the following provisions:

a.   The developer shall provide a description of the association, including its bylaws and methods for maintaining the open space.

b.   The association shall be organized by the developer and shall be operated with a financial subsidy from the developer, before the sale of any lots within the development.

c.   Membership in the association is automatic (mandatory) for all purchasers of homes therein and their successors. The conditions and timing of transferring control of the association from developer to homeowners shall be identified.

d.   The association shall be responsible for maintenance of insurance and taxes on undivided open space, enforceable by liens placed by the township on the association. The association may place liens on the homes or houselots of its members who fail to pay their association dues in a timely manner. Such liens may require the imposition of penalty interest charges.

e.   The members of the association shall share equitably the costs of maintaining and developing such undivided open space. Shares shall be defined within the association bylaws.

f.   In the event of a proposed transfer, within the methods here permitted, of undivided open space land by the homeowners' association, or of the assumption of maintenance of undivided open space land by the township, notice of such action shall be given to all property owners within the development.

g.   The association shall have or hire adequate staff to administer common facilities and properly and continually maintain the undivided open space.

h.   The homeowners' association may lease open space lands to any other qualified person, or corporation, for operation and maintenance of open space lands, but such a lease agreement shall provide:

(1) that the residents of the development shall at all times have access to the open space lands contained therein (except croplands during the growing season);

(2) that the undivided open space to be leased shall be maintained for the purposes set forth in this ordinance; and

(3) that the operation of open space facilities may be for the benefit of the residents only, or may be open to the residents of the township, at the election of the developer and/or homeowners' association, as the case may be.

i. The lease shall be subject to the approval of the board and any transfer or assignment of the lease shall be further subject to the approval of the board. Lease agreements so entered upon shall be recorded with the County Recorder of Deeds within thirty (30) days of their execution and a copy of the recorded lease shall be filed with the township.

3. Condominiums. The undivided open space and associated facilities may be controlled through the use of condominium agreements, approved by the township. Such agreements shall be in conformance with the state's uniform condominium act. All undivided open space land shall be held as a "common element."

4. Dedication of Easements. The township may, but shall not be required to, accept easements for public use of any portion or portions of undivided open space land, title of which is to remain in ownership by condominium or homeowners' association, provided: (1) such land is accessible to township residents; (2) there is no cost of acquisition other than any costs incidental to the transfer of ownership, such as title insurance; and (3) a satisfactory maintenance agreement is reached between the developer, condominium or homeowners' association, and the township.

5. Transfer of Easements to a Private Conservation Organization. With the permission of the township, an owner may transfer easements to a private, nonprofit organization, among whose purposes it is to conserve open space and/or natural resources, provided that:

1. the organization is acceptable to the township, and is a bona fide conservation organization with perpetual existence;

2. the conveyance contains appropriate provisions for proper reverter or retransfer in the event that the organization becomes unwilling or unable to continue carrying out its functions; and

3. a maintenance agreement acceptable to the board is entered into by the developer and the organization.

C. Maintenance Standards

1. The ultimate owner of the open space (typically a homeowners' association) shall be responsible for raising all monies required for operations, maintenance, or physical improvements to the open space through annual dues, special assessments, etc. The homeowners' association shall be authorized under its bylaws to place liens on the property of residents who fall delinquent in payment of such dues, assessments, etc.

2. In the event that the association or any successor organization shall, at any time after establishment of a development containing undivided open space, fail to maintain the undivided open space in reasonable order and condition in accordance with the development plan, the township may serve written notice upon the owner of record, setting forth the manner in which the owner of record has failed to maintain the undivided open space in reasonable condition.

3. Failure to adequately maintain the undivided open space in reasonable order and condition constitutes a violation of this ordinance. The township is hereby authorized to give notice, by personal service or by United States mail, to the owner or occupant, as the case may be, of any violation, directing the owner to remedy the same within twenty (20) days.

4. Should any bill or bills for maintenance of undivided open space by the township be unpaid by November 1 of each year, a late fee of fifteen percent (15%) shall be added to such bills and a lien shall be filed against the premises in the same manner as other municipal claims.

Recommended Further Reading

Arendt, Randall, 1989. "Patterns in the Rural Landscape," *Orion Nature Quarterly,* Vol. 8, No. 4, pp. 22–27.

Arendt, Randall, 1992. "Open Space Zoning: What It is and Why It Works," *Planning Commissioners Journal,* No. 5, pp. 4–8.

Arendt, Randall, 1996. "Creating Open Space Networks," *Environment & Development,* May. Chicago: American Planning Association.

Arendt, Randall, et al., 1994. *Rural by Design: A Handbook for Maintaining Small Town Character,* Chicago: Planners' Press.

Bruce, Hal, 1976. *How to Grow Wildflowers and Wild Shrubs in Your Garden,* New York: Alfred A. Knopf.

Clarke, Michael G., 1992. "Community Land Stewardship: A Future Direction for Land Trusts," *Land Trust Exchange,* Land Trust Alliance, Vol. 11, No. 2, pp. 1–9.

Cox, Jeff, 1991. *Landscaping with Nature,* Emmaus, PA: Rodale Books.

DuPont, Elizabeth, 1978. *Landscaping with Native Plants in the Middle Atlantic Region,* Chadds Ford, PA: The Brandywine Conservancy.

Freed, Kent, Nat Goodhue, and Robert Speth, 1991. *The Flexible Development Amendment to Grafton's Zoning Bylaw: A Comparative Study of Conventional and Flexible Subdivision Zoning Applied to Two Sites for the Town of Grafton, Massachusetts,* Conway, MA: The Conway School of Landscape Design.

Harker, Donald F., and Natter, Elizabeth Ungar, 1995. *Where We Live: A Citizen's Guide to Conducting a Community Environmental Inventory,* Washington, DC: Island Press.

Harney, Kenneth R., 1995. "Community Living: Look for Bike Paths, Not Golf Courses," *The Washington Post,* January 7, 1995.

Jarvis, Frederick D., 1993. *Site Planning and Community Design,* Washington, DC: Home Builder Press.

Kellert, Stephen R., and Wilson, Edward O., eds., 1993. *The Biophilia Hypothesis,* Washington, DC: Island Press.

Kuntsler, James H., 1993. *The Geography of Nowhere: The Rise and Decline of America's Man-Made Landscape,* New York: Simon & Schuster.

Lacy, Jeff, 1991. "Clustered Home Values Found to Appreciate More," *Land Development,* Vol. 3, No. 3.

Leopold, Aldo, 1976. *A Sand County Almanac,* New York: Ballantine Books.

Little, Charles, 1990. *Greenways for America,* Baltimore: Johns Hopkins Press.

Little, Charles, 1992. *Hope for the Land,* New Brunswick, NJ: Rutgers University Press.

Martin, Laura C., 1986. *The Wildflower Meadow Book: A Gardener's Guide,* Charlotte, NC: East Woods Press.

McHarg, Ian, 1991. *Design with Nature,* New York: John Wiley & Sons.

National Park Service, 1993. *Economic Impacts of Protecting Rivers, Trails and Greenway Corridors: A Resource Book,* Rivers, Trails and Conservation Assistance Section.

Nelessen, Anton, 1994. *Visions for a New American Dream: Process, Principles and an Ordinance to Plan and Design Small Communities,* Chicago: Planners' Press.

Orr, David W., 1994. *Earth in Mind: On Education, Environment, and the Human Prospect,* Washington, DC: Island Press.

Petit, Jack, Debra Bassert, and Cheryl Kollin, 1995. *Building Greener Neighborhoods: Trees as Part of the Plan,* Washington, DC: American Forests and Home Builder Press.

Pitz, D. Andrew, et al., 1994. *Design and Management Handbook for Preservation Areas,* Media, PA: Natural Lands Trust, Inc.

Roddewig, Richard J., and Duerksen, Christopher J., 1989. "Responding to the Takings Challenge," Chicago: American Planning Association, Planning Advisory Service Report No. 416.

Schwab, James, 1994. "The Biology of Wildlife Migration Corridors," *Environment & Development,* April. Chicago: American Planning Association.

Schwab, James, 1994. "Planning for Wildlife Migration Corridors," *Environment & Development,* May. Chicago: American Planning Association.

Small, Stephen, 1992. *Preserving Family Lands,* Boston: Landowner Planning Center.

Steiner, Frederick, 1991. *The Living Landscape: An Ecological Approach to Landscape Planning,* New York: McGraw-Hill, Inc.

Urban Land Institute, 1991. *The Fields at Long Grove,* Project Reference File Series, Vol. 21, No. 10, April–June.

Urban Land Institute, 1993. *Farmview,* Project Reference File Series, Vol. 23, No. 7, April–June.

Urban Land Institute, 1994. *Hawksnest,* Project Reference File Series, Vol. 24, No. 10, April–June.

Van der Ryn, Sim, and Cowan, Stuart, 1996. *Ecological Design,* Washington, DC: Island Press.

Wann, David, 1996. *Deep Design,* Washington, DC: Island Press.

Westover, Peter, 1994. *Managing Conservation Land: The Stewardship of Conservation Areas, Wildlife Sanctuaries, and Open Space in Massachusetts,* Belmont, MA: Massachusetts Association of Conservation Commissions.

Wilson, Edward O., 1992. *The Diversity of Life,* Cambridge, MA: Harvard University Press.

Wilson, Edward O., 1994. *Naturalist,* Washington, DC: Island Press.

Yaro, Robert D., and Hiss, Tony, 1996. *A Region at Risk: The Third Regional Plan for the New York–New Jersey–Connecticut Metropolitan Area,* Washington, DC: Island Press.

Yaro, Robert, Randall Arendt, Harry Dodson, and Elizabeth Brabec, 1988. *Dealing with Change in the Connecticut River Valley: A Design Manual for Conservation and Development,* Cambridge, MA: Lincoln Institute of Land Policy.

Note: For additional house plans such as those illustrated in Appendix D, see the following publications:

- Historical Replications, Inc., 1991, *Classic Cottages,* Jackson, MS (1-800-426-5628).

- *Professional Builder and Remodeler* journal, 1991. *Affordable Plans,* Des Plains, IL: Cahners Publishing Co. (1-800-323-7379).

- *Southern Living,* P.O. Box 1748, Birmingham, AL 35201.

Numerous plan books are also available from Homestyles Plan Service, P.O. Box 50670, Minneapolis, MN 55405 (1-800-547-5570).

Index

ABOUT THE AUTHOR

Randall G. Arendt is a land use planner, site designer, author, lecturer, and an advocate of conservation planning. A *magna cum laude* graduate of Wesleyan University and a St. Andrew's Scholar at the University of Edinburgh, he is vice president of conservation planning at the Natural Lands Trust in Media, Pennsylvania. He co-authored the award-winning volume *Dealing with Change in the Connecticut River Valley: A Design Manual for Conservation and Development* and is the principal author of *Rural by Design: Maintaining Small Town Character.* An elected member of the Royal Town Planning Institute in London, Mr. Arendt has lectured in forty-two states and five Canadian provinces and has designed conservation subdivisions in ten states.